# THE DREAM THAT WOULD NOT DIE

## The birth and growth of the World Evangelical Fellowship
## 1846–1986

# The Dream that would not Die

## The birth and growth
of the
World Evangelical Fellowship
1846–1986

DAVID M. HOWARD

*Foreword by Samuel Kamaleson*

DISTRIBUTED BY
BAKER BOOK HOUSE
GRAND RAPIDS, MICHIGAN

0-8010-4320-4

AUSTRALIA
Bookhouse Australia Ltd.,
P.O. Box 115, Flemington Markets,
N.S.W. 2129.

SOUTH AFRICA
Oxford University Press,
P.O. Box 1141, Cape Town.

**British Library Cataloguing in Publication Data**

Howard, David
    The dream that would not die : the birth
    and growth of the World Evangelical
    Fellowship, 1846–1986.
    1. World Evangelical Fellowship——History
    I. Title
    269'.2'0601        BV3752

ISBN 0-85364-442-X

Typeset by Photoprint, 9–11 Alexandra Lane, Torquay, Devon
and Printed in Great Britain for The Paternoster Press,
Paternoster House, 3 Mount Radford Crescent, Exeter, Devon
by A. Wheaton & Co. Ltd., Exeter.

## Dedication

TO
TOKUNBOH ADEYEMO OF AFRICA,
THEODORE WILLIAMS OF INDIA,
AND JOHN LANGLOIS OF GUERNSEY,
OFFICERS OF THE WORLD EVANGELICAL FELLOWSHIP,
WHO HAVE BEFRIENDED, ENCOURAGED, AND CHALLENGED ME
IN THE LEADERSHIP OF W.E.F.

# Contents

# Acknowledgements

Special thanks are in order to a number of people who contributed significantly to the preparation of this book. First and foremost I wish to thank Mr David Conner who served as my research assistant. He spent long hours working closely with me in researching countless facts and events and in consulting hundreds of pages of documents that were indispensable to preparing this book. Without this help my task would have been immeasurably more difficult and lengthy. David—a hearty and enthusiastic word of thanks to you!

Also very helpful were the librarians at Wheaton College: Mr Paul Snezek, Director of Learning Resources and Mr Daniel Bowell, Head of Public Services. The staff at the Billy Graham Center Library at Wheaton College were extremely cooperative: Miss Ferne Weimer, Director, and Miss Judy Franzke, Public Services Assistant graciously provided a private study room where I could research and write. The staff of the Graham Center Archives were especially helpful in providing access to files and advice on research procedures: Mr Robert Shuster, Director, Mrs Frances Brocker, Supervisor of the Reading Room, and Mr Paul Ericksen, Associate Archivist.

Special thanks are also due to Mr Jeremy Mudditt of Paternoster Press and Mr John Allan, Publications Editor of WEF, for their expert and helpful editorial advice.

My personal secretary, Mrs Carol Messina, faithfully and cheerfully typed and retyped the drafts of this manuscript and was always a constant encouragement. My colleagues on the staff of WEF, especially Mr Harry Genet and Dr Robert Youngblood, were patient and helpful in relieving me of some administrative duties in order to release me for this project. My warm thanks are also due to Pat Langlois for her help with the index.

Every writer feels that special thanks are due to his or her spouse in the preparation of a book. I am no exception to this. So at the risk of sounding pedantic (and knowing full well that Phyllis will deny any active share in the book's preparation) I want it to be known that her love, encouragement, good humour, unselfishness, and patience all contributed immensely to my completing this project. Were my children still living at home (they are all married and living elsewhere) I would be tempted to add what a friend of mine once threatened to put in the acknowledgements of his book, ". . . and to my children, without whose presence and help this book would have been written two years sooner." But my children gave encouragement and showed interest along the way, for which I am grateful.

*David M. Howard*

# Preface

One of the most difficult tasks of the historian is the matter of selectivity. Sifting through the massive amount of potential material, and then selecting those parts which are indispensable to the history, finds the historian in a constant dilemma.

A certain amount of subjectivity inevitably comes into play. I am fully aware that what I have chosen to include and exclude in this book may appear to some unbalanced. In many places another writer would have chosen a different emphasis. For this I can only ask for the indulgence of the reader.

I have tried hard to be as fair and as comprehensive as possible in view of the necessity of selectivity. There were many people who played significant roles in the history of the World Evangelical Fellowship, however, whose names do not appear in these pages. There are some events that were important to WEF that have not been included. To have included all of this detail would have made the volume too cumbersome for practical use. I have attempted to find a balance between comprehensiveness and readability.

Historical accuracy has been a primary concern. Wherever feasible I have tried to check my facts with persons still living who could provide material relevant to this history. The number of footnotes reflects the attempt to authenticate the accuracy of facts, quotations, and events recorded.

The writing of this book has been of immense value to me personally as General Director of the World Evangelical Fellowship. It has given me a far greater appreciation of our heritage and a broader perspective on our purposes. If it can serve to help others understand our evangelical roots and to appreciate the contribution of those who have gone before us, I shall be gratified.

It is my prayer that this book may make some small contribution to the ongoing ministry of strengthening our "fellowship in the gospel," our "defence and confirmation of the gospel," and the "furtherance of the gospel" in today's world.

David M. Howard

# Foreword

History teaches four Lessons, according to Charles Brand, the historian: When it gets darkest, the stars come out; when the bee steals from the flower, it also fertilizes; whom the gods would destroy, they first make mad; and the mills of God grind slowly but exceedingly small.

History does teach.

History, both personal and communal, has meaning. To learn from history, there must be a chronological record of significant events. It takes commitment and special skills to be a student before one can synthesize the events of history.

Dr David Howard, as I have known him, is a man of deep commitment to Jesus Christ and His church. I have known him for many years, and travelled in Asia with him expressing his commitment in many ways. He has translated this commitment to me as a deep, personal, outgoing interest, which misses no relevant details. There is always openness and acceptance. David Howard understands communication as a two-way process, because of his genuine interest in persons. When he recalls history, it is with interest that glows and never ignores details. His commitment to the content of the narration is genuine confidence that is a result of careful research. And the glow is contagious.

*A Dream That Would Not Die* glows with the same captivating rationality.

History teaches. But when it is our history that is being told, we want to be careful about the credentials of the person who tells it. For events translate into history in different ways, depending upon the vantage point of the one who narrates and relates them into a chronological and meaningful synthesis.

*A Dream That Would Not Die* is one story of the fellowship that evangelicals worldwide affirm. In the opening chapter, Dr Howard defines evangelicals in expanded terms that makes this story *our* story. My personal knowledge of Dr Howard as the Mission Director, and the Assistant to the President of Inter-Varsity Christian Fellowship, as the director of URBANA '73, and URBANA '76, the IVCF Missionary Convention attended by 17,000 delegates, as the Director of the Consultation on World Evangelization held at Pattaya, Thailand, sponsored by the Lausanne Committee for World Evangelization, places him inside "the family." His vantage point is as a family member.

But Dr Howard is a family member "who has been around." I know his broad exposure to those who are not of the family of evangelicals. Hence, in his task as the compiler of this chronicle, he assesses inside material accessible only to those who think from within the "mindset" of the family, with creative objectivity. Sometimes it stings. But then it ought to. For history has lessons to teach.

They who fail to learn from history, repeat historical mistakes.

This is the story of "our family"—may I say, yours or mine! As participants, we know that there were moments of clarity and confusion, moments of triumph and of apprehension. We have laughed and cried, hesitated and even moved boldly—all in their respective order within this chronicle. Read on. This is our story.

But this family story is *"A Dream That Will Not Die."* Praise be to God! Hallelujah!

Samuel Kamaleson
Vice-President, World Vision International

xiv

# Abbreviations

| | |
|---|---|
| AABC | American Association of Bible Colleges |
| ACTEA | Accrediting Council for Theological Education in Africa |
| AEAM | Association of Evangelicals of Africa and Madagascar |
| ATA | Asia Theological Association |
| BEST | Bangui Evangelical School of Theology, Central African Republic |
| BGEA | Billy Graham Evangelistic Association |
| BMMF | Bible and Medical Missionary Fellowship |
| CEEFI | Christian Education of the Evangelical Fellowship of India |
| CETA | Caribbean Evangelical Theological Association |
| COWE | Congress on World Evangelization (Pattaya, Thailand, 1980) |
| CRESR | Consultation on the Relationship between Evangelism and Social Responsibility (June 1982) |
| DAS | Development Assistance Services |
| EAC | Evangelical Association of the Caribbean |
| EEAA | European Evangelical Accrediting Association |
| EFI | Evangelical Fellowship of India |
| EFK | Evangelical Fellowship of Kenya |
| EFMA | Evangelical Foreign Missions Association |

| | |
|---|---|
| ICA | International Christian Assistance |
| ICAA | International Council of Accrediting Agencies |
| ICMC | International Christian Media Conference (Holland, 1986) |
| ICOWE | International Congress on World Evangelization (Lausanne, 1974) |
| IDAC | International Development Assistance Commission |
| IFEW | International Forum of Evangelical Women |
| IFMA | Interdenominational Foreign Mission Association |
| IIDI | International Institute for Development, Inc. |
| IRDA | Inter-church Relief and Development Alliance |
| IWY | International Women's Year |
| IVCF | Inter-Varsity Christian Fellowship |
| LCWE | Lausanne Committee for World Evangelization |
| NAE | National Association of Evangelicals (USA) |
| NCCK | National Christian Council of Kenya |
| PACLA | Pan-African Christian Leadership Assembly |
| SIM | Sudan Interior Mission |
| TAP | Theological Assistance Programme |
| TEAR Fund | The Evangelical Alliance Relief Fund (Great Britain) |
| TEE | Theological Education by Extension |
| TRACI | Theological Research and Communications Institute (New Delhi, India) |
| WEA | World's Evangelical Alliance |
| WEF | World Evangelical Fellowship |
| WHEATON '83 | Conference on "The Nature and Mission of the Church", Wheaton, I11., USA, 1983 |
| WRC | World Relief Corporation (of NAE) |

CHAPTER ONE

# Who is an Evangelical?

A definition of the word "evangelical" and how that word has been used over the years is indispensable to a study such as this. "The word is derived from the Greek noun *euangelion* translated as glad tidings, good or joyful news, or gospel (a derivative of the Middle English *godspell*, a discourse or story about God), and verb *euangelizomai*, to announce good tidings of or to proclaim as good news."[1] The noun and verb forms appear nearly one hundred times in the New Testament.

Historian John Gerstner has pointed out that:

> Despite the dominant usage of *euangellismos* [sic] in the New Testament, its derivative, evangelical, was not widely or controversially employed until the Reformation period. Then it came into prominence with Martin Luther precisely because he reasserted Paul's teaching on the *euangellismos* as the indispensable message of salvation. . .
>
> Although Luther himself disliked the name evangelical being applied to his followers precisely because he saw the evangel as absolutely essential to all Chistianity the term did become associated with Lutheranism. But in time . . . evangelicalism was freely applied to Protestants in general.[1]

Those known as evangelicals have always held to the centrality of certain basic beliefs related to salvation. Harold Lindsell summarized these as: "(1) man's sinful condition before a holy God; (2) man's need for salvation; (3) the revelation of the grace of God in Jesus Christ; (4) the authority of the inspired Scriptures; (5) the necessity for a birth from above or regeneration; and (6) justification through faith alone, apart from works."[2]

While all evangelicals have held the above beliefs, it is important to note that evangelicals have also been known for their social concern. This was especially true during the nineteenth century when men such as William Wilberforce (1759–1833), Lord Shaftesbury (1801–1885), and others led the fight for such social reforms as abolition of slavery, child labour laws, justice for the poor, alleviation of the condition of the insane, improved housing for the indigent. These men were all evangelicals whose personal beliefs in salvation by faith alone in Christ were unquestioned.

Another great characteristic of evangelicals since the eighteenth century has been a strong missionary vision. Many of the great missionary movements of the nineteenth century, which Latourette called "The Great Century" in terms of missions, were led by evangelicals. Their commitment to proclaim the evangel to the uttermost parts of the earth was prevalent in all their conferences, their writings, and their statements of faith.

## Fundamentalists and Modernists

During the early part of the twentieth century the great fundamentalist-modernist debates ensued, resulting in a somewhat modified use of the term "evangelical". Those who held firmly to the fundamentals of basic evangelical doctrine became known as "fundamentalists." The word was often applied to all opponents of "modernism," although there were great differences between the attitudes of moderate conservatives, militants, and such Reformed scholars as J. G. Machen. The term itself derived from the publication between 1910 and 1915 of a series of booklets entitled *The Fundamentals*, which defended a wide variety of basic biblical doctrines which were considered to be fundamental to Christianity. Reacting strongly against increasing emphasis on the social gospel, as expounded by those known as the "modernists" or "liberals," the fundamentalists swung the pendulum away from social activity in favour of a more inward-looking emphasis on personal relationship to Jesus Christ and holiness of life. Thus in the first half of the twentieth century those who were the legitimate offspring of the evangelicals of the previous century narrowed their focus in such a way that their opponents dubbed them as obscurantist, anti-scholarly, schismatic, and anti-social.

While such epithets were not wholly justified, there was some basis for the feeling that the fundamentalists had redefined the parameters of evangelicalism. A strong emphasis on eschatology, especially the premillennial viewpoint, became a hallmark of most fundamentalists, as a reaction to the social gospel emphasis which was primarily postmillennial in outlook. The belief that the world would get better and better, and that the church would usher in the kingdom of God, had dominated the first half of the nineteenth century and was still popular with leading churchmen prior to World War I. This, of course, was shattered irretrievably by two devastating World Wars, but prior to World War I it was a popular belief among many leading churchmen. Many evangelicals, however, increasingly saw this as unbiblical and reacted accordingly, turning away from political involvement and some aspects of social activity.

Matters of personal lifestyle came to hold almost an equal place in some fundamentalist thought with basic doctrinal beliefs. A certain standard of "dos" and "don'ts" became a *sine qua non* for some. This writer has studied the doctrinal statement of a mission society in Latin America, drawn up by fundamentalists during the 1930s and 1940s, which spent long paragraphs defining "worldliness" in terms of proscribed taboos such as the use of cosmetics for women, attendance at theatres, social dancing, use of alcohol and tobacco, modesty of dress for women—all an integral part of a statement of faith which placed them on the same level as belief in the substitutionary atonement and the resurrection of Christ.

However, many evangelicals were never at ease with this narrowing of outlook. There had been a "bunker mentality" among many fundamentalists, who seemed to withdraw from the world and from the painful theological debates of the first decades of this century. A great gap widened between liberals and conservatives with a breakdown of communication. But some were uneasy and felt that evangelicals must continue to stress the full message of the gospel as it had been understood by former generations of evangelicals.

## The New Evangelicals

In 1947 Harold J. Ockenga coined the term "the new evangelicalism" to identify this movement away from the negative connotations which had come to characterize fundamentalism.

> The new or "neo" evangelicalism took issue with the older fundamentalism. Ockenga argued that it had a wrong attitude (a suspicion of all who did not hold every doctrine and practice what fundamentalists did), a wrong strategy (a separatism that aimed at a totally pure church on the local and denominational levels), and wrong results (it had not turned the tide of liberalism anywhere nor had it penetrated with its theology into the social problems of the day).[3]

Other young theologians such as Edward J. Carnell and Carl F. H. Henry began to speak out along the same lines. Thus "neo-evangelicalism" came to be a good term for some and a negative term for others of the more narrow outlook.

The rise in America of the National Association of Evangelicals in 1942 and on the world scene of the World Evangelical Fellowship in 1951 brought the term "evangelical" back into favour. The concurrent rise to world prominence of an evangelist named Billy Graham, who gladly identified himself as an evangelical, focussed the word again in terms commensurate with its meaning in the previous century.

It was not until the decade of the 1970s that the social concern of evangelicals became widely accepted and began to make an impact again. The scars of the debates over the social gospel were still fresh for some, and a cautious temperament pervaded much evangelical thought. The recognition that missions had always been engaged in social activity, even during the decades of fundamentalist withdrawal from such arenas, together with a series of significant conferences on social concern, a renewed understanding of the full-orbed ministry of Christ himself and of the teachings of the Scriptures on responsibility to the world,—all of this caused evangelicals to feel more comfortable once again with being involved, as their forebears had been, in social concerns. Thus by the mid-1980s it was an accepted fact that evangelicals should be very much a part of the movement to emphasize again the second great commandment to love our neighbour as ourselves.

In spite of the fact that the term had been used with slightly different connotations over the years, those who claim the name of evangelical have consistently held to the same basic body of beliefs. A comparison of the statements of faith of the Evangelical Alliance drawn up in 1846 (see p. 11) and of the World Evangelical Fellowship accepted in 1951 (see p. 31) will demonstrate that there has never been much deviation from what evangelicals believe. The fact that these statements of faith have never been changed is also signifi- cant. It indicates that those who call themselves evangelicals are satisfied that the doctrinal statements to which they adhere are accurate expressions of their understanding of biblical truth.

Thus Pierard could write in 1984 that "evangelicalism has now come of age and is truly a global phenomenon."[4] This book tells the story of how evangelicals around the world have attempted to create a structure to hold that "global phenomenon" together. It was an ambitious dream, an unlikely achievement. But it proved to be a dream that would not die.

CHAPTER TWO

# The Evangelical Alliance

It was an impressive sight. 800 Christians, who had gathered in Freemasons' Hall, Great Queen Street, London, in August, 1846, were standing to shake hands and sing the Doxology. They had just voted to establish what has been called "a new thing in Church history—a definite organization for the expression of unity amongst Christian individuals belonging to different churches."[1] They called it "The Evangelical Alliance."

They came from England, Scotland, Ireland, Wales, France, Switzerland, Holland, Germany, Sweden, Canada, and the United States. While 84 per cent of them were from England, another 6 per cent were from other European countries and 10 per cent from the United States. (Many of this last group, because of the travel conditions of those days, had needed to invest in this endeavour six months of their time and considerable sums of money.) Although the composition of the gathering was almost exclusively Anglo-Saxon their target was clearly the world, as will become evident in the succeeding pages. "They represented fifty-two different branches of the Church of Christ. It was a meeting of remarkable enthusiasm, hailed as if it were the beginning of the Millennium, spoken of by delegates as the crowning moment of their lives."[2]

In his opening remarks the Chairman, Sir Culling Eardley Smith, reflected the optimism and vision surrounding this unique gathering:

It is the first experiment which has been made to combine together the interests of truth and love. In former times endeavours have been made to maintain the interests of truth, but never yet has there been a systematic endeavour to combine the interests of truth and those of love, as I hope they will be combined on this occasion.[3]

What was the conference that evoked such euphoria?

Primarily it was the culmination of a growing conviction in the hearts of many Christian churchmen—Establishment and Dissenters, High Church and Low Church—that the prayer of our Lord in John 17 concerning the unity of his followers must be answered in a way that demonstrated that unity and allowed for channels of cooperation in fulfilling the mission of his church.

## Preparatory Conferences

For some years, various church leaders in different countries had been advocating the need for true unity in the body of Christ. Among these were Revd J. H. Stewart of Liverpool; Dr Samuel S. Schmucker (1799–1873), a founder of the Lutheran Theological Seminary in Gettysburg, Pennsylvania; Dr Merle D'Aubigné (1794–1872) of Geneva; and Dr Kneiwel, archdean of Danzig. Revd John Angell James of Birmingham was apparently the first one to make a definite suggestion for the formation of a union, at a meeting of the Congregational Union held in May, 1842.

As a result of Mr James' proposals a committee was formed which organized a great rally at the Exeter Hall in London in June 1843. So great was the interest that 11,000 tickets were sold, nearly three times more than the hall could hold, and many were turned away disappointed. All seven men who helped lead the meeting were later to play a prominent part in the Evangelical Alliance and the meeting itself was evidence of the longing for more unity.[4]

As a result of this London meeting a more definitive preparatory conference was held in Liverpool from 1–3 October, 1845, with 216 leaders from 20 denominations participating. The emphasis in this conference was on unity and love rather than on controversy. There was an attempt to avoid involvement in issues which were internal to specific denominations or which were primarily political in tone. In fact, statements of opposition to certain movements or people within Protestantism were removed from the conference proceedings as being inappropriate. However, there was a definite posture of strong opposition both to Roman Catholicism and also to infidelity.

Three basic problems concerned organization, membership, and doctrine. Was the proposed union to be visible and organizational or merely invisible and "of essence?" Were the members to be individuals or denominations? What was to be the doctrinal basis of this union? Extensive discussion was precipitated on each of these points. It was not until the founding conference the following year that they were finally resolved. The name "Evangelical Alliance" was chosen for the organization which was envisioned for the immediate future.

"The importance of the Liverpool conference," wrote one historian, "did not lie only in the love which was manifested, but in the fact that it was shown that the keynote of Christian union had to consist of truth as well as love, and that these two could be combined in the practice of an interdenominational gathering."[5] Two further preparatory meetings were held in Birmingham in January and April of 1846.

Finally, as the culmination of a long-standing vision, a clearly articulated concern for unity, and meticulous preparations, the 800 delegates gathered in London to organize the Evangelical Alliance.

## Formation of the Evangelical Alliance

In spite of doctrinal, ecclesiastical, and political differences, all of which reared their heads at this founding conference, the delegates were able to work together in the spirit of love and unity that had been so evident in Liverpool. The major problems of structure, membership, and doctrine occupied most of the business sessions.

The question of Christian unity was embodied in the first resolution presented at the conference by Dr Wardlaw, Congregational minister from Glasgow:

> . . . that the church of the living God, while it admits of growth, is one church never having lost, and being incapable of losing its essential

unity. Not, therefore, to create that unity, but to confess it, is the design of their assembling together. One in reality, they desire also, as far as they may be able to attain it, to be visibly one: and thus, both to realize in themselves, and to exhibit to others that a living and everlasting union binds all true believers together in the fellowship of the Church of Christ.[6]

This was accepted unamended, indicating that the primary concern in unity was to be spiritual rather than institutional.

These words have played a vital role in the whole development of the Evangelical Alliance . . . Essential unity was the invisible bond existing eternally between all believers, whereas visible unity was that which these believers had to create among themselves as a testimony to the world . . . A spiritual unity, which had nothing to do with organization, became the great object of the movement, with the inevitable result that "aloofness from plans of reunion might almost be said to have become an Alliance article of faith."

Akin to this declaration on unity was the decision that membership in the Alliance would be individual rather than institutional or denominational. This was a major formative factor in the future development of the Alliance and colours much of its influence and activities in subsequent years. The emphasis on individual membership determined its structure as being primarily a voluntary alliance of individuals, rather than a confederation of churches.

It was an organization of individual Christians, not of churches. It aimed at making the "Invisible church visible," "that the world may know" . . . At the greatest conference it ever held, in New York in 1873, though it recorded Dr Samuel Schmucker's plan in its report, the Alliance refused to discuss his appeal for an official confederation of Protestant denominations, as being alien to the objects of the Alliance as "a voluntary union of individual Christians of different churches."[8]

The result was that

. . . it had no central organization whatever. Its conferences were arranged for as and when proposals were made by one or other of the national organizations. Most of the national branches of the Alliance looked to the British Alliance to take the lead in organizing the conferences; this it usually did, though not without exciting criticism from other nations. Not until the 1890s did it develop even the simplest form of central committee for arranging conferences, and then, rather curiously, on the demand not of activist America or Britain, but of Switzerland and Germany. Its secretaries were usually busy ministers. The day of full-time salaried secretaries was still far away in the 20th century.[9]

## *Doctrinal Basis*

On the third day of the conference, after the vote to organize formally the Evangelical Alliance had cemented the spirit of unity, the delegates began to debate the doctrinal basis which would undergird the Alliance. There were fears that disagreement here could fracture all that had so far been accomplished. After three days of debates the proposed statement was finally passed "unaltered and without a dissenting voice"[10] on the evening of the fifth day. The doctrinal statement, including the introduction and supplementary clause, reads as follows:

"That the parties composing the Alliance shall be such persons only as hold and maintain what are usually understood to be evangelical views, in regard to the matters of doctrine understated, viz:

1. The Divine inspiration, authority, and sufficiency of the Holy Scriptures.
2. The right and duty of private judgement in the interpretation of the Holy Scriptures.
3. The Unity of the Godhead, and the Trinity of Persons therein.
4. The utter depravity of human nature in consequence of the fall.
5. The incarnation of the Son of God, his work of atonement for sinners of mankind, and his mediatorial intercession and reign.
6. The justification of the sinner by faith alone.
7. The work of the Holy Spirit in the conversion and sanctification of the sinner.
8. The immortality of the soul, the resurrection of the body, the judgment of the world by our Lord Jesus Christ, with the eternal blessedness of the righteous, and the eternal punishment of the wicked.
9. The Divine institution of the Christian ministry, and the obligation and perpetuity of the ordinances of baptism and the Lord's Supper.

It being, however, distinctly declared; First, that this brief summary is not to be regarded, in any formal or ecclesiastical sense, as a creed or confession; nor the adoption of it as involving an assumption of the right authoritatively to define the limits of Christian brotherhood, but simply as an indication of the class of persons, whom it is desirable to embrace within the Alliance; Secondly, that the selection of certain tenets, with the omission of others, is not to be held as implying that the former constitute the whole body of important truth, or that the latter are unimportant."[11]

When the vote was taken on this crucial and fundamental issue, the sense of relief and thanksgiving was so great that

"Mr. Bickersteth broke forth in a peroration of rapturous joy and the whole conference sang 'All Hail the great Immanuel's name, let angels prostrate fall' . . . "with a depth of devotional feeling, which even during the meetings of this conference had never been surpassed."[12]

It is both curious and interesting to note that, although point 8 in the doctrinal statement refers to the consummation of history, there is no direct reference to the Second Coming of Christ. This seems to indicate that in 1846 this was not the issue that it certainly became sixty years later. The great Fundamentalist-Modernist controversies of the first half of the twentieth century forced that issue to the fore in such a way that a detailed statement on eschatology became an indispensable part of every doctrinal statement drawn up by evangelicals during that era.

*The Question of Slavery*

The practical outworking of doctrine and its effect upon the behaviour of Christians became an issue later in the week, as the delegates were beginning to grow weary with long business sessions. The question of whether or not a slaveholder could become a member of the Alliance was brought to the floor. "The subsequent debate occupied no less than four days and filled 180 closely printed pages of the magnificent report, not to mention many more days of debate at the separate conferences which were held later in Great Britain and the United States."[13]

The British, who had already abolished slavery through the noble efforts of men like Wilberforce, were adamantly opposed to allowing any slaveholder to be a member of the Alliance. The Americans, on the other hand, were just entering the period when slavery would become a major issue and would be debated hotly in the public fora of the nation. Many southern Christians were still holding slaves, and among some there was not only an absence of guilt of conscience about this, but actually a continued attempt to find Biblical justification for the practice. Most of the Americans present at the founding of the Alliance in 1846 were opposed to slavery in their practice and beliefs, but they were nonetheless sensitive to the social situation which surrounded them in the United States.

> To the Americans it was unacceptable that the British should force on them a general measure of discipline which took no account of the involuntary situation in which some slaveholders found themselves. To the British it was intolerable that a considerable proportion of evangelicals in America should try to justify slavery on biblical grounds, while the rest, who disagreed with slavery, should be so timid in their protest. As no further progress could be made it was decided to refer the matter to a sub-committee.[14]

The report of the sub-committee recommended a resolution strongly condemning slavery and excluding slaveholders from membership in any Alliance. While this was at first adopted, the Americans later reconsidered, and a new debate ensued which lasted for two more days.

> A fresh sub-committee was appointed, but as no agreement could be reached, it was eventually decided to abandon the idea of an ecumenical alliance and adopt the British suggestion of loosely linked national organizations which were not responsible for each other's actions . . .
>
> All felt at the close of the proceedings that the definitive organization of the Alliance must be adjourned to another conference. Humanly speaking the undertaking was a failure. As the Alliance which was constituted in the summer of 1846 has never again called an international conference with legislative powers, the Alliance proper, which must be distinguished from the national organizations which were established shortly afterwards, has long since died out. When one thinks of how nearly the founders' conference succeeded in its aim it is sad to think that for over a hundred years no further attempt was made in this direction.[15]

The "further attempt" referred to here did not come until 1951 with the founding of the World Evangelical Fellowship. It is sobering and saddening to realize that disagreement on a social issue such as slavery, which today would not occupy five minutes of debate in a worldwide evangelical forum, should scuttle the attempt to build a truly representative body of evangelicals on a global basis.

*National Alliances*

Thus the Evangelical Alliance settled for the establishment of national alliances, each one to be autonomous and only loosely related to the others through the Evangelical Alliance. In subsequent months several of these were formed. The British met in Manchester in November 1846, and formed the Evangelical Alliance (British Organization). Other alliances were formed in Canada at Montreal in November 1846; in Germany in 1847; in Sweden at Christiansand in April 1847; in India in 1849; and in Turkey in 1855. The American branch, however, did not come into being until 1867, after the Civil War in the United States had settled the issue of slavery.[16]

The branches of Evangelical Alliances founded in 1846–1847 in Great Britain and various European countries have remained active to this day. The American Branch, however, did not survive, despite prospering under the capable leadership of men like William Dodge, Philip Schaff, Irenaeus Prime, and Josiah Strong during the last three decades of the nineteenth century.

> Although the Alliance (American Branch) continued to exist on paper until 1944, when the corporation was dissolved and the funds were transferred to the Federal Council, it was largely a dead letter after 1900. Strong resigned in 1898, his activist policy opposed by the conservative directors, who were more interested in the theological *status quo* than in the invigorating winds of the Social Gospel. Schaff had died in 1893; the organization of the Federal Council in 1908, going several steps further than the Alliance in the direction of closer unity, made the latter a back number. As the early leaders died, little remained for the Alliance to manage other than the Annual Week of Prayer, and even this was finally taken over by the Federal Council.[17]

Internationally, however, the creation of Evangelical Alliances was to lead to more permanent and significant gains . . . as we shall see.

CHAPTER THREE

# Contributions of the Evangelical Alliance

And so the Evangelical Alliance came to be—an international, loosely-knit confederation of autonomous national branches. But what were its achievements? What contributions did it make to the life and progress of the church in the world?

*Some Achievements*

Unity
The first and most significant contribution of the Evangelical Alliance was its emphasis on uniting Christians of all denominations and groupings. Historian Stephen Neill refers to the Alliance as "the first society formed with a definite view to Christian unity" and adds that it "rapidly grew to international status."[1] There is no doubt that the desire for unity within the body of Christ was the primary motivating factor in the minds of the founders, as Kenneth Scott Latourette testifies:

> Multiform and fissiparous though Protestantism was, it also gave rise to efforts for union . . . The Evangelical Alliance, formed in 1846, endeavoured to draw together in fellowship all those in the stream of the Protestant Reformation who held to the authority of the Bible, the incarnation, the atonement, salvation through faith, and the work of the Holy Spirit. The movement for union gathered momentum and had its main fruitage in the twentieth century . . . but it was already in existence . . . before 1900.[2]

15

It is also interesting to note that the word "ecumenical," often used today in contradistinction from the word "evangelical," was used freely by the founders of the Evangelical Alliance as descriptive of their goals. In tracing the history of the ecumenical movement Norman Goodall says, "The word ecumenical was frequently used within the Alliance to denote the fact that it transcended national and denominational divisions."[3]

## Universal Week of Prayer

Undoubtedly the second most significant and tangible contribution of the Evangelical Alliance was the establishment of the annual universal week of prayer. This was established at the very outset, during the first week of January, 1847, to ask God to give direction and wisdom in overcoming some of the obstacles (such as the issue of slavery) that had plagued the founders. From there it became an annual event with growing worldwide impact. Kessler notes that "in 1858 for the first time, the appeal for a week of prayer was directed not only to Alliance members, but to all Christians throughout the world."[4]

About that time a group of missionaries in Ludhiana, India, were also meeting for a week of prayer as an annual event. When they discovered that the Alliance was calling for a similar week, they proposed that there should be a universal appeal.

> On March 28th, 1860, one of the Ludhiana missionaries wrote Lord Kinnaird explaining that if they of Ludhiana had known that the Alliance called for prayer during the first week of January, they would have chosen the same week. This missionary therefore proposed that in January, 1861, the Evangelical Alliance send out a combined call to prayer to all the churches. This suggestion was agreed to, so that the first universal week of prayer was held in 1861, starting on Sunday, January 6.[5]

Rouse and Neill speak of this week of prayer sponsored by the Alliance as "its most significant achievement."[6] Writing a century after the week's initiation, Norman Goodall says,

> One of the most far-reaching contributions of the Evangelical Alliance to the ecumenical movement was its initiation over a century ago of the annual week of prayer normally held in the first week of every new

year. Its support and vitality vary greatly in different countries and areas, but it represents a point of meeting in worship and intercession that ought not to be neglected or treated casually.[7]

The universal week of prayer is still a major activity of the Alliances in many countries, especially the European countries where it originated. It comprises one of their primary activities and emphases.

## Missions

A third contribution of the Evangelical Alliance was the development of a strong vision for world missions. William Richey Hogg states that

> From the first it was strongly missionary and tried to foster a co-operative, united missionary endeavour. The monthly journal of the Alliance, *Evangelical Christendom*, from its first issue in 1847 carried considerable news of missionary work everywhere. Missionaries in widely scattered parts of the world read the publication, especially for its global "Intelligence." Each of the great Alliance conferences devoted much attention to the subject of missions and missionary cooperation. There can be no doubt that through its broad appeal and that through the many missionaries who belonged to it, the Evangelical Alliance laid a foundation that greatly facilitated later developments in missionary cooperation.[8]

Arthur Johnston confirms this by saying that the

> . . . development of the Evangelical Alliance reveals two principle concerns of pietism so apparent in the seventeenth century: doctrinal fidelity to the authority and the infallibility of the Scriptures, and a concern for evangelism at home and in non-Christian lands . . . the unity of the Evangelical Alliance was not conceived or thought of as an end in itself, but rather as a means to promote evangelism through fellowship, prayer, and practical cooperation.[9]

Another historian, J. H. Ewing, has also highlighted how this missionary vision of the Evangelical Alliance was present from the earliest days of the movement.

> Although the Alliance was not founded as a missionary society, its spirit has always been intensely missionary, and it has worked in warm fellowship with the missionary societies of the various denominations . . .
>
> The warm feeling of the Alliance towards missions was expressed at its founding in a resolution proposed by the Rev. W. Arthur . . . In this resolution the members of the conference declared their longing for the universal spread of Christ's kingdom; gave praise to God for the grace whereby, in late years, Christians had been moved to missionary effort;

offered fraternal congratulations and sympathy to all evangelical missionaries; and prayed that through the out-pouring of the Holy Spirit both Israel and the heathen might receive the light of God.

In moving this resolution Mr. Arthur referred to the loneliness of many a missionary, to whom he trusted the message of the conference would bring encouragement. He believed that the movement towards Christian union had been largely stimulated through the coming together of Christians for missionary effort.[10]

Throughout its history the Evangelical Alliance has had a salutary influence in promoting missions through cooperation, especially with the national alliances developed in other lands. This will be seen particularly in the developments of the post-World War II era when alliances began to proliferate throughout the world.

## Publications: "Evangelical Christendom"

Beginning in January, 1847, a journal was published entitled "Evangelical Christendom." This appeared monthly until 1893, and then it became a bi-monthly until it ceased publication in 1954. The masthead describes it as "a monthly journal established and conducted by members of the British organization—in connection with the Evangelical Alliance." A note on p. 3 of the first issue, however, states:

> This work, therefore, is not officially the organ of that body (the British Organization of the Evangelical Alliance). It is an independent journal . . . It is the property of private individuals, by whom all its expenses are defrayed, and all its liabilities incurred.[11]

Despite that disclaimer the journal continued to carry the masthead statement of its connection with the Evangelical Alliance, and it was generally understood throughout its history to be the voice of the Alliance.

Its purposes were clearly enunciated in the first issue:

> *Evangelical Christendom* will advocate and exalt these common and uniting truths. Rejecting what is sectarian and partial, its pages will exhibit only the Catholic faith of God's elect. It thus enters upon the theatre of public life, the friend of all truly Christian communions, and the adversary of none. Its only controversy will be with Romanism and Infidelity. Against these common foes it will aim to unite the scattered forces of all EVANGELICAL CHRISTENDOM, and to incite them to the conflict under the deep conviction, that in its issue are involved the highest interests of the human race, and the final triumphs of the LAMB . . .

We are anxious to institute friendly relations and multiplied bonds of Christian love, as far as our means of effecting it may enable us amongst all the faithful of every land; that having common solicitudes, and common hopes, they may stand together "companions in tribulation," if it should be so, "and in the kingdom and patience of Jesus Christ."[12]

The references to "Romanism" and "Infidelity" are elaborated with pejorative language in other parts of the first issue with such phrases as "the paralyzing influences of the Romish Antichrist, and the strong whirlwinds of Pantheistic infidelity." The conflict, thus, with Rome was a major factor in the thinking of those early founders, and repeated references to this are found in the pages of the journal.

Strong tribute is paid to the influence of this journal by almost all historians who record the work of the Evangelical Alliance. It had a profound influence in the growth of the Alliance, in promoting unity and missions, in encouraging the universal week of prayer, in highlighting theological and missiological issues of the times, in giving news of worldwide missionary advance, and in providing a forum for evangelical spokesmen. Rouse and Neill speak of it thus:

> But the most valuable historical record of ecumenical thinking in all these changing phases and emphases is to be found in Christian journalism . . .
> From 1847 onwards the British branch of the Evangelical Alliance has published *Evangelical Christendom*, usually as a monthly. Although in the 20th century it has confined itself more closely to the affairs of the Evangelical Alliance, for many years in the 19th century it steadily provided a real instrument of ecumenical education by making available information about the churches and religious conditions in many countries, as well as about movements of cooperation or reunion between churches.[13]

## Revival

The Evangelical Alliance also played a part in revival movements through its emphasis on prayer, through reporting in *Evangelical Christendom* what the Holy Spirit was doing in the churches, through encouraging cooperation in evangelism and "deeper life" conferences, and in other ways. J. Edwin Orr in writing of the Great Awakening of 1859 speaks of

. . . the part which the Evangelical Alliance played in the commence-

ment and extension of the remarkable Awakening, a part of a great
importance, for the Evangelical Alliance not only prepared the ground
for the seed of cooperation between Christians of various loyalties, but
once the plant had sprung up, watered it most thoroughly.

When in 1846 the Evangelical Alliance was founded to enable
Christians of all nations to realize in themselves and to manifest to
others the living and essential union which unites all believers in the
fellowship of Christ, a score of distinguished leaders of the Church
Universal attended the sessions. The majority of them are recognizable
as promoters of the 1859 Awakening. Thus the Alliance identified with
the Awakening in its personalities.[14]

## Religious Liberty

One of the primary functions of the Alliance throughout its
history has been to defend and strengthen the church which
is passing through suffering and persecution. Its records are
filled with cases of efforts to alleviate the pressures placed on
Christians in many parts of the world. The pages of
*Evangelical Christendom* in almost every issue reflect this
concern. Reports are given regularly of oppression of the
church in lands where Christianity was a despised religion,
in places where persecution broke out in physical and
violent form, and where Protestantism was attacked or
suppressed by other branches of the Christian religion.

The suffering of Christians in Russia under the Czarist
regime, of Armenian Christians slaughtered by the Turks, of
Christians in Greece oppressed by the state religion, of
Protestants in Colombia and Spain under open attack from
the Roman Catholic Church, fill the pages of the journal year
after year. These efforts to give publicity to the mistreatment
of the followers of Christ throughout the world, to encourage
them in their sufferings, and to defend them in the public
and governmental fora of the day, were some of the finest
contributions which the Evangelical Alliance has made to the
church of Christ.

## International Conferences

From the earliest days of the Alliance, international conferences played a significant role in its ministry. These
usually lasted from a week to ten days and were spent in
inspirational study of the Scriptures, prayer, praise, and
discussion of the key issues facing the church at that time.

Eleven such conferences were held, as follows: London, 1851; Paris, 1855; Berlin, 1857; Geneva, 1861; Amsterdam, 1867; New York, 1873; Basel, 1879; Copenhagen, 1884; Florence, 1891; London, 1896; and London again, 1907. This was the last such conference held prior to the formation of the World Evangelical Fellowship in 1951. These conferences served to bring together Christians from many countries (albeit largely European and North American, with smaller numbers from other nations), for fellowship and comparison of ideas. They gave visibility to the ministries of the Alliance and allowed for exchange of views and news of God's work in many areas.

## Multi-lingual Hymnbook
One little known and seldom mentioned contribution of the Evangelical Alliance was the publication of a multi-lingual hymnbook. Rouse and Neill in recounting the development of such hymnbooks state: "The pioneer in multi-lingual hymnbooks was a collection of twenty-nine *Psaumes et Cantiques*, prepared by the Evangelical Alliance for its Conference in Geneva in 1861."[15] Because of the importance of music in revival and the development of the church, this hymnbook, and subsequent ones published by different branches of the Alliance, have unquestionably played a quiet, largely unnoticed, yet important part in the life of the church.

## *The World's Evangelical Alliance*

In 1912 the Evangelical Alliance incorporated itself in England in order to gain the legal status needed to acquire and hold property for their headquarters. At that time the name "World's Evangelical Alliance" was chosen as the legal name for the organization which had existed since 1846. No explanation appears to be known for this addition of the word "World's" to the title, except that this was apparently a recognition of the international scope which the Evangelical Alliance had always maintained. Occasional references prior to 1912 are found when someone will refer to the Alliance as the "International Evangelical Alliance" or the "World's Evangelical Alliance," but the title was not official until 1912.

The change is reflected in the masthead of *Evangelical Christendom*. The issue of July-August, 1912, carries the name "Evangelical Alliance (British Organization)," while the next issue, September-October, 1912, carries the title "World's Evangelical Alliance (British Organization)." There is no explanation in the pages of the journal for this change.

Years later the following explanation appears in *Evangelical Christendom:*

> It is not always realized that the World's Evangelical Alliance is not an internationally controlled organization. Its title is, in fact, somewhat misleading. When the Alliance was founded in 1846 its name was simply the Evangelical Alliance, and the alteration of title to its present form was not made until 1912. Despite this change, the w.e.a. centered in this country remains a British Organization only, and its Executive Council has no jurisdiction over any other branch. The European branches of the Alliance are entirely autonomous, the only real link between them and the British organization being a common adherence to the Doctrinal Basis as formulated in 1846, and the observance of the Universal Week of Prayer. There is no council or committee representative of the different overseas branches."[16]

When the World Evangelical Fellowship was founded in 1951 with roots in the Evangelical Alliance it was recognized that some confusion could result with the use of a similar name. Therefore in 1953 action was taken to revert to the original name. This is recorded as follows:

> At the Annual General Business Meeting held on May 28th, 1953, a resolution was unanimously passed to the effect that the organization known since 1912 as the World's Evangelical Alliance (British Organization) should revert to the original name given it by its founders in 1846, namely that of the Evangelical Alliance. This change was made for two reasons. In the first place, the formation of the World Evangelical Fellowship made it desirable to change the name of the Alliance in order to avoid the inconsistency of having two "world" bodies in direct association with each other; and secondly, the coming into being of the European Committee of the Evangelical Alliance made it advisable to alter the name of the British organization in order to bring it into line with the other branches.[17]

## Conclusion

Let us conclude this historical survey with the words of Ruth

Rouse, which summarize beautifully the development of the movement:

> In a class by itself must be placed the continuous work of the World's Evangelical Alliance, which for more than a hundred years has based its membership and its activities on the central conviction of the unity of individual Christians who, though belonging to many churches, hold the same faith. During the 20th century the Alliance has pursued its traditional unitive activities in stimulating missionary activity, in rousing a consciousness of unity amongst "Evangelicals," and above all in the Universal Week of Prayer. In recent years it is more and more realizing itself as a *World* Alliance, is initiating new methods of drawing evangelicals of all nations together, and seeking new ways of promoting evangelism and missions.[18]

# CHAPTER FOUR

# The Founding of the World Evangelical Fellowship

As World War II drew to a close the world was rapidly and irrevocably changing. Harbingers of the space age had already been seen in the powerful rockets that Germany had developed to carry the devastating V-II bombs which terrorized London in the final year of the war. The mushroom clouds over Hiroshima and Nagasaki changed the face of the world and the course of diplomacy in a way unparalleled by any other single event since the invention of gunpowder. The amazing speed of jet travel was already on the horizon, threatening the development of jet planes of warfare. The idea that countries could continue to survive in isolation from each other was fast becoming obsolete.

The concept of "one world" was popularized in Wendell Wilkie's book of that title. The formation of the United Nations was an outgrowth of the same concept. On 1 January, 1942, the allied nations opposing the Axis signed a declaration signifying the uniting of nations in a common cause. This concept was developed during the war years, until on 26 June, 1945, fifty-one nations signed the United Nations Charter at San Francisco. No longer could nations live in blissful seclusion from the rest of the world.

These same ideas of unity and cooperation which formed the basis of the U.N. had already been developed and promulgated in the Christian world by the Evangelical Alliance since 1846. The growth of the ecumenical movement was another indication of the recognition of the need for cooperation and unity. World missions conferences in Edinburgh (1910), Jerusalem (1928) and Tambaram, Madras (1938), had led the way to the formation in 1948 of the World Council of Churches.[1]

The activities and influence of the Evangelical Alliance seemed to wane during the first decades of the twentieth century. The last international conference sponsored by the Alliance had been held in 1907, and attendance was considerably less than at previous conferences. The American branch of the Evangelical Alliance had, for all practical purposes, ceased to function after the turn of the century, although it continued "on paper" to exist until 1944.

*Moves Towards Unity*

Evangelicals, however, were increasingly recognizing the need for an outward demonstration of unity and for cooperative action on behalf of the gospel. In 1929 the New England Fellowship was formed under the leadership of J. Elwin Wright. Summer Bible conferences at Rumney, New Hampshire; camping programmes for boys and girls; daily gospel radio broadcasts; bookstores for distributing evangelical literature in New England; Christian education ministry in the public schools; and the opening of closed churches were some of the activities of this Fellowship.[2]

The annual conferences of the New England Fellowship in 1939, 1940, and 1941 "adopted resolutions calling for the organization of a national fellowship."[3] In 1941 Dr Wright made a tour of 31 states interviewing evangelical leaders with the purpose of forming a national fellowship.

On 27–28 October, 1941, a small group of men met at Moody Bible Institute in Chicago to consider the feasibility of such a movement. Out of this meeting came a call, signed by 147 evangelical leaders, to a National Conference for United Action Among Evangelicals held in St. Louis on 7–9 April, 1942. At this meeting the seed of the National Association of Evangelicals (NAE) was sown.

Historian Bruce Shelley lists three major reasons for the

creation of NAE: first, "a dissatisfaction with other expressions of Christian unity," such as the Federal Council of Churches of Christ, with its emphasis on the "social gospel;" second, "a sense of isolation among conservative Christians;" third, "the firm conviction that a positive witness could be given by united evangelicals and only by united evangelicals."[4]

The Call to the St. Louis Conference declared:

> It is our belief that something of this nature can become a basis for an effective cooperation among evangelicals by which our mutual interests may be conserved and aided. There are millions of evangelical Christians in this country who feel that at present they have no corporate means of making their wishes known in matters common to all. We believe the time has come to render God this service.[5]

In May, 1943, a Constitutional Convention was held in Chicago when NAE was formally organized. Its purposes were to encourage united action among evangelicals in evangelism, local and national use of radio for gospel preaching, public relations, representation of evangelical positions before the government, preservation of separation of church and state, Christian education, and the guarantee of freedom for home and foreign missionary outreach. These same purposes, together with others that have been added over the years, continue to characterize the ministry of NAE.

Dr J. Elwin Wright was chosen as the first executive secretary and Dr Harold J. Ockenga, pastor of Boston's Park Street Church, was chosen as president. Dr Wright established the office of NAE in Boston and was ably assisted by his long time colleague and secretary, Miss Elizabeth Evans, who had served with him in the New England Fellowship.

> Within two years after the National Association of Evangelicals was organized in Chicago in 1943 there was already interest in encouraging closer ties of fellowship with believers overseas. From various countries Christian leaders expressed a wish to join N.A.E. This was impractical as N.A.E. was exclusively a United States organization. However several outstanding evangelical leaders, including Dr T. Christie Innes and Dr Harold John Ockenga, visited England and discussed the need of international evangelical cooperation along the lines laid down by N.A.E.
>
> This was followed by Dr Wright's first visit to England in 1946. He conferred with leaders and visited the Evangelical Alliance as an official representative of the National Association of Evangelicals. He also conferred with leaders on the continent, visiting France, Switzerland,

Germany, Holland, and Belgium, explaining N.A.E.'s formula for
evangelical fellowship.[6]

As a result of these initial contacts a meeting was held in
Clarens, Switzerland, in 1948, to which NAE invited leaders
of the Evangelical Alliance of Great Britain. Two representatives from Great Britain attended, Prebendary Gough and
the General Secretary of the Evangelical Alliance, H. Martyn
Gooch. The possibility of calling a world conference of
evangelicals was discussed, but it was decided that the post-
war turmoil of Europe plus the shortness of time for
preparation of such a conference made it inadvisable at that
time.[7]

## Bringing the World Together

Two years later, on 7–10 March, 1950, an International
Delegate Conference was held at Hildenborough Hall in
Kent, England. Representatives from twelve countries of
Europe, including the Evangelical Alliance of Great Britain,
together with delegates from the NAE in America attended.
An International Committee was formed. and Lt. Gen. Sir
Arthur Smith—elected unanimously as chairman. It was
pointed out "that the basis of belief would be the foundation
stone on which all were to build, but that each movement
would be autonomous as to the details of the application of
this basis to their national situation."[8]

A similar conference was convened at Gordon Divinity
School in Boston, on 4–8 September, 1950, "at which it was
recommended to set up an International Association of
Evangelicals with a threefold purpose: 1) to witness to
evangelical and historic Christianity, 2) to encourage and
promote fellowship among Evangelicals and 3) to stimulate
evangelism and promote united evangelical action in all
spheres."[9]

At about the same time in 1950 the NAE formally organized
an NAE Commission on International Relations with Dr Harold
J. Ockenga as chairman and Dr J. Elwin Wright as executive
secretary. The purpose of this commission was to encourage
and foment evangelical cooperation on a worldwide scale. In

1956 the name of this commission was changed to the NAE Commission for the World Evangelical Fellowship, although even at later dates the former name appears in some NAE documents. This eventually became the board of the NAE USA Corporation of the World Evangelical Fellowship, which is the legal body in the USA responsible for the finances of WEF.

As a result of the two meetings of 1950 held at Hildenborough Hall and Gordon Divinity School J. Elwin Wright and Clyde W. Taylor were requested to make a world tour in the interests of evangelical cooperation. It was not be be an organizing tour but rather one to stimulate interest in united action. From 12 October 1950 to 28 January 1951 these two men undertook that responsibility. One is left somewhat breathless today in reading the accounts of the extent of their trip, especially when one realizes that this was before the days of jet travel. To give an idea of the scope of this trip it is worth mentioning the cities they visited: Tokyo, Manila, Hong Kong, Bangkok, Calcutta, Nagpur, Akola, Bombay, Fatehpur, Allahabad, New Delhi, Beirut, Damascus, Amman, Jericho, Jerusalem, Nicosia, Athens, Rome, Zurich, Geneva, Marseilles, Barcelona, Paris, Amsterdam, and London. They discovered, among other things, that evangelical fellowships were already being formed in other places such as Japan, India, and Cyprus.[10]

Because of these experiences the International Committee formed at Hildenborough Hall issued a call to an "International Convention of Evangelicals (of lands around the world)" to meet at Woudschoten, a student retreat hostel near Zeist in the Netherlands, on 5–11 August 1951. 91 delegates, visitors, and observers from 21 countries gathered for that week in a spirit of expectancy and hope.

*The Woudschoten Convention*

Since the opening day was Sunday, it was spent largely in worship, fellowship, and prayer.

In the morning worship service, Direktor Heitmuller of Hamburg,

Germany, spoke of the necessity of close fellowship with God and with each other, allowing God to lead us out into a new thing. In the afternoon, an address was brought by Rev. John R. W. Stott, of London, on the theme, "The Holy Spirit and the Church," an exposition of I Corinthians 12 . . . The evening was devoted . . . to brief reports on the three previous international meetings . . . Following this, Mr. John Bolten, of Lawrence, USA, brought a special message on the nature of the Church.[11]

At the opening business session on Monday, 6 August, greetings were read from Princess Wilhelmina of the Netherlands; Prince Oscar Bernadotte of Sweden; President and Madame Chiang Kai Shek of China; and Sir Henry T. Holland, president of the British organization of the World's Evangelical Alliance. Most of that day was spent in hearing reports from various areas of the world summarizing the situation of the church and the state of evangelical cooperation.

On Tuesday, 7 August, it was moved "that we proceed with constituting a worldwide fellowship".

A very strong feeling was expressed, especially by the delegates from the Orient, that the need for such a world fellowship is very great. In the third session of the day on Tuesday, the motion of the morning was carried by a large majority, but with four national delegates against it: Denmark, Norway, Sweden, and France. Delegates of all other countries favoured it.[12]

Several possible names were considered: International Association of Evangelicals, International Evangelical Association, World's Evangelical Alliance, International Evangelical Fellowship, and World's Evangelical Fellowship. However, the final vote established the name as The World Evangelical Fellowship.

Considerable work had already gone into drafting a constitution including a doctrinal statement, which, it was felt, would form an indispensable foundation on which to build the cooperation being sought. This did not precipitate nearly as much controversy or discussion as is sometimes experienced in such conferences when matters of policy and doctrine are hammered out. The official minutes simply state that:

The conference then proceeded to draft the constitution and by-laws, using as a basis the preliminary draft which had been prepared by the Interim Committee and previously circulated to all national movements. It was unanimously agreed:

. . . That the constitution and by-laws as adopted should be submitted to each national movement for ratification and that all qualified movements adopting the actions of the Woudschoten Conference on or before August 31, 1952, be charter members.[13]

The statement of faith included in the constitution was as follows:

We believe in the Holy Scriptures as originally given by God, divinely inspired, infallible, entirely trustworthy; and the supreme authority in all matters of faith and conduct . . .
One God, eternally existent in three persons, Father, Son, and Holy Spirit . . .
Our Lord Jesus Christ, God manifest in the flesh, His virgin birth, His sinless human life, His divine miracles, His vicarious and atoning death, His bodily resurrection, His ascension, His mediatorial work, and His personal return in power and glory . . .
The Salvation of lost and sinful man through the shed blood of the Lord Jesus Christ by faith apart from works, and regeneration by the Holy Spirit . . .
The Holy Spirit, by whose indwelling the believer is enabled to live a holy life, to witness and work for the Lord Jesus Christ . . .
The Unity of the Spirit of all true believers, the Church, the Body of Christ . . .
The Resurrection of both the saved and the lost; they that are saved unto the resurrection of life, they that are lost unto the resurrection of damnation.[14]

It is worthy of note that this doctrinal statement has remained unchanged since 1951 and today is, word for word, the doctrinal statement of the World Evangelical Fellowship.

The purposes of WEF were discussed and determined to be:

(a) The furtherance of the Gospel (Phil. 1:11)
(b) The defence and confirmation of the Gospel (Phil. 1:7)
(c) Fellowship in the Gospel (Phil. 1.5) 15

Bishop A. J. Dain, who was present at that conference, once told the author, in referring to these purposes, "John Stott dictated them; I wrote them down." Those of us who know John Stott can well appreciate that it might well be his incisive mind that would come up with the suggestion for these succinctly stated purposes.

In a personal letter to the author dated 1 August 1985, John Stott confirms this: "I remember suggesting that those three expressions about the gospel in the first chapter of Philippians would make a good summary of the WEF's three main purposes: Those were memorable days."

A General Committee was chosen which, according to the By-Laws, was to manage the affairs of the Fellowship. It consisted of the following members:

> Lt.-Gen. Sir Arthur Smith (England) *President*
> Mr John Bolten (USA) *Treasurer*
> Dr A. P. Guruswamy (Ceylon)
> Direktor F. Heitmuller (Germany)
> Revd K. S. Hiraide (Japan)
> Dr Clarence W Jones (Ecuador)
> Dr Harold John Ockenga (USA)
> Revd W. Zilz (Germany)

Mr F. Roy Cattell of London and Dr J. Elwin Wright of Boston were chosen as co-secretaries. It was agreed that:

> . . . the administrative work, from an office point of view should be largely carried on in London; Dr. Wright should be primarily responsible for visiting those countries where there is need of establishing national evangelical fellowships. It was understood that a close liaison should be maintained between London and Boston . . .
>
> Reference was made to the appointment of Mr. A. J. Dain to the staff of W.E.A. effective December 1951, and his responsibility in connection with the coordination of missionary interests in Great Britain and international aspects.[16]

Four standing commissions were established at the outset with the following leadership and purposes:

> EVANGELISM: Dr Harold J. Ockenga (USA), chairman; ". . . to stimulate evangelism by every possible means in every part of the world."
>
> MISSIONARY: Dr Clyde W. Taylor (USA), chairman; to promote "closer coordination and cooperation between missionary societies in different countries where greatly needed."
>
> LITERATURE: Dr Rene Pache (Switzerland), chairman; "for the coordination of supply and demand to ensure the maximum efficiency of all existing literature agencies."
>
> CHRISTIAN ACTION: The Rt. Revd Hugh R. Gough (England), chairman; "for action in defence of Christian liberty on behalf of persecuted minorities, and in other spheres of Christian life and witness."[17]

A closing service attended by 800 people was held on Friday, 10 August, in the Moravian Church of Zeist. A delegate from each country gave a text of Scripture in his own language, the Statement of Faith was read in French and Dutch, and Dr Ockenga brought the closing address, which was a challenge to the church for renewed evangelism in that hour of crisis.

## Moving into Action

The first major project undertaken by the newly-founded WEF was to sponsor a promotional tour of the USA by the president, Lt.-Gen. Sir Arthur Smith, and Dr Oswald J. Smith, pastor of The People's Church of Toronto. From 30 October to 9 December, 1951, these two men held 37 mass meetings in cities across the United States to introduce WEF to the evangelical public.

Then on 26 December, 1951, Dr J. Elwin Wright and Dr Paul Rees, president of NAE, embarked on a round-the-world trip on behalf of WEF. They travelled 31,000 miles and visited 24 countries. The purposes of their trip were, first, to have a spiritual ministry to evangelicals in other countries; second, to promote evangelical cooperation; and third, to learn of the needs of other lands where help could be provided through WEF. In reporting on this trip they wrote:

> We are convinced that the best methods of promoting the interests of WEF would be by a concern for the spiritual interests of those with whom we met, rather than by direct overtures to them regarding membership.[18]

The needs that impressed themselves most on the two men, according to their reports, were the need for training of national leadership and the need for adequate Christian literature.

In the course of this trip they were privileged to participate in the first annual meeting of the Evangelical Fellowship of India, held in Akola. EFI was one of the earliest national fellowships to be formed and has proved over the years to be one of the best organized and best led members of WEF. Dr Wright commented:

> EFI in its first year of existence has proven its great value. It is lifting a high standard spiritually, is tolerant and friendly to all groups, and is

attaining a great degree of respect among all organizations . . . I believe
it is destined to exercise a great influence on the spiritual life of India.[19]

One discordant note on the founding of WEF was that at
Woudschoten some of the European nations did not wish to
subscribe to the use of the word "infallible," in reference to
the scriptures, in the Statement of Faith. The result was that
in 1952 the European Evangelical Alliance was formed
completely independently of WEF. It was not until 1968 that
this breach was finally mended and the European Evangelical
Alliance became a member of WEF.

Apart from that one discordant note, there was a euphoric
sense of excitement and vision as the new body was
launched on its quest to promote unity and cooperation
among evangelicals around the world.

# CHAPTER FIVE

# Early Growth

One year after the founding of WEF, Dr J. Elwin Wright reported to the International Committee at its first meeting held on 26–28 August, 1952 at Pirbright Lodge in Woking, England. "The first year of the existence of WEF," he commented, "has definitely not been one of marking time, but rather of advance and progress . . ."[1] The trip which Dr Wright and Dr Rees had made around the world had laid the foundation for growing contacts and interest in the concept of evangelical unity. Plans were being laid for the first General Council meeting (in later years to be known as the General Assembly) to be held in 1953.

*General Council Meeting of WEF, 27–31 July, 1953*

The St. George's School in Clarens, Switzerland, on the shores of beautiful Lake Geneva, was the site of the first meeting of the General Council. Invitations were extended to all national evangelical fellowships that had been formed up to that time. 7 of these had become charter members of WEF by subscribing to the Statement of Faith prior to the first meeting of the International Committee (held one year after the Constitutional Convention of August, 1951, in Holland). These were the Evangelical Fellowship of Ceylon, Gospel Workers' Fellowship, Cyprus, the Evangelical Alliance of

Great Britain, the Evangelical Fellowship of India, the Japanese Association of Evangelicals, and the National Association of Evangelicals of the USA.

At Clarens 6 more bodies were received into membership. These were the national fellowships of Singapore, Hawaii (not yet a formal state of the USA), Switzerland, Germany, France and Holland.[2]

Although plans were laid for about eighty delegates to attend the conference in Clarens, registrations numbered 171 from 23 countries. This included a delegation of 52 who flew over from America on a KLM charter flight which had been arranged by Dr Wright and his secretary, Miss Elizabeth Evans. Every continent except Australia was represented. While official delegates came from the member bodies, attendance was also open to observers and visitors. A brochure announcing the conference said:

> All who are interested in the development of worldwide evangelical cooperation are invited to attend this conference. Many of the sessions will be open to all fraternal delegates and observers . . .
>
> All Christians desiring to attend as observers or fraternal delegates are cordially invited to the open sessions held daily.

The same brochure announces the purpose and platform for WEF by quoting directly from the constitution which had been adopted at Woudschoten in 1951. With respect to its purpose, the preamble of the constitution states the premise on which it is founded.

> God so loved the world that He gave His only begotten Son to be its Savior. It is His purpose, as revealed in His Word to call out for Himself from the world a people, the Church of Jesus Christ. This worldwide company of Christian believers, redeemed by the Son of God, indwelt by the Spirit of God, and being one in Christ Jesus, have a duty both to worship Him and to go into all the world to preach the Gospel.
>
> Those who become associated in this Fellowship declare their purpose to be:
> (a) The furtherance of the Gospel (Phil. 1:12);
> (b) The defense and confirmation of the Gospel (Phil. 1:7);
> (c) Fellowship in the Gospel (Phil. 1:5).

In establishing a platform for the organisation, the Constitution further declares that the fellowship is committed to:

> 1. Belief, without mental reservation, in the basic doctrines of our faith as expressed in the Statement of Faith;

2. Acceptance into active cooperation with us, and service for our Lord Jesus Christ, of all who hold these doctrines and give evidence of loyalty to them, though there may be differences in conviction on other points of doctrine or ecclesiastical government;

3. Obedience to the commands of Scripture by renunciation of all cooperation with unbelief in, and apostasy from, these doctrines;

4. Recognition of the complete autonomy of every constituent national or area-wide body within the Fellowship;

5. Dedication to a programme of mutual helpfulness in the propagation of the Gospel, the defence of Christian liberties and the attainment of objectives which are of common concern.

Daily Bible readings were given by Dr Paul Rees. Evening sessions for three nights centred on the three stated purposes of WEF, namely "Fellowship in the Gospel"— where the speakers were the Revd L. F. E. Wilkinson and Dr Rene Pache; "The Defence of the Gospel"—Direktor F. Heitmuller and Dr Frederick Curtis Fowler; "The Furtherance of the Gospel"—Revd John Savage and Revd Calvin Chao. On the final night, Friday, 31 July, a public rally was held in Lausanne with Dr Paul Rees and the Rt Revd Hugh R. Gough as speakers.

Dr Wright evaluated the conference with these words:

The harmony and understanding which existed from the very beginning was a remarkable evidence of the presence of the Holy Spirit in our midst.

General Sir Arthur Smith presided, with his usual efficiency, so that no time was wasted in pointless discussion . . .

. . . In Clarens the document (the constitution) was considered again in the light of our two years' experience and finally adopted with a few minor changes.

It was voted that World Evangelical Fellowship should establish a separate office with its own full time executive secretariat, as soon as arrangements could be perfected. Preference was expressed for Washington, D.C. as the location. As soon as this change can be brought about, each member organization will share in the expense of operation on an equitable basis, taking into consideration the ability of each.[3]

The plans for a full time executive secretariat were not to be fulfilled for over twenty years, when Waldron Scott became the first full time general secretary in 1975. Plans for each member organization to share in the expense of the operation have never fully materialized.

Prior to the conference in Clarens, Revd A. J. Dain of Great

Britain had replaced Mr F. Roy Cattell and was now serving as co-secretary of WEF with Dr J. Elwin Wright. The two offices in London and Boston were maintained with approximately the same division of duties that had originally been outlined. A new Executive Committee (referred to previously as "General Committee"), was elected with the following members:

Gen. Sir Arthur Smith (England) *President*
Mr John Bolten (USA) *Treasurer*
Direktor F. Heitmuller (Germany) *Vice President*
Dr A. P. Guruswamy (Ceylon) *Vice President*
Dr Paul S. Rees (USA) *Vice President*
Revd Calvin Chao (Singapore) *Member at Large*
Dr E. L. Cattell (India) *Member at Large*
Revd John Savage (South America) *Member at Large*
Revd J. Dordreuil (France) *Member at Large*[3]

The same four commissions established at Woudschoten were confirmed with the same chairman.

*Members, Ministries and Money*

Membership was defined in those days as follows:

Membership as defined in the following categories, is open to all who accept without mental reservation the Statement of Faith.
*Full Members:* National fellowship of believers in any country which represnts an adequate cross section of evangelical life and interests, always providing that they are truly interdenominational in character. These members alone have full voting powers.
*Associate Members:* Similar fellowships, or small evangelical denominations or churches which represent only a section of evangelical life and interests in the area. Such members have all the advantages of full membership except in voting.
*Individual Membership:* Where no organization exists for the drawing together of evangelicals individuals may be received into individual membership.[4]

Programmes that were being developed during that period of time included an emphasis on the following areas: *evangelism*, through encouraging the national fellowships in aggressive outreach; *prayer life*, through promoting the annual Week of Prayer begun over a century before by the Evangelical Alliance; *conferences and retreats*, through the ministry of special speakers who were sponsored by WEF, men such as Donald Barnhouse, Robert Munger, Harry Hager, J. Edwin Orr, Theodore Elsner, Herbert Mekeel, Paul Rees, Bob Pierce, whom WEF helped to make available to the church around the world for special ministries; *scholarship programmes* for students from the Third World to study abroad when no adequate training facilities were available in their country; *books for libraries* of Bible institutes and seminaries in Third World countries. In the first year of WEF Dr Wright's office shipped 8,000 volumes overseas to 48 Christian schools and three lending libraries in 26 countries.[5] There were also efforts being started to help in literature production and distribution, radio ministries, Christian education, government relations, and other areas where the church and national fellowships needed help.

In the area of finances WEF faced major difficulties from its very inception. By the nature of its structures it could not assess adequate fees from its membership to cover the costs of the organization, even though this was one of its goals. There was voluminous correspondence between J. Elwin Wright and many Christian leaders, business and professional people, and others in which he discussed the need for the financial underwriting of WEF. He initiated an ambitious programme called SHARE, which was to develop donors for WEF in order to make it financially solvent and viable. Generous help was given by several Christian businessmen such as Mr Herbert J. Taylor of Chicago and Mr John Bolten of Lawrence, Massachusetts, during the formative years of WEF. Without these men WEF never could have established itself. The files of WEF contain hundreds of letters concerning Dr Wright's vision for the SHARE programme. Sadly, this dream was never fulfilled and was finally dropped as unworkable.

Periodically there appear in the files of the period letters or reports of a crisis nature indicating that financial bankruptcy was just around the corner. On more than one occasion Dr Wright opted not to receive his own salary because of the lack of funds. Efforts were always made to reimburse him for lost salary, but it is possible that he bore personal losses that were never fully recovered. This same situation was true of other General Secretaries in later years.

In a 1966 report the following statements are found:

> Even though each fellowship is to pay a membership fee for belonging
> to the WEF, most are struggling financially and have given very little
> support to the international body. When a general secretary has been
> paid or projects have been supported, for the most part the support has
> come from Great Britain and the United States. The WEF has frequently
> been considered "nobody's baby" . . .
>
> The procurement of funds continue [sic] to be one of the great
> problems of the WEF. It has been found lacking in services to its national
> constituencies and their suggested programs, to a large degree it is due
> to the fact that it has been unable to support staff on the field. Until
> evangelicals awaken to the great threat inherent in the fact that their
> overseas churches are not being tied together internationally, it is
> predicted that the World Evangelical Fellowship will have a difficult
> time securing adequate financial support.[6]

Although written in 1966 this represents the type of
statement found in reports, letters, and minutes dating back
to the earliest days of WEF.

## The WEF *BULLETIN*

Another project that had been started immediately after the
founding of WEF and was continued for many years was the
publication of the *World Evangelical Fellowship* BULLETIN. The
first edition (Volume 1, number 1) was dated January, 1952.
It consisted of four pages in fold-over format containing a
letter from J. Elwin Wright, news "flashes" from around the
world, and the travel schedule of Dr Wright and Dr Rees for
their world tour. The second edition, dated April, 1952, was
expanded to eight pages. The July, 1952, edition had
progressed to glossy paper and contained six pages in fold-
out format.

Over the years the format changed from time to time, but
the content was generally similar. The *BULLETIN* contained
letters from the General Secretary, church and mission news
from around the world, itineraries of key WEF leaders who
were travelling, news of the fund raising efforts, news of
development of new projects in such fields as literature,
education, medicine, radio, and related ministries, reports of
national evangelical fellowships, and reports on the persecution of Christians in many parts of the world. It served a

valuable purpose in keeping WEF members and others informed of their mutual interests and ministries.

*Travels*

Dr Wright and other leaders of WEF continued to travel tirelessly to many areas of the world to promote the concept of spiritual unity and to encourage the development of national evangelical fellowships as well as to exercise a spiritual ministry to the church. On 9 December 1954, Dr Wright, accompanied by Mr Floyd G. Keck, a layman from Ohio who was a member of the NAE International Commission, took off on a 32,000 mile trip in which the two men visited 21 countries. They travelled through England, Europe, the Middle East, India, Southeast Asia, Northeast Asia, and back to the USA via Hawaii. They conferred with leaders of national fellowships, with mission leaders, and with churchmen of many backgrounds. They ministered in churches, schools, and conventions. It was also their privilege in a few countries to have interviews with high government officials, including President Syngman Rhee of Korea, who was about to celebrate his eightieth birthday.

One notation of special interest, in the light of more recent history, comes from Dr Wright's comments on their visit to Vietnam. He says,

> I also had an opportunity to visit some of the refugee villages which now have a population of over 600,000 refugees from the north. We also visited one of the large military hospitals, and watched the unloading of a refugee ship, on our final day in Saigon. These unfortunate people are still coming from the north at the rate of 10,000 weekly and constitute a grave problem. They are utterly without worldly goods, except what they were able to bring in their hands, and the government allowance has to be supplemented with food from private organizations in order to keep them from starving. We conferred with the leaders, both in regard to getting food and clothing to them, and also some provision for spiritual leadership in these refugee villages. The Roman Catholic priests and nuns are moving into Viet Nam in large numbers and occupying many of the refugee villages.[7]

This influx of refugees followed the battle of Dien Pien Phu when the Viet Minh forces under General Vo Nguyen Giap captured this French stronghold, forcing the French to surrender on 7 May, 1954. At a conference held in Geneva in July, 1954, Vietnam was divided into north and south sections. As the Viet Minh under Ho Chi Minh took strong and ruthless measures to consolidate control of the north, refugees began to pour across into the south causing the situation which Dr Wright and Mr Keck saw during their visit. Reports written twenty or twenty-five years later in the same area of the world would describe an identical tragic situation.

Also in 1954 Dr Clyde Taylor and Mr Dawson Trotman, founder and President of The Navigators, along with Mr John Savage of the Evangelical Alliance in Great Britain, travelled through South America.

> Numerous conferences were held in all the republics of Latin America, everywhere urging evangelical action and encouraging evangelical fellowship. Whereas, as yet, no associate members of WEF exist in Latin America there is a notable development of a very fine fellowship among evangelicals in this area.[8]

In 1955 Clyde Taylor was once again on the road for a lengthy trip to Africa. He visited 21 countries "encouraging closer evangelical cooperation in all of these countries."[9] This journey was sponsored by the Evangelical Foreign Missions Association of NAE, but Dr Taylor also represented WEF in the tour. This kind of travelling exploit, covering many weeks or months and including numerous countries, was typical of the activities of the early leaders of WEF. They seemed to be men of iron with tireless energy, limitless vision, and a spirit of self-sacrifice not often seen today.

## *Making Progress*

A sense of the progress being made in the years following the Clarens conference can be felt in the report of J. Elwin Wright given to the NAE convention in April, 1956. After reporting on finances he says:

> We have other financial needs, however. World Evangelical Fellowship is the sponsor of SHARE, which was created to provide a fund for

assisting our associated organizations around the world in their most pressing needs. In this way we are becoming a "sort of Red Cross" for spiritual emergencies, which have to do with nation-wide needs rather than those of individual missions or churches. Our information as to the greatest needs comes from the executives of those associated national fellowships. Between April 1 and December 31, 1955, $27,136.03 was received for these purposes.

We look with satisfaction on the practical results of our overseas ministry when we consider the institutions in several countries which would never have been organized had it not been for the Commission on International Relations and the American section of WEF. Also, we have sent more than 90,000 volumes abroad for lending libraries and libraries of evangelical schools.

Fifteen nationals of unusual promise from several foreign lands have received graduate education in America under our sponsorship. Still others will be coming this autumn.

Under our encouragement or sponsorship the finest leadership in America has gone abroad on special missions designed to assist in bringing spiritual revival.

But perhaps the greatest service has been rendered by the constant encouragement we have given to the leaders of overseas countries to get together in cooperative projects, to the end that the whole programme of world evangelism may be stepped up.[10]

The vision of 1846 was beginning to be fulfilled!

# CHAPTER SIX

# Emphasis on People

At the time of the International Conference of the General Committee in 1953, it was felt that such a conference should be held every three years. In the following years reference was frequently made to "the triennial conference."

Thus the next conference was held on 27–31 August, 1956, at Providence-Barrington Bible College in Barrington, Rhode Island, USA. There were official delegations from Ceylon, Cyprus, France, Great Britain, Greece, India, Japan, Korea, Singapore, Spain, Switzerland, Taiwan, and the United States. Observers came from Brazil, Canada, Costa Rica, Cuba, Haita, Indonesia, Japan, Korea, the Philippines, Thailand, and the United States. It is interesting to note that the largest single delegation (apart from the USA, which was the host country) came from Korea, with five delegates and two observers.

Actions taken at this conference decided the future policy of WEF in several areas. There was clear recognition of the autonomy of each national group.

> The Committee recognized with humility and profound thankfulness to God that the original aims of the Fellowship as set out in the Constitution were being steadily achieved and that the development of the Fellowship in many major areas had reached a stage where, within each area, on the basis of complete autonomy, a full measure of functional responsibility should be assumed.[1]

This point was reinforced in the By-laws at that time with this clause:

> Nothing contained in these By-Laws shall give any power to the Fellowship to control the activities of each area, national or regional group, which shall remain autonomous in the control and management of its internal affairs.[2]

There was also an agreement to work for the legal incorporation of WEF in the USA, especially for the purposes of tax exemption.

> It was agreed that ratification be accorded to the action taken by the executive committee members in London . . . to effect the incorporation of the W.E.F. in the U.S.A., and thus to secure recognition by the U.S. Bureau of Internal Revenue for tax exemption purposes; and further that the above mentioned American members of the International Executive, plus additional members to a total of nine, elected annually by the N.A.E. Board of Administration, be authorized to serve as the W.E.F. Incorporated Board.[3]

It was agreed that the interests of WEF could best be served by dividing the world into geographical regions. Each of these regions should be "invited to establish a representative committee and secretariat with a chairman who shall hold office for three years (or until a successor be appointed) and who shall be ex-officio Vice-President of the W.E.F."[4] The regions recommended were Asia, Europe, North America, Latin America, Africa and Australasia.

*New Developments*

The By-Laws reflect one additional category of membership beyond that which was established at Clarens in 1953.

> In areas where full or associate membership is not yet possible, groups may be admitted to correspondent membership.[5]

Resolutions were passed related to a variety of topics such as "the continuing relevance of the evangelical witness," the need for a treatise "on the doctrine of biblical inspiration and revelation," and "the vital importance of sound evangelical literature," with a recommendation that each national area appoint a Literature Committee for the purpose of production and distribution of Bible study books, Christian magazines and other "truly evangelical literature which is acceptable also from the point of view of the national cultures, languages and style."[6]

One rather interesting resolution listed under "Religious Liberty" asked "that Dr Clyde Taylor be instructed to investigate the possibility of W.E.F. becoming a corresponding member of the United Nations Organization; and that the Executive Committee be authorized to take necessary action to secure such representation."[7] Dr Taylor followed through on this resolution both in Washington and also with a trip to the United Nations headquarters in New York. After considerable study it was determined that such a step was not necessary or wise for WEF.

The International Executive Committee elected for the next three years consisted of most of the same men elected in 1953 with the following changes: the Rt. Revd Hugh Gough of England replaced Direktor F. Heitmuller of Germany as a vice-president, Revd J. Dordreuil of France was replaced as a member at large by Dr Rene Pache of Switzerland, and Revd E. A. Lee of Korea and Revd A. Kurumada of Japan were added. Dr J. Elwin Wright and Revd A. J. Dain were asked to continue as co-secretaries with the offices in Boston and London respectively.

## VIPS in Disguise

Perhaps the best summary of the results of that conference is given by the co-secretary, J. Elwin Wright, in October, 1956:

> Just a few weeks ago some of us gathered at the Providence-Barrington Bible College for the Triennial International Conference of World Evangelical Fellowship. All who were present will agree that it was an experience of Christian fellowship which we can never forget. It was also fellowship leading to action.
>
> Delegates and observers came from twenty-seven countries. Among them were some of the top executives of national fellowships which now exist in many countries. Not all of these have joined W.E.F. as yet, but undoubtedly are on their way to such action.
>
> Before reporting to you the important decisions made in the business sessions I would like to speak of other things of equal importance which characterized this unique conference.

To my mind the thing which mattered most was the fact that, regardless of nationality, we met as brethren in Christ. If there were any VIPs there (VERY IMPORTANT PEOPLE) I didn't meet them. That was something to be thankful for!

And yet, viewed from a heavenly standpoint, there may well have been several VIPs (very well disguised). I wonder if one of them might be that delegate from an Oriental country who had given many years of his life to be a missionary to another country. He spent much of his savings to make the long journey to America because he has a deep conviction of the significance of W.E.F. in the world picture. He couldn't speak English but it was not difficult to sense his deep devotion to our Lord and his dedication to the Great Commission.

There was another one, a man who is writing a new chapter in the history of Christian work in his country. A man who gave the only land he owned to make possible a Bible Institute for the training of national leadership to carry out the vision of a truly indigenous church. A man who even sold his most indispensable possession—his motor car—that the work of building might not be halted.

Yes, now that I think of it, there were several other VIPs in attendance, none of them wearing decorations, only scars for the Lord Jesus Christ. One was a young man of great promise in the work of Christ. He seems utterly unconscious of his own abilities. Only two generations removed from head hunter forebears, he was unanimously elected Secretary of the fellowships of the whole continent of Asia—an honor which left him somewhat in a state of shock because he felt he was unworthy.

Then we came to love another man of God, born in China but now, also a missionary to the nearly 90,000,000 people of Indonesia. His qualities of deep devotion, vision of a great work to be done, daring in undertaking the impossible, and selflessness, mark him as a leader who will play a large part in welding the evangelical movement in Asia into an irresistible force for the advancement of the work of God. All the above are but samples of God's handiwork in the development of evangelical stalwarts who are taking their places of responsibility in the Orient—the most strongly represented area in the Conference. Others of equal spiritual stature were present also and did much to assist by their wise counsel in laying foundations for united evangelical action.[8]

Following the conference at Barrington some key leaders of WEF remained in the USA for a period of several weeks for speaking engagements. These included Mr A. J. Dain, co-secretary of WEF, Dr A. P. Guruswamy, president of the Evangelical Fellowship of Ceylon, Revd D. Jose Martinez, secretary of the Evangelical Alliance of Spain, and Mr I. Ben Wati, assistant executive secretary of the Evangelical Fellowship of India. Mr Wati was to play a prominent role in the succeeding years both in EFI and in WEF.

It was recommended at Barrington that the next triennial conference of WEF be held in Asia in one of the following countries: Japan, Singapore, Ceylon, or Formosa. The decision was left to the International Executive for subsequent decision. As it turned out six years were to pass before the next conference was held, and, although it was held in Asia, the venue was Hong Kong.

# CHAPTER SEVEN

# Changing the Guard

By the middle of the 1950s Dr J. Elwin Wright had given a quarter of a century to promoting evangelical cooperation through the New England Fellowship, the NAE, and then WEF. It was only natural that he should request to be relieved of his responsibilities in WEF and that a younger person should be named in his place.

At the NAE convention on 9 April, 1956, in Cleveland, Ohio, Dr Wright closed his report with these words:

> I would like now to return to a subject which I have mentioned on several other occasions—that of my retirement from my present responsibilities to a subordinate relationship, at least.
>
> I am encouraged to believe that much more adequate leadership is becoming available to us. I not only wish to resign my secretarial post but I believe it is essential. I have already stayed on for many months beyond the limits which I long ago set as the deadline, because it seemed necessary.[1]

He then went on to request that a successor be appointed immediately. He stated that he was "willing to make any reasonable sacrifice for the work," but insisted that the replacement be arranged as rapidly as possible.

Intensive search was made to find a replacement for Dr Wright. This was no easy task, as few people had the experience, the background, the qualities of irenic leadership, or the stamina to assume such a position. Several attempts were made in different directions, but nearly two years passed before a final choice was made.

*The New Secretary*

On 4–6 December, 1958, Dr Wright and Revd A. J. Dain as co-secretaries met in Stroudsburg, Pennsylvania, with Dr Clyde Taylor, of the NAE office, and Mr Fred Ferris, executive director of the NAE Commission for WEF. As a result of their consultations they produced a list of fourteen recommendations to the WEF Executive Committee and the NAE. The substance of their recommendations was that the time had come to consolidate into one International Office for WEF and that this should be located in the USA with Revd Fred G. Ferris as International Secretary.

They requested that Mr Ferris continue to serve as executive director of the NAE Commission for WEF, and that his assistant, Mr Verle Nietzel, be asked to carry the bulk of the Commission business, thus freeing Mr Ferris to give more time to WEF. It was also recommended that "with the establishment of the International Office in the USA, provision be made to appoint an Assistant WEF Secretary for Europe, probably in London, and later in other major areas, for the coordination and implementation of regional WEF business."[2]

These recommendations were circulated through Gen. Sir Arthur Smith, President of WEF, to the membership requesting confirmation of such action. As a result Mr Fred Ferris was named International Secretary of WEF at the end of 1958. He had previously been in charge of Mr R. G. LeTourneau's projects in Liberia, and since December, 1957, had been serving as executive director of the NAE Commission for WEF.

Mr Ferris was already acquainted with many of the leaders and members of WEF. From 26 December, 1956, to 12 April, 1957, he had travelled around the world in the interests of WEF, even though he did not at that time hold the official position to which he was later named. He visited England, Lebanon, India, Ceylon, Singapore, Thailand, Vietnam, Hong Kong, Taiwan, Okinawa, and Japan.

*Assessing the World Scene*

It is enlightening to compare his comments from that trip

with certain recurring themes that emerge in WEF reports over the years. In England he met Gen. Sir Arthur Smith and Revd Gilbert Kirby and found their insights helpful.

> They both believe [he reported] that England has not accomplished much by way of a WEF Program these past three years. Lack of finances has been a hindering factor. Both men emphasized a spiritual rather than a material ministry. On this we were entirely in agreement.[3]

This reference to lack of finances represents perhaps the most common refrain found throughout the history of WEF. More will be said about it later, but it should be noted that there has been no era in WEF history when this problem has been absent.

In Lebanon he found "tremendous needs of the refugees, both with regard to their physical needs, and educational needs."[4] One is reminded of how that sad theme of refugees has characterized the land of Lebanon now for so many decades.

In India he found the Evangelical Fellowship of India to be "well organized . . . doing a grand job. Every area of Christian effort is included in its programme."[5] Reports of EFI over the years repeat this same sort of enthusiastic indication of a well organized and active fellowship. He visited the Union Biblical Seminary in Yeotmal, recently founded by EFI, and reported that it was "considered the best in Asia, although it is only five years old."[6]

In Vietnam he saw "staggering needs" in refugee work, again a reminder of the long-drawn-out agonies of that land. In Hong Kong he found "a strangely divided and muddled situation." Because of the uncertainty of the future for the church in Hong Kong at that time it seemed "unwise for any Chinese to affiliate with anything that has the stamp of Americanism upon it." Therefore, he recommended that "this is not the time for any W.E.F. move in Hong Kong."[7]

He reported that Japan was "another muddled situation," with three dominant groups among the evangelicals "riddled with sectarianism, suspicion and misunderstanding."[8] The possibilities of much cooperation in Japan at that time seemed remote. He found Japanese and mission leaders confessing that "the evangelical cause is more widely split and shattered in Japan than in any other country."[9]

Mr Ferris concluded this report with recommendations that regional offices of WEF be established and that the WEF *Bulletin* should be issued at least quarterly and circulated to members around the world. Again these are themes that have recurred throughout WEF's history, and represent areas of concern where efforts have been made at different stages but never with permanent results. The lack of finances invariably has been the major reason for failure to progress in such programmes.

*Further Journeys*

Immediately following his appointment as International Secretary of WEF Mr Ferris was in contact with Dr Clyde Taylor concerning a trip around the world to visit WEF members and leaders. Dr Taylor was at that time planning a trip on behalf of EFMA (Evangelical Foreign Missions Association) of which he was executive secretary. Plans were rapidly made for the two of them to travel together and funds were provided. Thus from 3 January to 25 March, 1959, these two men visited 18 countries in Europe, the Middle East, and Asia. Their reports and conclusions were similar to the findings of Mr Ferris on his trip two years earlier to many of the same countries. In some countries, such as India and Taiwan, they found continued vigorous leadership and growth. Some lands such as Japan and Korea showed continued divisions. Many other areas did not yet have national evangelical fellowships but were working towards forming one.

In reporting on this trip to the NAE Commission for WEF on 6 April, 1959, Mr Ferris concluded by saying:

> There are yet large areas of the world that have not been adequately informed regarding W.E.F. One or two inquiries have come from Africa, but on the whole, the African Continent is as yet outside the orbit of our ministry. Central and South America, Canada and the Scandinavian countries also present large areas as yet unreached by us.[10]

He went on to speak of "the importance of establishing a sound financial programme for underwriting the operational budget."[11] This was a continued burden to him, as he was spending much of his time in fund raising and promotional work rather than out in the field in ministry. "This has proven to be the failure of our W.E.F. effort in the past."[12] Once again a recurring theme is heard that has come through in the reports of every person who has held the responsibility for leadership in WEF. The difficulty of building a sound financial base for the operations and programmes of WEF has plagued it from the beginning.

Mr Ferris was clearly a well-organized administrator. His office and files were orderly and logical. His ability to perceive problems and to analyse perplexing situations were evident in his procedures and reports. Because he lived in Muscatine, Iowa, the International Office of WEF was moved to that town in 1959, a move which had been previously agreed by the Executive Committee. This led to some good-humoured comments occasionally, along with some concern that it was hardly the best place for an international office. Comments such as "I'm sure Muscatine must be a lovely town, but is it really the crossroads of the world?" appeared in correspondence from time to time. Mr Ferris expressed his willingness to move to Chicago or Washington if requested, but pointed out the heavy financial implications of such a move.

### Developments under Fred Ferris

In the summer of 1959 Mr Ferris began publishing *The WEF Witness*, a continuation of the WEF *Bulletin* which had been published since the early days of WEF. The summer issue of 1959 contains a letter from the secretary plus news from various areas of the world. For some unexplained reason Mr Ferris is identified in this publication as "executive secretary," whereas the title of "international secretary" is consistently used elsewhere, on his letterhead and in the signing of letters.

Later in 1959 Revd A. J. Dain, who since 1952 had been co-secretary of WEF with J. Elwin Wright, and who had been named Associate Secretary with Fred Ferris, accepted appointment as federal secretary of the Church Missionary Society of

Australia and moved to Sydney. The pressure of these new responsibilities made it difficult for Mr Dain to continue to be as active as he had previously been in WEF. Consequently, by 1960 the WEF letterhead listed him as "Hon. Advisor, W.E.F." and Revd Gilbert W. Kirby of England as "Consultative Secretary." Mr Kirby would later succeed Mr Ferris as International Secretary.

Mr Ferris' administrative nature and business abilities caused him to chafe under some of the limitations of a small organization with limited funds. Writing to A. J. Dain in July, 1960, he aired some of these frustrations:

> I had a very frank talk with Brother Gilbert Kirby while in London and he is of the opinion that we ought to do something immediately to convene at least an Executive of the WEF to face ourselves. I am certain you realize the almost impossible position I am in at present in which I have no Board to represent me and no Executive Committee meetings, due to the fact that our Executive members are scattered all over the world and most of them are deeply engrossed in their own work and have very little time or thought for WEF. The WEF can never be all that it ought to be as long as it is a one-man proposition, and yet the very nature of our organization makes it almost impossible for an Executive Committee to meet to plan, to make decisions and to in some measure direct the work.[13]

This is one of the difficulties faced by every Secretary of WEF from the beginning, and it is inherent in the structure of the organization. In order to be a truly international organization WEF must have a broad geographical and cultural representation on its Executive Committee; that is, the members must represent all major areas of the world. But for a group such as this to meet very often would require expensive travel and consumption of time to an extent which has never been feasible within the financial restrictions which constantly have bound WEF. The other alternative, of having a Board or Executive Committee composed of men who are located reasonably close to the Secretary, is unacceptable for the simple reason that this would make it largely a one-nation operation. Regardless of where the Secretary was located, his Board would have to be made up of people primarily from the same geographical region. This would not do justice to the international nature of the organization . . . Mr Ferris and others felt this frustration keenly.

Mr Ferris also took pains not to allow WEF to appear to be an arm of the NAE of the USA. He was sensitive to the fact that, having consolidated the International Office into one operation in the USA (combining the previous London and Boston Offices), the idea could become prevalent that WEF was primarily an American organization linked to the NAE. In actual fact NAE was (and is) a member of WEF, not *vice versa*. But there was always the danger of misunderstanding on this point, especially since the NAE had a Commission on International Relations which existed primarily to promote the interests of WEF in the USA. As long as the Secretary was an American, and the office was located in the USA, some would look upon WEF as an American body. This has been a danger throughout its history, as all secretaries have been Westerners in spite of strong efforts on various occasions to recruit leadership from the non-Western world. In writing to Mr John Bolten, who had participated in the founding of WEF and had been a generous contributor, Mr Ferris said,

> I am sure you gathered from our conversation at the time I was with you in Andover that we are very much in agreement regarding "Americans" and their effectiveness and acceptability as leaders overseas. I do believe, however, the WEF is really a free association of national movements, which in themselves are fully autonomous and sovereign. At no time do we seek to dictate to them or to implant our will or authority over them. This is a policy we hold inviolate.
>
> The location of the International Office admittedly should be outside the U.S.A. However, the WEF affiliates themselves voted its location within the United States. This is a matter we want to present when and if we meet in January.[14]

## Hong Kong, 1962

The by-laws of WEF accepted in Holland in 1951 suggested (not mandated) that, conditions permitting, the General Committee should meet once every three years, and the Executive Committee once a year. This suggestion was fulfilled only once. Three years elapsed between the meeting of the General Committee in Switzerland, in 1953, and the 1956 meeting held in Rhode Island. As we have seen, it was recommended in 1956 that the next meeting be held in Asia.

Various places were proposed over the next couple of years, and suggested plans for the meeting were put forth at different times.

However, for a variety of reasons, it did not appear that the time was ripe for such a meeting in 1959 or 1960. Correspondence between the leaders of WEF expressed doubts about the proper timing for the next meeting. A. J. Dain wrote from Australia to Fred Ferris, "I certainly question rather seriously whether the W.E.F. is, at this stage, ready for a further worldwide conference."[15]

The result was that the General Committee did not meet again until April, 1962, in Hong Kong. This lapse of six years seemed to set the precedent which has been followed ever since. Every subsequent meeting of the General Committee (now referred to as the General Assembly) has met at intervals of six years.

As plans for the next meeting were being laid Mr Ferris outlined the purposes of the conference in a letter to Mr Bolten:

> We do not envision a large meeting, nor will there be wide publicity— we do not need that, nor are we ready for it. We do seek to convene a "Work Conference" to which each affiliate will send two delegates. The purpose of the meeting is to study needed changes in WEF Constitution which will make the organization more effective and functional—to elect new officers—to review and discuss the aims and purposes of the WEF—and to do real spadework in developing the kind of organization and program so desperately needed to give evangelicals unity and leadership across the world today. This meeting will be attended only by delegates of our affiliates—no outsiders![16]

The meeting was convened from 25 April to 2 May, 1962 in Hong Kong. The host was Dr Timothy Dzao, founder and president of the Ling Liang World-Wide Evangelistic Mission, an indigenous mission society centred in Hong Kong with outreach to various parts of the world. All expenses in Hong Kong, including board and room, were covered by the local church members.

It was a small conference with seventeen delegates coming from eleven countries (Ceylon, England, India, Indonesia, Japan, Okinawa, West Pakistan, Switzerland, Taiwan, Vietnam, and the USA). There were also eight observers and a few guests.

Daily Bible readings were led by Dr Rene Pache of Switzerland. The rest of the day was spent in business sessions and times of prayer and sharing of what God was doing in different parts of the world. Much time was dedicated to revising the constitution.

6 commissions were named to function on behalf of WEF:

| | |
|---|---|
| Spiritual Ministry | – Timothy Dzao |
| Religious Liberty | – Gilbert Kirby |
| Missions | – Clyde Taylor |
| Literature | – Harold Street |
| Communications | – Bob Bowman |
| Youth | – C. Stacey Woods |

It was also decided to start the regional committees that had been suggested for some years. The first one to be named was the committee for Asia, to be called the "Asia Fellowship". The following were named to the committee:

| | |
|---|---|
| Chairman: | B. E. Fernando (Ceylon) |
| Vice Chairman: | J. B. Kawet (Indonesia) |
| Secretary—Treasurer: | K. Thirumalai (India) |
| Members: | D. V. Mieng (Vietnam) |
| | Ernest Tak (Pakistan) |

In the report of the International Secretary Mr Fred Ferris stated that he saw three possible positions WEF could adopt regarding evangelical unity and cooperation: first, *total isolation*, which requires no effort and ignores all others; second, *limited cooperation and unity*, which provides for a more effective coordination of effort, and presents fewer problems on major doctrinal issues, but brings into focus present divergences between evangelicals; third, *full cooperation*, which poses the very real difficulties of agreement on major doctrinal issues, with the possibility of compromise on spiritual convictions.

He also raised again the severe problem of finances for an organization such as WEF.

> Failure to establish an adequate program for financing the WEF has largely proven its undoing. Admittedly, the ideal is for the affiliates to largely provide the finances for the World Organization. Practically, this is impossible at this stage . . .
>
> The WEF has proven to be most difficult to finance. Had we had finances to convene regular stated meetings, the organizational weaknesses plaguing us today would have been faced and solved . . .

Had we had adequate financial support your International Secretary would have been free to spend much more of his time and effort in overseas ministry. As it is, most of his time has been used in the raising of funds.[17]

He also continued to recommend the establishment of regional boards or committees to assist the worldwide work of encouraging the national fellowships.

Although his report contains no hint of this, Mr Ferris presented his resignation at Hong Kong. The minutes record the tendering of the resignation to be effective from 31 May, 1962. As a result Mr Gilbert Kirby of England was appointed General Secretary, with a request that the Evangelical Alliance loan Mr Kirby for this purpose. It was also decided to close the office in Muscatine, Iowa, and move it to London under Mr Kirby. No reasons are recorded for this resignation, which was accepted with reluctance, and with great appreciation for the sacrificial and valuable service Mr Ferris had rendered during a very difficult period in the life of WEF.

The newly elected Executive Committee was composed as follows:

| | |
|---|---|
| President: | Everett Cattell (India/USA) |
| Vice President: | I. Ben Wati (India) |
| Treasurer: | William D. Rottschafer (USA) |
| Members at Large: | James Dickson (Taiwan) |
| | B. E. Fernando (Ceylon) |
| | Rene Pache (Switzerland) |
| | John Savage (England) |

The delegates ministered in local churches in Hong Kong on Sunday, and a closing meeting was held with pastors and leaders for a time of inspiration, prayer, and fellowship. While the conference was small in numbers, there seemed to be a spirit of oneness and a desire to move ahead with the goals of WEF. The future seemed promising.

CHAPTER EIGHT

# "Spiritual Unity in Action"

When Gilbert Kirby took over as International Secretary, he added this job to his position as General Secretary of the British Evangelical Alliance. Thus for the next four years he carried a dual responsibility. The international office of WEF was accordingly moved to London and included in the headquarters of the British Evangelical Alliance.

Early in his term of office Mr Kirby wrote to his American friends and colleagues an open letter published in the NAE periodical *United Evangelical Action* under the title "A Britisher Writes A Letter to Americans." He begins by expressing appreciation and joy at the prospect of working more closely with his American friends. He also promises, in spite of his heavy commitment as General Secretary of the British Evangelical Alliance, to "give all of my strength, under God, to promoting the interests of WEF."[1]

He then comments on the difference in American and British viewpoints on the relationships between evangelicals and non-evangelicals. "I gather that the line between the evangelical and the non-evangelical is much more clearly drawn there than here."[2] There is, he observes, a much larger evangelical population in America than in Britain, and the influence of the ecumenical movement has been felt more keenly in America than in Britain. Thus, he surmises, the Americans have given more thought to this problem than the English.

He goes on to assure his friends that the primary purpose of WEF is to strengthen the work of the church in such places as Africa, Asia, and the Far East, and Europe. The omission of any reference to Latin America is notable, since it seems to reflect the situation which had been prevalent from the founding of WEF. Not much emphasis had yet been placed on the Latin American continent, and thus very little participation had come from that area of the world. Even Africa had barely begun to be noticed in the activities of WEF at this time.

Kirby then comments that "we are not concerned with building a strong central organization, but rather strong national fellowships which are self-sufficient and self-supporting."[3]

He also sounds an affirmative note in stating:

> While we reserve the right to criticize in love those who differ from us, we should remember that primarily we have a positive witness to bear. The World Evangelical Fellowship must never exist for its own sake. We are essentially a service organization and will gain the respect of our evangelical brethren across the world only as we are able to offer a practical service.[4]

He outlines his thinking on how this can be done. He suggests the sharing of gifted Bible teachers from the Western world for pastors' and leaders' conferences elsewhere. He notes the need for studying the scriptural foundations for unity. He sees the possibility of scholarship funds to help worthy candidates from the non-Western world receive theological education in schools outside their homelands when necessary.

He also raises the ever-present spectre of the financial limitations of WEF. He expresses appreciation for the great debt owed to the Americans, who had, up to this point, carried the major burden of financing WEF. He states, however, that this is not a healthy state of affairs, and he hopes to see it corrected.

### Spiritual Unity in Action

The major concern of his work, as he repeatedly stated at

other times during his term of office, was to translate concepts of spiritual unity into concrete action. He says

> We have so often protested that we already know the meaning of spiritual unity and that we do not need to strive for it. Now it is high time that this unity be expressed in effective action. As I visualize the WEF program in the years ahead, I feel the phrase "spiritual unity in action" would be as fitting as any to describe our objectives.[5]

This emphasis on "spiritual unity in action" was to be picked up in later years and used as a slogan to describe the purpose and ministry of WEF. It appears that Mr Kirby here coined a phrase which was to give cohesion and expression to the movement.

He concludes his open letter with a reaffirmation of the three principles on which WEF had been founded in 1951, namely, the need for fellowship in the gospel, defence and confirmation of the gospel, and the furtherance of the gospel.

Mr Kirby reiterated his dreams for WEF in the WEF *Bulletin* in early 1964, in an article entitled "My Vision for WEF." He wrote:

> 1. It should devote all its energies towards the encouragement of *National* Fellowships which shall be truly representative of evangelical life and witness, and which have a positive and effective programme.
> 2. It should avoid developing cumbersome organizational machinery, but should remain a loose federation of national evangelical fellowships, and avoid all unnecessary expenditure.
> 3. It should encourage national fellowships by making it possible for acknowledged Bible teachers to visit different countries from time to time for spiritual ministry.
> 4. It should build up a Scholarship Fund to assist a limited number of potential evangelical leaders to get further theological training where necessary outside their own country.
> 5. It should be prepared to accept, whenever practicable, invitations to send observers to ecumenical gatherings, and should always maintain an attitude of Christian courtesy in its dealings with other bodies.
> 6. It should adopt as its slogan—"Spiritual unity in action."[6]

These goals were obviously the ones which he pursued during his time in office.

A strong right arm to Mr Kirby was given by Dr Everett Cattell, the president of WEF. He had reluctantly agreed in Hong Kong to accept the presidency, writing to Kirby on 31 May, 1962:

I am considerably embarrassed to find myself in the position of president as I had strongly urged that Ben Wati be made the president in order to get the center of gravity away from the United States. It was only after Ben Wati's firm refusal to take the office that I finally succumbed to pressures, and so for the present will try to do what I can.[7]

This letter marked the beginning of a voluminous correspondence between Cattell and Kirby which was to continue throughout most of Kirby's tenure in office. Dr Cattell took a keen and intricate interest in every phase of the work of WEF, writing to Mr Kirby on every conceivable topic related to WEF, commenting intelligently on all reports from Kirby, and giving wise advice and counsel. Dr Cattell, having been one of the founders and leaders in the formation of the Evangelical Fellowship of India, now proved his abilities and wisdom in promoting unity on a world-wide basis through his energetic involvement in WEF.

In January of 1964 Mr Kirby spent three weeks in India where he attended the annual conference of the Evangelical Fellowship of India and brought the daily Bible readings as well as the main evening addresses. This was attended by a record number of 536 participants from all but one of the states of India. Eight new churches or groups were admitted to membership in EFI bringing its total membership to 65 affiliated groups.[8]

Following the EFI conference Mr Kirby ministered in a Leaders' Conference near Madras and in churches in Madras itself, met with leaders in Delhi, spoke at Union Biblical Seminary in Yeotmal, ministered in a conference of missionaries of the Poona and Indian Village Mission, and finally preached at a pastors' retreat in Nasrapur. He was accompanied on this trip by Mr I. Ben Wati, Executive Secretary of EFI and Vice President of WEF. He was greatly impressed with the strength of EFI and the leadership given by Mr Ben Wati. He said in a subsequent report

Undoubtedly EFI has much to teach the various fellowships and Alliances already in existence, as well as those in process of formation in different parts of the world. It expresses the slogan, "Spiritual Unity in Action," very effectively . . . Unquestionably it owes a very great deal to the wise leadership which it has enjoyed, and particularly to its Executive Secretary, Mr. I. Ben Wati.[9]

*Important Decisions*

In the summer of 1964 the WEF Executive Committee met in London under the chairmanship of Dr Everett L. Cattell. Others present were Mr I. Ben Wati, vice-president; Mr W. D. Rottschafer, honorary treasurer; Dr James Dickson, Dr Rene Pache, Dr Clyde Taylor, and Revd Gilbert Kirby. At this meeting plans for expansion in Asia were discussed.

As early as 1962 there had already been extensive discussions about establishing a WEF secretariat in Asia. At the Hong Kong meeting of the General Council in 1962 consideration was given to naming a man from Singapore as Asian secretary. After lengthy exchanges, this particular person was dropped from consideration. Approaches were begun with Revd Samuel Kamaleson, pastor of the Emmanuel Methodist Church in Madras. Kamaleson was a rapidly developing young evangelist and singer whose impact was to grow to worldwide proportions in later years.

Dennis Clark, a missionary in India of the Bible and Medical Missionary Fellowship (BMMF), was also becoming involved in WEF Asia concerns during these years. Clark was working part-time with the Billy Graham Evangelistic Association in Asia, and served as a consultant for the David C. Cook Publishing Company, along with his BMMF responsibilities. In April 1962 the BMMF had agreed to release him for about four months per year of work with WEF. Clark, Kamaleson, and the executives of WEF remained in contact during the next two years.

Gilbert Kirby expressed his enthusiasm for Kamaleson in a letter to Dr Everett Cattell on 6 May, 1963, as follows:

> I should tell you that the Revd Sam Kamaleson is a young man, presently pastor of the thriving Emmanuel Methodist Church, Madras. He is a qualified veterinary surgeon, but trained for the ministry at Asbury Theological Seminary, USA. He has worked with the Inter-Varsity Fellowship of India and is a particularly gifted singer . . . We all feel that the interests of WEF would be well served by Mr. Kamaleson should he feel able to accept our invitation.[10]

Thus during the period of 1962 to 1964 both Samuel Kamaleson and Dennis Clark were bring drawn into more WEF activities. In 1965 a letterhead was printed for the "WEF

Asia Secretariat" showing Clark and Kamaleson as "co-secretaries."

In July, 1965, Clyde Taylor of the USA joined Clark and Kamaleson for a trip to Japan, Taiwan, and Hong Kong, with Taylor and Kamaleson continuing on to the Philipppines while Clark travelled elsewhere in Asia. The purpose of the trip was to strengthen the existing national fellowships and encourage their growth and outreach.

By the end of 1965 Clark was feeling the pressures of carrying too many diverse responsibilities. In a letter to Clyde Taylor dated 17 November, 1965, he says that he is facing the problem of handling both the BGEA and WEF, and that the two jobs are too much. He, therefore, requested his supervisor in the BGEA, Walter Smyth, to release him for more time with WEF. This was granted in January, 1966, and Clark began giving more attention to WEF.

In March, 1966, the BMMF released Clark from some of his responsibilities for them, in order to give nearly his full time to WEF, based now in Toronto. Thus he was able to travel in Asia from May to July, visiting Japan, Korea, Taiwan, Hong Kong, Vietnam, and the Philippines.

The 6 commissions which had been appointed at the Hong Kong Assembly in 1962 had not really been functioning and so it was agreed that a different approach would be desirable. The report of this Executive Committee meeting states:

> It was felt that at the present time the various Commissions which had been set up were not in a position to function effectively. Instead, it was agreed that the WEF should be in a position to call upon men with specialized knowledge in various departments of evangelical work and witness, who could be consulted from time to time and serve as liaison officers with national or international organizations operating along the lines of their own special interests.[11]

More than a decade was to pass before most of the WEF commissions really began to function as originally conceived, although, as will be seen later, the Theological Commission did get started and became an effective instrument before the others were operative.

It was also decided to invite Dr Clate Risley of the USA to become WEF Secretary for Christian Education. Known to many as "Mr Sunday School" Dr Risley had been for 12 years the executive secretary of the National Sunday School Association in the USA and had been leading Sunday School training conferences in other countries. An office was opened in Oak Park, Illinois, and Dr Risley began to function on behalf of WEF under the guidance of the American board of WEF, which was the Commission on International Affairs of the NAE.

## Looking at Africa

It was during Mr Kirby's term of office that WEF began to concentrate more of its attention on the continent of Africa. Mr Kirby had a special interest in Africa through serving on the boards of several mission societies such as the Sudan United Mission and Sierra Leone Mission. In 1962 two cooperative mission alliances in the USA, the Interdenominational Foreign Missions Association (IFMA) and the Evangelical Foreign Missions Association (EFMA) cooperated in sending Mr Kenneth L. Downing of the Africa Inland Mission to Nairobi, Kenya, to set up an Africa Evangelical Office. The Evangelical Missionary Alliance of Great Britain, of which Mr Kirby was executive secretary, also took a close interest in this venture. Its goal was to promote greater cooperation among evangelicals in the countries of Africa. At that time there were known to be three evangelical fellowships in existence: the Sierra Leone Evangelical Fellowship, the Evangelical Federation in Upper Volta, and the Ivory Coast Evangelical Fellowship.[12] Other fellowships were soon to be formed, and the ultimate goal was to establish an evangelical fellowship of all Africa under African leadership. This was realized with the formation of the Association of Evangelicals of Africa and Madagascar in 1966 which was to become a significant member of WEF. Without doubt Mr Kirby's interest in Africa played a role in encouraging these developments.

In a significant article published in *Christianity Today* in January, 1965, Dr Cattell spelled out the visions and problems of WEF. Admitting that some of its early goals and aspirations had not been reached, he spoke of the failure of the commissions to become operative, of the decision not to seek representation at the United Nations, and the difficulty of establishing an adequate financial base.

In dealing with the financial problems which WEF had constantly faced, he explained how, in the post-World War II era, a number of new mission bodies had been formed which had been more attractive to donors.

> They tended to emphasize technical programs such as aviation, literature, orphan care, relief projects, radio ministry and gospel records. These are much easier to dramatize than the slogging work of bringing churches to maturity and have therefore won out in the competition for evangelical dollars. This is said without bitterness; it is a plain fact. It has always been true that the most strategic phases of Christian work are the most difficult to "sell" to the rank and file, and that the most dramatic appeals often have the least strategic value. At any rate, the great dream of WEF based on large income never materialized.
>
> The real genius of the World Evangelical Fellowship, however, has come to light through its poverty . . .
>
> WEF operates on something less than a whole shoestring. It has not been able to do even the most basic thing, namely, to keep a man in the field for spiritual ministry and to assist the weaker fellowships and organize new ones. Financially the great strength of WEF is its lack of funds to distribute and its emphasis upon helping existing agencies to do more with what they have. Much of the staff work of WEF and indeed of some of the national fellowships is done by people lent part or full-time by other agencies.[13]

He then goes on to speak in a positive way of the great contribution which WEF makes in the spiritual realm and in promoting renewal in the churches.

> The highest importance of WEF and its members lies in its spiritual impact rather than in its handling of material resources . . . WEF's primary concern is to foster spiritual renewal of all the churches . . . The main task of WEF is to labor by prayer and ministry for the renewal of the spiritual life of the churches, both old and new . . .
>
> Spiritual renewal, a strengthened evangelical witness in all the churches, and the benefits of cooperative action—these are the major goals of WEF.[14]

Surely Dr Cattell's warmth of heart and breadth of vision did much to keep alive the ministry of WEF during a time when financial restrictions were limiting its activities. While Mr Kirby was only part-time in his capacity as International

Secretary, he also contributed greatly to forming the foundations on which WEF could continue to minister.

The problem of finances mentioned by Dr Cattell continued to plague Mr Kirby throughout his term of office. At a meeting of the Executive Committee of WEF held in London in September, 1965, he reported on:

> The disappointing financial situation—there had been no improvement over the past twelve months, apart from the generous gift from the Eli Lilly Foundation (Lilly had given a grant of $30,000 over a period of three years) . . .
>
> The present unsatisfactory financial situation. Apart from generous gifts from the USA, the income of WEF is virtually nil.[15]

Nearly twenty years later Mr Kirby told this author over a luncheon in London, with a shaking of his head, that he wished the best for WEF but that finances had always been the major roadblock for advance.

In 1966 Gilbert Kirby responded to a call to become Principal of London Bible College. In doing so, he left his two posts at the British Evangelical Alliance and the World Evangelical Fellowship to concentrate his energies full-time on the new responsibilities placed upon him. But his impact on WEF is still felt today, as the concept of "spiritual unity in action" continues to express the purposes and goals of WEF.

# CHAPTER NINE

# Tensions and Progress

In October 1966 Billy Graham convened the World Congress on Evangelism in Berlin, bring together over 1200 evangelical leaders from around the world so that they could consider the future of world evangelism. This proved to be a propitious time for the WEF Executive Committee to meet, as many of its members were invited in any case to the Congress. Thus they met on 27 and 30 October, and 1 November, 1966, in Berlin.

The first item on the agenda was to accept the resignation of Gilbert Kirby. This was done with expressions of deep appreciation to the British Evangelical Alliance for making his services available to WEF for the past four years, and to Mr Kirby for his ministry through WEF.

Mr Dennis Clark was then appointed as International Secretary with the office to be located in Toronto (where Mr Clark was then based under BMMF). He assumed these responsibilities in December, 1966. At the same meeting Mr A. Morgan Derham of England (who had replaced Gilbert Kirby as Secretary of the British Evangelical Alliance) was named International Editorial Secretary, and Mr Sam Kamaleson of India was named Asian Secretary, having already served as co-secretary for Asia with Dennis Clark.[1]

In preparation for the Berlin meetings Dennis Clark had drawn up a paper on the "The Ethos and Objectives of WEF" in which he outlined his vision for what God might do through WEF in the years ahead. In this paper he presented his feelings, which were to come increasingly to the fore during his term of leadership in WEF, that the time had come to recognize the emerging leadership of the church in the non-Western world. Up until now WEF leadership had largely come from Europe and North America (with a few exceptions such as Ben Wati and Sam Kamaleson). Clark stated:

> During the 1960s a moving of the Holy Spirit is evident in the growth of evangelical groupings in Africa, Australasia and Latin America; and a strengthening of evangelical groups in Asia. The period in which we now find ourselves—1966/67—is characterized by leadership from evangelicals in the newly emerging nations, and a new concept of world operation, in which the previous "sending countries" accept a proportionate place as partners in work of Jesus Christ on a global basis. At this juncture, therefore, several important trends are pointing the way to WEF developments.[2]

He then went on to spell out these developments. Some of his key points were:

> 1. WEF now has the potential of development into spiritual fellowship of evangelicals on a truly world basis . . .
> 3. The WEF is concerned to assist the younger churches in areas where they express their need for help.
> 4. WEF is a forum for discussion and action in areas of need . . . especially in the context of Africa, Asia and Latin America.
> 5. WEF can become a voice for evangelicals to the nations and to Christian church groupings . . .[3]

He saw the WEF objectives for the next few years as being:

> 1. Encourage unaffiliated Alliances/Associations/Fellowships to affiliate with WEF, provided they are of one mind with the WEF Statement of Faith, objectives and ethos.
> 2. Provide an extension ministry to nations where no formal Alliance/ Association/Fellowship exists, with a view to encouraging such a development. This extension ministry will be planned in the closest consultation with evangelical leaders of the nations visited.[4]

Clark was thus sounding a strong note for internationalizing the ministry of WEF in a way which, up to this point, had not been realized. A major emphasis in his ministry in the coming years was to encourage this development of leadership from the emerging nations.

*Tensions and Misunderstandings*

One of the first things he did to implement his vision was to issue a new logo for WEF in three languages—French, English, and Spanish—to demonstrate the truly international character of WEF and to counteract the impression that WEF was primarily a North American-European organization. This logo undoubtedly did a lot to help promote the international-ization of WEF.

The emphasis on the emerging nations which Clark brought into focus sometimes led critics in some circles to characterize Clark as "anti-American" and "anti-missionary." He was not averse to criticizing Western missionaries publicly and privately, often undoubtedly with some justifi-cation. In large public fora, such as the Inter-Varsity student missionary convention at Urbana, he sometimes gave the impression of being very negative about missions and missionaries. A student at an IVCF conference asked him if he was not himself a missionary. His reply was, "I never use the word." While he was admittedly a missionary of BMMF, such statements as this gave him an unfortunate reputation.

This attitude towards missions, amongst other things led inevitably to growing tensions between Mr Clark and some other mission leaders, not the least of whom was Clyde Taylor. In an exchange of correspondence with Clark, Everett Cattell, president of WEF, expressed his concern for what appeared to be a "growing rift" between Clark and Taylor. A lengthy letter from Taylor to Clark of 12 May, 1967, reveals some of Taylor's concerns that Clark was not representing WEF in the proper way before missions and national churches. He says:

> The International Secretary of WEF *is* Mr. WEF. His is the official voice, his statements are taken as official. Where he goes, the WEF goes . . . Snap judgements or startling opinions (given in an effort to challenge people to think or reconsider) must not be used by the International Secretary. These become official opinions of the WEF even though they were not so intended.[5]

That final statement describes how some mission leaders felt Dennis Clark was presenting himself in his public pronounce-ments.

While Clark was accused by some of being anti-American, he apparently felt that some of his friends were anti-British. One American missionary in Africa stated, "My relations with Dennis Clark from my first acquaintance with him at Winona Lake in 1962 have been very friendly, but I do not think it could be denied that from the outset of our 'encounter' with him at Berlin he was hostile and had prejudged us as being anti-British (that is, against British missions and churches)."[6]

## African Difficulties

Tensions and misunderstandings came to a focus in Africa with the development of the Africa Evangelical Office (see p. 67) under the leadership of Kenneth Downing of the Africa Inland Mission. Dennis Clark planned to visit Africa with the purpose of encouraging national evangelical fellowships to affiliate with WEF. The Africa Evangelical Office (forerunner of the present day AEAM—Association of Evangelicals of Africa and Madagascar), however, felt that WEF should visit only those nations which already had affiliated with WEF, and that the other African nations should be allowed to develop at their own speed, relating *first* to the Africa Evangelical Office before relating to a world body such as WEF.

A meeting was held on 13 and 14 July, 1967, in New York between Dennis Clark and Everett Cattell of WEF and eighteen representatives of IFMA (Interdenominational Foreign Missions Association) and Evangelical Foreign Missions Association. Discussions ranged over the purpose of WEF, its constitution and membership requirement, and its relationship with some of the African fellowships. Dr Cattell read a statement of WEF which was well received as being a fine clarification of the purposes and positions of WEF. It was agreed that this, along with the WEF constitution, should be circulated to all IFMA and EFMA missions to apprise them of what WEF was aiming to accomplish.

Subsequently a small EFMA/IFMA committee was named to follow through with some suggestions to WEF arising out of this meeting. Their major recommendation was presented to WEF to be considered for inclusion in their by-laws:

The presence of thousands of evangelicals who are aggressively proclaiming the gospel within denominations which are members of conciliar organizations is acknowledged. Many of these evangelicals are desirous of organizational relationships with others who are maintaining a clear testimony to the basic doctrines of the Christian faith. It is, therefore, the policy of the World Evangelical Fellowship to encourage its constituent members to offer membership to such individuals, local churches, and organized segments of denominations: However, it is understood that no national fellowship may have dual membership in WEF and any international conciliar organization which is not committed to the principles outlined in the WEF Constitution.[7]

This proposal was presented to the WEF General Council meeting in Lausanne in May, 1968, for consideration. It was accepted for inclusion in the by-laws with the exception of the last sentence. This is significant, because the last sentence clearly includes the heart of what the IFMA/EFMA men were trying to say. But WEF was not ready to state "that no national fellowship may have dual membership in WEF and any international conciliar organization which is not committed to the principles outlined in the WEF Constitution."

Mr A. Morgan Derham, representing both WEF and the Evangelical Alliance of Great Britain, visited Kenneth Downing of the Africa Evangelical Office in Nairobi, Kenya, 4 to 7 October, 1967. At that time there was disagreement as to the need of a separate evangelical fellowship in Kenya. Mr Morgan Derham maintained that the National Christian Council of Kenya was controlled by evangelicals and there was, therefore, no need for a separate fellowship. Mr Downing held that the evangelical fellowship had purposes of spiritual renewal that were distinct from some of the projects of the NCCK, such as representation before the government of Christian interests, and that there were leaders in the NCCK who were also affiliated with the World Council of Churches, causing confusion in the minds of evangelicals.

The differences of opinion seemed to rotate around two areas: differences between American and British outlook, and between IFMA/EFMA and WEF viewpoints. A further meeting was held in New York City on 27-28 November, 1967, between Everett Cattell, Dennis Clark, and Morgan Derham together representing WEF, and twenty-three representatives of IFMA and EFMA missions. This was an "off the record" meeting with no formal agenda and no minutes kept. Reports prepared afterwards by various representatives of the mission groups seem to agree on several observations. Dennis Clark came across as "very conciliatory," "very temperate and pious in almost all of his remarks," "self-effacing," and more amenable than he had been in July.

Morgan Derham, on the other hand, reportedly, "alienated himself" from the others, came across as "intransigent," with his mind already made up, deepening the suspicion of WEF which some already had. Some felt that there was more suspicion and reluctance towards WEF after this meeting than before; that the goodwill which had been generated in the July meeting had been damaged by the November one.

Morgan Derham's viewpoint was obviously different. He reported confidentially on this meeting, using such phrases as "deep feelings underneath," "a very unpleasant experience," "totally unyielding attitude," "the experience left me very depressed." He also stated that "Dennis . . . stood manfully for internationalism. Everett asked some shrewd questions. Clyde did not say much. I felt that I was the object of the evident hostility."[8]

One refreshing reference is to Wesley Duewel of OMS International who, Derham states, "was an exception . . . He pleaded eloquently for fellowship in a broad sense."[9]

Derham also stated, in referring to the situation in Kenya,

> My report, suggesting that an EFK was not necessary since the evangelicals could take over the CCK, was sent on to USA in advance of my arrival, so the IFMA men had seen it before I got there—the result was a most unpleasant confrontation. What I was wanting to avoid was what has in fact happened—the exclusion of the largest evangelical group in Kenya, the Anglicans, from EFK. Dennis Clark was in advance of his time, and his "internationalist" approach undoubtedly provoked some of the hostility to WEF . . . which has taken a lot of overcoming. But he was right.[10]

The WEF representatives felt that the American missions were guilty of exporting their own problems to Africa, that is, problems of ecumenical relationships. They also felt that the Americans were trying to control what happened in Africa, rather than allowing the African church to determine its own directions.

At the same time the American representatives felt that the WEF men were doing exactly the same thing. A case in point was the choosing of African delegates who could attend the forthcoming WEF General Council meetings to be held in Switzerland in May, 1968. The WEF men requested the mission leaders to recommend Africans who could be invited to the General Council. The mission men steadfastly refused to do so, saying that under no circumstances would they do such a thing, because the naming of delegates must be done by the national fellowships and not by an outside world body. Some felt that Dennis Clark and Morgan Derham already had their minds made up about who should come, and would go ahead with this anyway. This was highlighted by one mission leader as follows:

> Another point of tension was the matter of naming an African delegate for the WEF committee which is to meet at Lausanne in May. They not only are determined to have one, regardless of any missionary opinion, but it finally came out in discussion that Dennis had already pretty well made up his mind who this man should be and was bringing the name forward to their executive committee. The debate centered on the matter of how such a man would be selected—by mission societies, by choice of national groups on the field, or by their executive committee. The right way seemed clear, but time and pragmatic considerations made it infeasible to follow it.[11]

Over the years, these suspicions and tensions, fortunately, were diminished greatly, and the AEAM eventually became one of the most supportive and active members of WEF. In fact, as this history is being written the present executive secretary of AEAM, Dr Tokunboh Adeyemo, is also chairman of the Executive Council of WEF.

## Evangelicals and Social Action

Another area where Dennis Clark's progressive outlook became a forerunner of later developments was in the matter of social action. Before the decade of the 1970s it was highly suspect for evangelicals in general to become involved in "social action" activities. Such things seemed to smack of the "social gospel" from which fundamentalism had veered away in the earlier decades of the twentieth century. During the 1960s, however, there were a few glimmers of hope that evangelicals would begin again to recognize their responsibility to the physical and social needs of mankind. Examples of this were some parts of the Wheaton Declaration (a statement drawn up at the Congress on the Church's Worldwide Mission held in Wheaton, Illinois, in April, 1966) and some of the messages given at the Congress on Evangelism in Minneapolis in 1969. But in general it was a lonely voice among evangelicals that would speak out in favour of social action.

Dennis Clark was one of those lonely voices. In March, 1967, on a tour of Latin America he became heavily burdened for the social needs he was seeing in Bolivia, Chile, and Argentina. He studied some of the programmes that were being developed by evangelicals in those lands to help raise the health, economic and social levels of the poor, hungry, and oppressed. In a report written during that trip he described projects of chicken farming, alpaca wool manufacture for export, medical work, angora rabbit raising for wool, and others. He commented that "all evangelicals I have met . . . state that they think it is inadequate to have a spiritual programme without a correlative concern and compassion for the poor and hungry where Communism breeds. Even among Christians this is a relevant issue."[12]

While today such action is taken for granted as being essential, and is promoted vigorously in most evangelical circles, it raised the eyebrows of some of Clark's WEF colleagues. Concern was expressed that he was deviating from the purposes originally established by WEF. Everett Cattell, as President of WEF, wrote to him,

> I, of course, am fully in sympathy with the idea that evangelicals must be involved in social action. But it appears that you are projecting a programme here which we have not discussed as an executive committee and which raises the question in my mind as to whether we are not in danger of abandoning our purpose at this point. In other words, we have always held that we were not the body to carry on the action but we are to be a stimulus to the local groups toward their

getting into action. Our primary function is to coordinate and bring into cooperation those at the national level who are doing these things.[13]

It is important to note here that Dr Cattell was not opposing involvement in social action but rather raising the procedural question of the purpose of WEF. He favoured the action; he questioned whether WEF should be directly involved in carrying out such projects rather than stimulating others into the action and coordinating those who were involved. (However, it is also true that many evangelicals in 1967 would have questioned the validity of such actions as a part of gospel witness). But Dennis Clark was not fearful of speaking out on such an issue, even though he doubtless knew it could be controversial in some quarters.

## *The Office of Christian Education*

Another area that caused some initial tension for Mr Clark was the office of Christian Education under the direction of Dr Clate Risley which had been opened in Oak Park, Illinois, during Gilbert Kirby's administration. Clark expressed doubts about the function of this office and its relation to WEF. Writing to Clyde Taylor immediately after taking office he said:

> I would appreciate your guidance concerning his (Clate Risley's) partic-
> ular brief for operation . . . what exactly is his function internationally?[14]

This confusion as to the function of Clate Risley had increased a few months later when Clark wrote again to Taylor:

> I am replying at once concerning Clate Risley. I have given considerble
> thought to this matter, and would like to point out:
> 1) That Clate has been a concern of the WEF USA Committee until the
>    present date. There are no records on the file. I have not had any
>    reports. There is no approved budget, and as International Secretary,
>    to this date there is [sic] no relationship between Clate Risley and the
>    Secretariat.
> 2) Therefore the USA committee should deal with the matter, as they
>    employed Clate, and have to date negotiated everything with him. I,
>    as International Secretary, would prefer not to become involved in a
>    problem of this nature.

3) During the present interim period until the Beirut Council we are trying to present an international image of WEF, and we must avoid any suggestion that WEF is an American ancillary with an American staff member operating on his own, with a letterhead and fund raising program. WEF International Executive appointed three secretaries at Berlin, and that is the position as I see it at the moment.

If our brother Clate has a vital ministry in Christian Education, could it not be related to NAE, the national affiliate of WEF, or some missionary body.[15]

Finally on 16 May, 1967, a meeting was held of the U.S. Committee of WEF in Chicago, in which both Clate Risley and Dennis Clark were present. There was discussion of the ministry of Dr Risley in Sunday School and Christian Education training. Dennis Clark expressed his concern that this rightfully belonged among the concerns of a USA committee and should not be a part of WEF. Therefore, it was agreed:

In light of the restructuring of the organization of the World Evangelical Fellowship, and

In the interest of a more simple and efficient operation, and

In view of the separate financial arrangements of the office of the Secretary of Christian Education by which the World Evangelical Fellowship assumes no financial responsibility and the United States committee has been unable to adequately support the office;

It is agreed that the WEF Executive Committee be requested to dissolve the present relationship, and

That the Secretary of Christian Education continue the present services under a board of directors to include, where desired, members of the present United States committee and the advisory board;

That the proposed transfer be completed no later than December 31, 1967, and that a change of name be effected as soon as possible and

That the committee express its deep appreciation to the Secretary of Christian Education for the excellent services he has sacrificially rendered in the name of the World Evangelical Fellowship.[16]

Both Dennis Clark and Clate Risley were reportedly satisfied with this arrangement, agreeing that it was probably the best solution. Mr Clark assured Dr Risley of his complete cooperation and fellowship through WEF.

Mr Clark continued his extensive travels on behalf of WEF during these times of tension and development. One of his most significant trips was taken in October and November, 1967, when he travelled through the USSR, Poland, Czechoslovakia, and Yugoslavia. He had a ministry of Bible teaching to believers in those lands, and reported confidentially and in great detail on the situation which he observed in the churches. He was encouraged by the fidelity of the believers and challenged by their desire for serious Bible teaching and personal growth.

# CHAPTER TEN

# Internationalizing the WEF

The most important milestone during Dennis Clark's tenure of office was the meeting of the General Council of WEF held in Lausanne, Switzerland, in May, 1968. Originally scheduled to be Beirut, Lebanon, the venue was changed to Switzerland because of the political turmoil in Beirut at that time and because of the plan to move the WEF office to Lausanne.

Clark worked hard in preparation for this General Council meeting. The last one had been held in Hong Kong in 1962, and he felt the time had come for a major thrust to make WEF genuinely international. The adoption of a tri-lingual logo had been a tangible expression of the international nature of WEF, but the General Council must now demonstrate that nature by its composition and actions.

Writing to Dr Carl Henry in November, 1967, Clark said:

> WEF is gaining a momentum I could hardly have hoped for a year ago
> . . . I am caught in the squeeze of being spread all over the world with a
> new momentum in WEF.[1]

A second letter written just two weeks later to Henry said:

> I do not think there is a room for WEF to jog along in a third class way
> any longer. For some of us either Lausanne (1968 General Council
> meeting) will be a movement into something that with rapid momentum
> can take the world scene, or we should close it down. I personally
> would not be interested in giving the best of my last years to what is
> only a name, and which [sic] has no substantial backing from the
> evangelical community around the world.[2]

In his report to the General Council Dennis Clark referred to his past activities and summarized his views on the future of WEF. He said:

> The Council will debate in detail the role of WEF. Your International Secretary notes two divergent trends:
> 1. That from WEF's early beginnings in 1846 the main concern has been for spiritual renewal, unity and evangelism.
> 2. That the main thrust of WEF could be diverted from spiritual and practical concerns for men and women, so that WEF becomes a pseudo "political" grouping in conflict with or as a counter to the World Council of Churches.
>
> It is recommended that WEF continues to maintain its spiritual emphasis, as referred to under No. 1 above, and a positive openness to ALL EVANGELICALS wherever found. We must decline to become involved in "power structure politics" or fixed attitudes which would exclude fellow members of the body of Christ.[3]

Then as he focussed attention on the need to internationalize WEF, both structurally and in terms of its ministries, he said:

> Much time has been spent in consultation with a wide range of evangelical leaders in a number of countries . . .
> An attempt has also been made to hold in balance three evangelical forces often ignoring each other or in conflict:
> 1. The North American missionary task force
> 2. The European and Commonwealth task force
> 3. The national church force
>
> It is the considered opinion of the International Secretary that one of the important functions of WEF in its declared concern for spiritual unity is to enable each of the above three groupings to recognize and esteem the other, and particularly to counsel aliens in a host nation to CONSULT NATIONAL EVANGELICAL LEADERS on a broad scale BEFORE taking any initiative or action in the nation to which they have come as visitors. There is deep concern and unrest among evangelicals in a number of nations because of the insensitive operation of alien evangelicals with financial backing from a more affluent sending country.[4]

In the conclusion of his report Clark gave forceful expression to the feelings which characterized his desire to lead WEF into an international sphere.

> WEF stands at a new watershed. The challenge is to move forward with a positive programme that is truly international in scope and operation. Anything less than this is unthinkable, and if the challenge is not tenable the Council should consider dissolution of what could only be termed a facade. WEF must NOT operate like a "mission," it must truly reflect a synthesis of international concern and opinion and action born and financed from the convictions of its affiliates.[5]

*The Meeting in Lausanne*

The General Council gathered in Lausanne, Switzerland, from 4 to 10 May, 1968, with 65 delegates from 36 countries. It is noteworthy that, in contrast to previous meetings, only three Americans were present—Clyde W. Taylor, Hudson T. Armerding, and Arnold T. Olson, all representing the NAE. There was a breadth of representation and a new sense of purpose not seen before in WEF.

A number of significant actions were taken at this meeting over the course of the week. It was decided to open the office of WEF in Lausanne, closing the Toronto office which Dennis Clark had kept. His plan was to use a small staff located on the same premises as the office of the International Fellowship of Evangelical Students, headed by Mr C. Stacy Woods. Clark, while remaining in Toronto, would travel to Lausanne periodically for contact on his world travels.

Clark was reappointed as International Secretary for a period of three and a half years, seconded by BMMF on a half-time basis. The budget approved by the Council was based on his half-time work.

Two major papers were read at the Council. One was by New Zealander Bruce Nicholls, a missionary in India of BMMF, on "Theological Confession in the Renewal of Asian Churches." This was a detailed study of the theological scene in Asia in 1968 dealing with critical issues such as the eternal state of those who have never heard the Gospel, inter-religious dialogue, the indigenization of the Gospel, unity and cooperation, the secularization of society, and related matters.

The second paper was presented by C. Stacey Woods on "The Role of the World Evangelical Fellowship in Relation to Youth." This covered the crisis among youth in the late 1960s, the responsibility of the church to meet this challenge, and the role which WEF should play in the process.

As a result of these two papers the Council adopted *Theology* and *Youth* as two major emphases to be addressed during the next five years. Bruce Nicholls was appointed as Theological Coordinator of WEF, and Stacey Woods was appointed Youth Coordinator. In subsequent years Bruce

Nicholls aggressively developed the theological dimension and ministry of WEF and became executive secretary of the WEF Theological Commission. (More of this later.) The emphasis on youth, however, never was fully developed in WEF, and the recommended commission on youth did not materialize.

In the financial realm a budget was adopted, totalling $29,963 for the fiscal year of 1968–69. It was also agreed that each member fellowship would contribute one per cent of its annual income to WEF. This was a noble gesture, but it never happened to any effective degree. In fact, there is little evidence that most of the member bodies ever contributed anything to the international office. These expenses continued to be borne largely by contributions from the USA and Europe.

The priority of evangelism in the ministry of WEF was reiterated, but apparently no specific steps were taken to implement this other than to encourage the member bodies to be engaged in aggressive evangelism and to exchange gifted evangelists from country to country.

In discussing an interchange of Bible ministry an interesting new emphasis emerged. The minutes record that the Council discussed

> the desirability of assisting gifted Bible teachers from Asia and Africa to visit and minister to fellow-believers in nations other than their own. It was hoped that some Asian and African Bible teachers would be able to visit and minister to churches in Eastern Europe.[6]

This is a marked departure from previous assemblies where action was taken to encourage gifted Bible teachers from North America and Europe to minister in non-Western countries. At Lausanne the emphasis switched to encouraging teachers from non-Western countries to minister cross-culturally, including some ministry in Western nations. The lack of any mention of teachers from Latin America underlines the fact that WEF's focus of attention continued to be primarily directed towards Asia and Africa, as well as Europe and North America.

This was a forerunner, in evangelical circles, of the emergence of leadership from the non-Western world. Such leadership was certainly there, but it had not yet come to the surface in most international circles. It was not until the decade of the 1970s that non-Western leadership became more prominent in international gatherings of evangelicals. But Dennis Clark deserves credit as one of the early pioneers and prophetic voices calling for a recognition of talented leadership from all nations.

## The Infallibility Issue

Another significant development at this Council meeting was the opening of the door for the European Evangelical Alliance finally to become a member of WEF. At the founding of WEF in 1951 in Holland there had been an unfortunate misunderstanding, as we have already noted, between some of the European alliances and WEF. This was based on a different understanding of the doctrine of Scripture, especially the use of the word "infallible" in the WEF Statement of Faith. Apparently some of the Europeans felt that "infallible" implied a dictation theory of inspiration, that is, that God literally dictated his message, word for word, to the writers of the Holy Scriptures. While this was never the idea held by those who framed the Statement of Faith, it was interpreted in that way by some European theologians. This kept many of the European alliances from joining WEF.

In 1962 Gilbert Kirby had dealt with this issue on several occasions. On July 30, 1962, he wrote to Everett Cattell:

> You will be interested to know that I have been asked to go to Berlin at the end of September to meet the Executive Committee of the European Evangelical Alliance and to talk over WEF matters with them. As I think you will know we have always been embarrassed by the attitude of these brethren in Europe. Many of them at the time when the WEF was formed went off to form this European Evangelical Alliance rather than join up with WEF. We always felt in Britain that in some cases their motives were definitely mixed. We are quite sure that in several countries there was a fear that members of WEF, would be required to subscribe to a definitely evangelical basis, whereas in some of these Alliances some of the members, at least, had somewhat departed from such a basis. However, I think now things are beginning to clarify themselves and in some countries, at least, there is a revived interest in WEF, particularly, I would say, in Germany where the Alliance is quite

strong. I hope to be able to answer some of their queries at this meeting in September and shall value your prayers.[7]

Following his visit to Berlin Kirby wrote again to Cattell on 2 October, 1962,

> I listened patiently to the various points of view that were expressed and I did feel that by God's grace I was able to answer most of them, I hope, convincingly. It does seem that one of the stumbling blocks in some of their minds is the use of the word "Infallible" in relation to the Scriptures. I assured them that this did not imply a mechanical theory regarding inspiration but did, in fact, refer to the nature of the truth revealed in Scripture. They did ask me whether or not I could produce an official WEF Statement as to what that word is intended to convey. They would like then to translate this Statement into German and French and bring it to the notice of the Conference meeting later this month in Berlin. I am wondering whether you would feel able to draft a simple Statement which we could quickly get translated. I do not think a long article is called for but a straightforward elucidation of the meaning of "Infallible" in this context. I did stress that in WEF we do require that those who serve on the Committees of the National Fellowships shall be of one mind regarding the evangelical faith. I think that some of these Alliances in Europe are in the process of "putting their houses in order" and when this has been done, I do sincerely hope some will apply for membership, but things do not move very fast. Looking back I can see that a number of mistakes were made by different people at Woudschotin but that is now past history and we need to face things are they are today.[8]

Now in 1968 the time seemed ripe to resolve this problem and bring the Europeans wholeheartedly into WEF. The European Evangelical Alliance brought to the General Council a detailed "Statement on Holy Scripture" which represented their position. This covered three pages, but the most pertinent part for our purposes reads as follows:

> We accept the whole of Holy Scripture as the divine revelation inspired by the Holy Spirit, and Word of God with absolute authority determining the doctrine and the conduct of the believer.
>
> Therefore we must reject any view which regards the Bible merely as another historico-religious document, seeing in it only the testimonies of gifted men but without binding or continuing importance.[9]

After due consideration and discussion of its implications for WEF the General Council was satisfied that the European statement was not in contradiction to the WEF Statement of Faith. The following actions appear in the minutes:

> The exception in the European Alliances' application permitting a

variance in wording in the Statement of Faith Clause 3, Section I, was brought up for clarification. Does this allowance of variances mean a revision of the constitution—no. [sic]

They were granted the privilege of submitting their statement on "The Scriptures" and subscribing to the World Evangelical Alliance Statement of Faith, plus agreement with the ancient Christian Creeds, as equivalent to subscribing to the World Evangelical Fellowship statement, thus eliminating the use of the word "infallible." By common consent of movers and delegates, the motion was amended to approve all but (d), which was referred to the Executive Committee for drafting and re-submission to the council.[10]

Statement of Faith—The motion prevailed that a statement be drafted by the Executive Committee for insertion in the minutes when the membership of the European Alliances are [sic] ratified, explaining the reasons for and basis of the permission to be a member on a variant but equal statement of faith and limited to Alliances that had been members of the WEA on the basis of the old statement of faith of the World Evangelical Alliance.[11]

To implement the above action, special consideration was given to European Evangelical Alliances which were originally members of the World Evangelical Alliance of which the World Evangelical Fellowship is an outgrowth.

Since some of these have recently reaffirmed their faith in the historic creeds, and the original statement of faith of the World Evangelical Alliance, and in addition have subscribed to the statement of faith of the British Evangelical Alliance, and in addition have drawn up a fresh and detailed statement of their position on the authority of scripture, all of which documents were circulated to our membership, we have concluded that these are equivalent to our constitutional statement of faith for purposes of membership.

We recommend therefore the ratification of this action in the case of those European Alliances which were members of the World Evangelical Alliance and not to be taken [sic] as a precedent for others.

Motion prevailed that statement be ratified.[12]

Thus after seventeen years this issue was laid to rest and the European Evangelical Alliance became an active and participating member of WEF. It has continued to be one of the prime movers of WEF to the present time.

## Preparing for the Future

A new Executive Committee was elected at Lausanne with the following membership:

| | |
|---|---|
| President: | I. Ben Wati (*India*) |
| Vice President: | Clyde W. Taylor (*USA*) |

Treasurer:          Ernst Beck (*Germany*)
Members at Large:   George Chen (*Taiwan-China*)
                         A. Morgan Derham (*Britain*)
                         Daniel Jonah (*Sierra Leone*)
                         K. Liddle (*New Guinea*)

A Finance Committee was also appointed consisting of the following men:

Chairman: Ernst Beck (*Germany*)
B. E. Fernando (*Ceylon*)
Stan Izon (*Canada*)
C. Stacey Woods (*Switzerland*)

The election of Ben Wati of India as President marked the first time that a non-Westerner held this position of leadership in WEF. It was the fulfillment of a dream for Dr Everett Cattell who had worked closely with Ben Wati in the formation and development of the Evangelical Fellowship of India and who had promoted him for the presidency of WEF in 1962 at Hong Kong. It also was directly in line with the desires expressed so strongly by Dennis Clark for emerging leadership from Asia and Africa.

Reporting on this General Council meeting *Christianity Today* entitled a news column "Housekeeping—In Private." It was a short article, less than one column in length, indicating that "most of the week was spent on housekeeping matters for the WEF, which stresses a minimum of central organization."[13] The reporter apparently failed to grasp the significance of the new ground which WEF was now breaking in the emergence of leadership from nations other than the USA and Britain, or the momentum gained by the resolution of the theological misunderstandings that had previously kept some Europeans from active participation in WEF.

As the General Council came to a close, there was evident among the delegates a new vision for the international ministry which WEF could exercise, a new sense of purpose, and a renewed concern for spiritual renewal in the church. Special time was spent in prayer for revival. The delegates returned to their homes with optimistic anticipation of increasing momentum in fellowship, renewal, and cooperation in the outreach of the church.

But clouds were gathering on the horizon.

# CHAPTER ELEVEN

# From Lausanne to London to Washington

In the aftermath of the problems faced by Dennis Clark, as described in our last chapter, (some might cynically say "*caused* by Dennis Clark!") he began to feel that it was futile for him to fill out his term of office. He had been appointed at the Lausanne General Council meeting in May 1968 for a further three-year term. However, by May 1970 he was expressing increasing frustrations in the work.

On 2 May, 1970, he wrote from Seoul, Korea, "An Open Letter to the Executive, Co-ordinators, and Close Friends of WEF." In this he reflected upon his involvement in WEF since March 1966. He spoke at length of the problem of finances, saying that he had "proceeded on the basis of a solemn pledge of a minimum of one percent from the major Western bodies of their national income . . ." but that this had not materialized. He added that "previous attempts to get WEF off the ground by my predecessors ran into stalemate due to lack of financial backing." He said that he had been unable to attract major donors apart from BGEA (Billy Graham Evangelistic Association).

Then he raised an absolutely fundamental question.

> As we again arrive at an impasse it is necessary to ask the same old questions. Do members really want WEF? How is it to be financed?
>
> At the Lausanne Council all present agreed to the need for WEF and voted against dissolution. Members pledged themselves to do all possible financially, but this pledge in the first year brought in only

$2,000 and in the first seven months of the second year only around $150.00. It is not possible to operate in this way.

It is demoralizing . . . to see the disinterest [sic] by member bodies and lack of financial responsibility . . . The International Secretary cannot operate in the field with all the pressures this entails if the centre is not supplied.[1]

Clark then went on to propose two possible courses of action. One was to name as his successor, at the end of his term, someone who would be more able to attract finance and interest than he had been. The second course would be to close the Lausanne Office, keeping only a Swiss postal box at low cost, and encourage the growth of projects such as TAP (Theological Assistance Programme), ICA (International Christian Assistance) and Bible ministries. He favoured the latter alternative.

Clark felt keenly that member bodies of WEF had not lived up to their commitments. This was especially true of the Americans, in his opinion, even though the Americans had always provided the lion's share of funding for WEF. He stated categorically to the author that "the Americans reneged on their budgetary commitments when they saw they lost control of it . . . The Americans would furiously deny this, but it is a fact. So, when the money was not available, I closed down the office in Lausanne."[2]

Clark decided, after continued frustrations, to return to the work that he had been doing with BMMF and the David C. Cook Publishing Company, leaving his WEF responsibilities by the end of 1970.

A press release was sent out on 10 July, 1970, stating:

The WEF central Lausanne Office closes with this announcement. As an economy measure the Lausanne Office was closed at the end of June. Mr Dennis Clark continues to serve from his Canadian home base until the end of 1970 as International Secretary, during which time he will provide a reduced service to member bodies and the functional ministries. The Lausanne bank account and post box address has been retained while negotiations for a low cost secretariat service by one of the WEF member bodies is being negotiated.

The functional ministries of WEF continue at field level and finance will be directed to these important emphases.[3]

*Gordon Landreth*

Dennis Clark continued to serve as International Secretary

until the end of 1970. At that time Mr Gordon Landreth, General Secretary of the British Evangelical Alliance, was asked to become interim International Secretary until the Executive Committee of WEF could find a successor to Mr Clark. There was a degree of confusion for a few months as to the division of responsibilities. The Lausanne office having been closed, records and office functions were moved to the London office of the British Evangelical Alliance where Mr Landreth was located. Landreth wrote to Clark early in 1971 asking for all current receipts and payments, so that he could "be a proper acting secretary."

Clark responded on 22 March, 1971, indicating that he was continuing to function until his successor was named, and that the London office existed only to receive membership renewals.

> Your office in London coordinates the annual membership renewal for which you received 100 pounds. This is your only function, so you have nothing else to worry about. Everything else should be referred to me. I continue to serve from my home base in an honorary capacity until not later than September 30, 1971 . . .
>
> There has never been any change in the Secretary's function, and your letter is the first intimation that you thought you were to be "a proper acting secretary."[4]

(In the same letter he spoke of the need for proper procedures in the naming of his successor, indicating that there must be sensitivity to the feelings of non-Western leaders. "We must at all costs avoid the old Western colonial manipulations where a few Western leaders make their own decisions for the rest of the world.")[5]

Apparently the other WEF leaders, including the president Mr I. Ben Wati of India, disagreed and clarified that Mr Landreth was, indeed, the interim International Secretary. Thus in April, 1971, Mr Clark turned over to the London office of the British Evangelical Alliance the files and records of WEF to be kept there until a more permanent office was established. Gordon Landreth wrote to Clark on 7 May, 1971, acknowledging receipt of papers and accounts.

*Decisions in Doorn*

The Executive Committee of WEF met in Doorn, Holland, from 26 to 28 August, 1971, for urgent business, especially the naming of a new International Secretary. After due consideration the role was given to Dr Clyde Taylor of the USA. Dr Taylor already held three positions: he was General Director of NAE of the USA, Director of Public Affairs of NAE, and Executive Secretary of EFMA. WEF requested NAE to allow him to spend up to one third or one half of his time on WEF business. In October 1971 the NAE Board of Administration granted this request, and Dr Taylor's appointment became official. The WEF office was thus officially transferred from London to Washington, D.C., where Dr Taylor was located. Gordon Landreth was appointed Treasurer of WEF replacing Mr Ernst Beck of Germany. Accounts were thus split between London and Washington.

Following the meeting in Holland there was a new sense of direction and vision for what WEF could accomplish. In an unsigned and undated report of the Executive Committee meeting, prepared "by the editors," a sense of renewed outreach comes through enthusiastically. Board members were reported to be "a bit overwhelmed at the prospects of unifying 14 new evangelical organizations from Africa, Asia, and Latin America with their present 16 member countries. Five or six more countries are setting up their organizations, a potential addition to WEF's growing membership."[6]

Another thing that raised hopes for renewed vision within WEF was the suggestion of a possible congress on world missions.

> The members "called for a world congress of missions, possibly in connection with a Second World Congress on Evangelism, to bring together for serious study the leaders of evangelical missions from the older sending countries and the many new missions raised up by the younger churches in the so-called "mission lands" . . .
>
> The Netherlands meeting may be a turning point for the World Evangelical Fellowship. Although most of its members have been quite willing to go along with the plans and operations of the world body, only a few of them have been able to muster significant strength and leadership to help make WEF a strong world organization. Now with the possibility of increasing its membership in the next year or so, WEF's future appears bright.[7]

Once again, however, the ever present spectre of financial limitations is raised.

The procurement of funds continues to be one of the great problems of the world organization. If it has been found lacking in services to its national constituencies and their suggested programmes . . . to a large degree it is because it has been unable to support staff on the field. Until evangelicals awaken to the great threat of their churches not being tied together internationally . . . it is predicted that WEF will have a difficult time securing adequate financial support.[8]

Nevertheless, in spite of the financial problems, the report ends on an optimistic note by saying, "Expectations are high among WEF leaders that the organization may become a dynamic, viable fellowship which will enable the millions of evangelicals around the world to display their oneness in Christ."[9]

## The New Secretary

Clyde Taylor had already been fully involved with WEF for many years, and so it was not much of a change for him to add one more side to his many-faceted role in evangelicalism. He had already been travelling extensively around the world in the course of his EFMA duties, and sometimes these trips had been related to WEF. Now he would continue to travel but with the official title of International Secretary of WEF.

Early in his term of office he drew up a detailed list of "Proposed Goals for the Future of the World Evangelical Fellowship." These were ten goals with another fifteen subpoints showing the breadth and depth of his vision for WEF. These goals were for strengthening the existing national fellowships where they did not exist; encouraging others to become members of WEF; emphasizing evangelism; furthering the development of non-Western mission societies; strenthening the efforts of TAP (Theological Assistance Program) and TEE (Theological Education by Extension); circulating exchanges of information among member fellowships; sponsoring Bible conferences and seminars where requested; and implementing the structure of WEF through regional committees and secretaries.

WEF *World News*, a quarterly news sheet which had begun under Dennis Clark's leadership, was continued. It carried regular news of evangelical alliances and the church in general from all around the world. The news was not limited to WEF members, although it focussed primarily on WEF activities.

In his annual report for 1972, the first full year of his tenure as International Secretary, Clyde Taylor was able to report that there were now 18 national members with two other national bodies being considered for membership. All of these member bodies, with one exception, had been visited by the Secretary or one of the officers of WEF during the past year. He reported that:

> Most of the fellowships have active programs and are structured to meet the needs of the evangelical constituencies of their nation. With the establishment of regional offices it will be possible to more adequately visit [sic] and serve the national bodies.[10]

Taylor was able to report that WEF had met its financial responsibilities during 1972, but this was only because no meeting of the Executive Committee was held during that year. Had the committee met, there would have been a deficit at the end of the year.

Taylor stated in his report that the Executive Committee must meet during the coming year. He was experiencing the same difficulty faced by his predecessors in convening a widely scattered board, with all the expense and time involved,

When Billy Graham began the thinking and planning for the International Congress on World Evangelization to be held in Lausanne, Switzerland, in July, 1974, Clyde Taylor became very actively involved. Much of his time and effort for two years prior to this event went into trying to work out the implications of such an event for WEF and the ways in which WEF might help in the follow-up process. It is probably accurate to say that the event was constantly in the background of Dr Taylor's thinking as he attempted to lead WEF into a stronger worldwide ministry on behalf of evangelicals.

CHAPTER 12

# International Ambassador

When a man wears four "hats" administratively, it would not be surprising if he were to neglect one or more of them in his daily duties. Clyde Taylor seemed to have the remarkable capacity to wear all four hats at one time without neglecting any. His worldwide perspective, his long background in WEF, and his boundless energy combined to WEF's benefit, even though he was responsible for three other offices at the same time.

The years of his tenure in office (1971–1974) were characterized by vigorous activity in a number of areas.

First, there was the ever present problem of raising funds for WEF. Early in 1972 he reported that

> since the last meeting of the Board most of the effort expended on the part of WEF has had to do with concentrating foundations and individuals in an endeavor to raise the budgets for WEF and TAP. Up to the present time as indicated in the report a little over $10,000 has been received. Requests are out to meet the budget if only the money is received from the foundations and other donors. Prayers of the Board were requested on this behalf.[1]

Second, Dr Taylor's tireless travels were continued. In 1972 he travelled to Africa for six weeks in July and August, and then to Europe and Asia in October and November in the company of Mr and Mrs E. L. Frizen, Jr., of IFMA. On this trip they visited England, Germany, Lebanon, Iran, Pakistan, India, Sri Lanka, Singapore, Indonesia, Thailand, the Philippines, Hong Kong, Taiwan, Korea, and Japan.

In May 1973, along with Mrs Taylor, Clyde travelled to Jamaica, Haiti, Venezuela, Colombia, Panama, Honduras, El Salvador, and Guatemala, with the purpose of encouraging local evangelical fellowships to form and to become members of WEF. He reported his hopes that perhaps four of the eight or nine fellowships in that region would soon join WEF.

Third, a great deal of time was spent in preparation for the International Congress on World Evangelization to be held in Lausanne, Switzerland, in July 1974. Dr Taylor participated in the planning committee for this great event and took an active part especially in plans for the post-Congress follow-up. (This will be discussed below.)

Fourth, the interests of WEF were being broadened at this time to include development in the Third World as an important and integral part of the mission of the church and, therefore, of WEF. An organization called Development Assistance Services (DAS) had come into being. Known originally as "Help for a Hungry World," it had changed its name to DAS when it came under the umbrella of International Students, Inc. Its purpose was to study the needs among evangelicals in Third World nations for small business, industry, and agricultural activity; then to match up with situations of need the personnel in Western nations who could evaluate such needs and provide the expertise and funds to help get programmes moving. The plan was to work closely with the International Institute for Development, Inc. (IIDI), turning over to them the programmes for follow-through after the initial explorations had been carried out.

In 1971 International Students, Inc., was planning to move its headquarters from Washington, D.C., to Colorado and was re-evaluating its ministries, including DAS. They requested that DAS should come under the jurisdiction of WEF, which as an international body could help carry out its vision.

Clyde Taylor saw this as an opportunity for WEF to show its concern for the total needs of men and women. He wrote to the WEF/USA Board:

> [IIDI] will work with the successor of the DAS to promote industry, businesses, and other programs in the "third world" where jobs and food are in short supply, as a Christian expression of concern that goes along with our spiritual concern for their salvation. However, these businesses

are not to be run by missions or churches, but by the private segment. The ultimate concern is to start industries that will be a joint enterprise between Westerners with the know how and the funds and national leaders who will be taken into the management as they learn and also become shareholders in the business. It is hoped that eventually the national Christian laymen will take over the business.[2]

Early in 1972 several meetings were held between members of DAS and WEF to discuss the possible turnover of the ministries of DAS to WEF. By-laws were drawn up stating the purpose of a newly formed group, to be called International Development Assistance Commission (IDAC), as follows:

1. Its purpose is to supplement the work and outreach of missions, churches, evangelical fellowships in economically underdeveloped countries by assisting evangelical business men in the establishing of businesses and projects that will provide economic opportunity in these areas.
2. It will inform concerned Christians overseas and at home of the need, opportunities, and available resources and services.
3. It will receive, document, and seek evangelical business men to evaluate the requested projects sent from the field.
4. It will seek businessmen competent and willing to start and operate businesses overseas.[3]

On 12 April, 1972, at its meeting in St. Louis, Missouri, the WEF/USA Board ratified these By-Laws and accepted IDAC under the umbrella of WEF. An executive secretary was appointed located in Grand Rapids, Michigan. However, by the middle of 1973 there was an increasing dissatisfaction with the operation of this office. Finally in July 1973 the WEF Executive Committee requested that IDAC become a commission of the NAE rather than of WEF. At its meeting of 8 October, 1973, the WEF/USA Board voted

that the International Development Assistance Commission be considered a Commission of NAE, but remain under the direction of the WEF-NAE (read "USA") Board, with Secretary Clyde W. Taylor acting as IDAC Secretary.[4]

It was also decided to close the Grand Rapids office and move it to Washington to function under the WEF and NAE. Thus Clyde Taylor added another "hat" to his many responsibilities!

From the beginning of his term of office it had been understood that Clyde Taylor would not be able to give full attention to WEF due to his manifold duties in other areas of responsibility. Thus a search was being made for a full-time International Secretary to replace him. The WEF Executive Committee met in Atlanta, Georgia, 2–4 July, 1973, and considered this matter.

> A report indicated that there was complete inability to secure even a good prospect for the position. The instructions had been to seek a person from the Third World if at all possible and this is where the search has centered. However, any person that might be capable of this position is so essential to the ongoing of the church in his area, that he would not consider an international position.[5]

The matter was left at this point for future consideration.

## WEF *and Lausanne*

The International Congress on World Evangelization (ICOWE), to be held in Lausanne, had been in the planning stages for several years. Its roots actually went back to 1960 when in Montreux, Switzerland, Billy Graham had convened a small select group of evangelical leaders from around the world to consider greater cooperation in evangelism. Out of this meeting grew the World Congress on Evangelism held in Berlin in 1966. From that congress several regional congresses on evangelism were spawned, in Bogota, 1968; Singapore, 1968; Minneapolis, 1969; and Amsterdam, 1971. Now the time had come for a much larger and more representative gathering to consider the entire scope of world evangelization. This had been a dream of Billy Graham's for many years, and at last it was to come to fruition in Lausanne.

Enthusiasm for ICOWE grew rapidly and with great intensity during 1973 and 1974. As early as 1972 Clyde Taylor had reported, following his trip to Europe and Asia, that the follow-up to this congress could well produce some new world-wide structure for evangelism. Referring to meetings held with evangelical fellowship leaders in many countries, he wrote:

> The thought was discussed that out of the ICOWE there might come, as part of an on-going strategy, a simple worldwide structure of some kind to implement the strategy agreed upon as the means to finish the task of world evangelism. I expressed the hope that this might be the WEF if it becomes strong enough and viable enough.[6]

Considerable correspondence was carried on between the

planners of ICOWE and the WEF leadership to see if by any means WEF could be the umbrella under which the follow-up could be structured. Because of the importance of this issue, Billy Graham called twenty leaders from around the world to meet in Atlanta, Georgia, in June, 1973, for a "Post-Congress World Organization Consultation." The purpose was to consider the best possible means of conserving and continuing the vision to be given at ICOWE.

Dr Donald Hoke, director of ICOWE, wrote to these twenty invitees expressing the purpose of the consultation:

> At that time, after a period of waiting upon the Lord for divine wisdom and guidance, we will discuss:
> —the need for such a world organization of evangelicals;
> —all the various possibilities or organization and structure for such a world organization (such as the World Evangelical Fellowship, etc.);
> —the steps to be taken to bring such an organization into being, etc.
> May I emphasize that we will all come to this consultation with open minds. We are not committed to any program or plan. It may be the Holy Spirit will lead us to decide against such an organization. But as a key evangelical leader in your nation and continent, you are needed to consider this vital need.[7]

Clyde Taylor was one of those invited. To the letter of invitation to him Dr Hoke added a P.S. saying, "In preparation for the above consultation, it would seem to me to be wise to have some kind of an official presentation by you or Hudson [Armerding] on the history, specific genius, and future reasonable expectations of WEF."[8]

Bishop A. Jack Dain, Executive Chairman of the ICOWE Planning Committee, also wrote to Clyde Taylor concerning the possibility that the WEF Executive Committee could hold its forthcoming meeting in Atlanta immediately after the ICOWE meeting. He said, "Finally, regarding the W.E.F. Executive Committee, there would seem to be very real value in using the presence of two or three of the members and I am wondering whether this could not assemble on the evening of Monday 2nd . . ."[9]

Each person invited to this consultation was asked to prepare a paper with his views on how the ICOWE follow-up should be handled and whether or not a new organization might be necessary. A wide variety of opinions was expressed in these papers.

G. Aiken Taylor of the USA was one who did not feel that WEF was the adequate vehicle for such a work. Philip Teng of Hong Kong was non-committal but requested that the discussions be held wisely in relation to WEF. He felt that WEF was good but needed strengthening. Paul McKaughan of Brazil felt that "the establishment of a world organization for evangelicals in Brazil might cause a very unfortunate polarization."[10] Gordon Landreth of Great Britain felt that

> it is better to build on an existing foundation (if this is sound) rather than to start up completely from scratch . . . If anything else is set up, it will need to be so like the present WEF that the question must be asked whether this present structure cannot be taken over and given new life in a fresh initiative at the ICOWE. Here is a ready-made framework for future body building.[11]

John Stott wrote rather a full and thoughtful paper saying, among other things,

> My own hope is that the WEF will be revived and restructured . . . I have very considerable hesitations about the wisdom of launching yet another world body. It would not 'kill' the old WEF, and the two would surely exist side by side resulting in embarrassment and wastage . . . Nevertheless a radical overhaul of the WEF would be necessary, both to meet the new and wider needs envisaged and to win the confidence of the worldwide evangelical constituency.[12]

Perhaps the strongest statement against forming another worldwide body came from the German Evangelical Alliance. Peter Schneider, Executive Secretary, wrote a paper entitled "German Evangelical views about a possible post-Congress Evangelical organization." He pointed out that "WEF has not made any impact yet within Germany and is hardly known to anybody outside the main Board of the German Evangelical Alliance." Therefore, the Germans were hesitant to limit the possible follow-up to WEF. Yet at the same time he went on to say:

> We do believe that there is an absolute must for having a worldwide organization for Evangelicals which will be strong and effective enough to not only articulate evangelical convictions, but also to act in various fields of evangelistic, theological, social, and maybe even political areas.
>
> If WEF does not find worldwide support to be this desired worldwide organization of evangelicals then there should be organized something else. But by no means we would like to see another worldwide evangelical organization alongside or a parallel to WEF. . . . So, whatever the name

would be, we must only have one evangelical world organization. Otherwise the German evangelicals would not be willing to contribute either thought or action of finances.[13]

No final action was taken at this consultation, as it was felt that the congress itself should express its desires concerning how and by whom the vision of ICOWE should be carried on.

## *The Role of WEF: Conflicting Opinions*

Immediately following this consultation the WEF Executive Committee met in Atlanta. Considerable discussion ensued about how WEF could relate to the post-ICOWE follow-on programmes. Bishop Jack Dain, who was both a member of the WEF Executive Committee and also executive chairman of ICOWE's Planning Committee, expressed his feeling that WEF was a unique organization with a distinct role to play in the evangelical world, and that it should continue with its present programmes. It was agreed that some of the functions of WEF, especially of its commissions, might be taken over by the post-Congress planning.

> It was noted that WEF should stress its functional work and this is to be done through the commissions. We should seek the position of a servant body and develop a servant image.[14]

As ICOWE drew nearer, the discussions of the follow-up plans and the possibility of a new organization became more intense. Clyde Taylor was hopeful that a Commission on Evangelism could be developed that might relate to WEF. On 6 March, 1974, he wrote to Bishop Dain saying,

> I am still very hopeful that out of the congress there may come the structure of a Commission on Evangelism that will be set up with regional offices, and then break down into national committees, that could have a central chairman and reporting center without a lot of machinery. I think that this is possible, and, if so, it should fit in perfectly well with what we have in WEF. Since WEF is still a flexible entity and quite viable, I believe it can be adapted to anything that is going to be thoroughly evangelical.[15]

On 19 March Taylor wrote to Donald Hoke along the same line, expressing his hopes as follows:

> A possible solution might be the formation of an Evangelism Committee

or Commission which would specialize in evangelistic efforts and thrusts in all parts of the world . . .

It seems to us that it would be unfortunate to have Lausanne form a competing organization to WEF at a time when it is showing progress . . .

If the congress seeks to develop an organization which could develop along the lines of WEF in its structure and ministries, confusion could very well develop and set back the whole evangelical cooperative movement.[16]

Some weeks later Donald Hoke wrote to Taylor very positively expressing his own hopes along similar lines. He then added a significant word:

> Now I have some good news for you. I saw Billy [Graham] over the weekend in Chicago. We discussed briefly a post-Congress world organization. In the course of the conversation, Billy himself came out with the thought that he felt that the best thing to do would be to try to revitalize and reorganize the World Evangelical Fellowship, building upon that foundation.[17]

Hoke seemed to feel that this would be the direction in which the congress would go. In a later confidential letter, "not be be quoted," he spoke in a similar vein.

About this time a forcefully-worded statement came from the German Evangelical Alliance. Mr Wilhelm Gilbert, president of the German Evangelical Alliance, wrote to Bishop Dain on 17 April, 1974, stating that the Germans strongly opposed the formation of any new worldwide evangelical organization. He enclosed a press release drawn up by the Alliance in which this was spelled out.

> *German Evangelical Alliance does not wish for a new evangelical world organization.*
>
> Berlin (idea)—As on the German level (German Evangelical Alliance), so also on a worldwide level (World Evangelical Fellowship), one can only ever expect initiatives from the Evangelical Alliance, but not executive or legislative measures. This opinion was advocated by the Main Board of the German Evangelical Alliance at its spring session in Berlin-Schwanenwerder. The Main Board has also decided to warn the directors of the International Congress for World Evangelization in Lausanne officially against aiming at a new worldwide organization—in accordance with the desires of some individual Christians—as a result of the Congress. Much rather, the present loose form of the Worldwide Evangelical Fellowship should be retained. With its various specialist commissions it is fully sufficient as a platform for the articulation of evangelical conviction, i.e. conviction with the Gospel, and up till now has not been fully turned to account.[18]

This evoked a three page letter in response from Bishop Dain in which he expressed grave concern that the German brethren should be making such statements. He said that the congress must be able to meet "without such warnings as your press release contains." He also said that questionnaires which had gone out to all participants in ICOWE indicated that the large majority of them felt that "the WEF cannot itself meet the total demands of the present situation in world evangelization."[19]

Others continued to express their concern that the follow-up of ICOWE should be carefully considered on a cooperative basis. Dr Hudson Armerding, president of Wheaton College and vice president of WEF, wrote to Bishop Dain on 3 May, 1974, saying,

> . . . it would seem to be time-consuming and wasteful to set aside one organization and then create another. I strongly favor necessary modifications rather than complete replacement . . .
> . . . I trust we can seriously consider the feasibility of programs growing out of the Congress that will be cooperative with or even a part of the ministry of the World Evangelical Fellowship.

Bishop Dain continued to express his personal support of WEF and its ministry while at the same time he maintained his feeling that it might not be wise to limit the follow-up of ICOWE to the one structure of WEF. He wrote to Clyde Taylor on 13 May, 1974, indicating that as chairman of the Executive Committee he had tried to ensure the fairest and fullest exchange of views. He also said it would be dangerous for him to make any public statements regarding what would happen after Lausanne, since it was vital that the Spirit of God be given freedom to direct the congress itself. "Nothing could be more damaging than the suggestion that we had attempted to force a particular pattern on the Congress."[20] He went on to express his hope that whatever happened after Lausanne would serve to "strengthen WEF and enable it to expand its ministry both geographically and functionally."[21]

He also pointed out that there were some areas of the world where, for various reasons, evangelicals would not wish to accept membership in WEF but might be willing to work with a WEF commission without actually joining. He added, "I am afraid if we attempt to create a tight structure we shall only run into serious difficulty."[22] He quoted Billy Graham who had "shared his conviction that we should not act precipitately in

Lausanne but explore guidelines, directions and concerns and then have a meeting perhaps in the latter part of the year."[23]

On the eve of ICOWE Clyde Taylor still had hopes that, whatever was set up following Lausanne, it could be loosely related to WEF. He had received a letter from Arnold T. Olson, president of the Evangelical Free Church of America, saying, "The word on the continent is that the powers that be plan to start a new International Fellowship which might possibly replace the World Evangelical Fellowship."[24] In replying to this Taylor wrote,

> . . . there is a tendency to believe that whatever comes out of Lausanne will probably be a committee, that, in turn, will propose the setting up of an International Evangelism Fellowship, which will encourage evangelism, exchange information, and this type of thing. They want this set up on a regional basis. They have now discovered that that is the way the WEF plans to be set up. Therefore, we are exchanging a lot of information with the leaders of the Lausanne Congress, and Billy Graham told me personally that he thought perhaps the best thing that could come out of it would be cooperation with the WEF.[25]

This is where the matter stood when ICOWE was convened during the dates of 16–25 July, 1974. At the congress itself a questionnaire was circulated to all participants asking their feelings about how the follow-up should be handled. Two question especially pertinent to this discussion, with their respective answers, were:

1. Is there a need for a post-Congress fellowship to assist in implementing the vision of the Congress?

   | | | |
   |---|---|---|
   | *Great need* | 993 | 63% |
   | *Some need* | 381 | 24% |
   | *Doubtful* | 117 | 7% |
   | *No need* | 95 | 6% |

2. How much do you know of the World Evangelical Fellowship?

   | | | |
   |---|---|---|
   | *A good deal* | 277 | 14% |
   | *Some* | 944 | 48% |
   | *A little* | 436 | 22% |
   | *None* | 301 | 15% |

It was, therefore, against this background that the WEF met immediately after ICOWE to hold its sixth General Assembly in Chateaux d'Oex, Switzerland.

CHAPTER THIRTEEN

# Is there Life after Lausanne?

On the day that ICOWE concluded a group of over one hundred of the participants travelled for about an hour and a half up into the mountains of Switzerland to the village of Chateaux d'Oex. That evening, 25 July, 1974, 114 delegates, observers and official visitors were called to order for the sixth General Assembly of the World Evangelical Fellowship. Snuggled in a beautiful valley surrounded by stone cliffs and pine forests, Chateaux d'Oex provided an ideal setting for the gathering.

WEF President I. Ben Wati of India opened the assembly with greetings and a presidential address in which he put WEF into historical perspective. He reviewed its roots going back to 1846, its official founding in 1951, its purposes, and its present status. He spoke of the uncertainty concerning WEF's role and function as expressed at the General Assemblies held in Hong Kong in 1962 and Lausanne in 1968. He recognized that this assembly could be somewhat anticlimatic following the great enthusiasm and vision demonstrated by the 4,000 who had attended ICOWE.

At the same time he spoke of the fact that "WEF provides the only visible unity and solidarity among evangelicals." He recognized that "our programme in this General Assembly and our decisions together will have much to do with our experience in Lausanne and what may come out of it." In spite of the possibility that the assembly could be considered

107

an anticlimax, he stated that "it may be the Lord's time to conserve what has been achieved so far and move forward much further in our WEF." He encouraged the delegates to "harness our spiritual unity to evangelical actions." He concluded by expressing his "confidence that this assembly can be the beginning of deeper fellowship, and a more meaningful role under new leadership, giving a new image, not for the sake of WEF but for the Glory of the Lord Jesus Christ and for the sake of the increasing millions of evangelicals around the world."[1]

Greetings were brought to the assembly by Dr Harold J. Ockenga, who spoke briefly of the founding of WEF in Holland in 1951, and by Dr Billy Graham, Dr Donald Hoke, and Bishop A. J. Dain on behalf of ICOWE. Several new fellowships were received into membership: The South Africa Evangelical Council, The Evangelical Fellowship of Rhodesia, The Evangelical Fellowship of Zambia, and The Council of Evangelical Churches of Haiti.

In his report to the assembly the International Secretary, Dr Clyde Taylor, indicated that "the main task of this assembly will be to determine the future goals, strategy, and structure of the WEF, as well as its leadership, its funding and its outreach through its commissions." He went on to ask "What do we want the WEF to be? What do we want it to do? What world image should it have?"[2] This summarized well the direction which the assembly was to take.


*Deciding on the Future*

The major items considered during the next four days were the significance of ICOWE and the ways in which WEF could relate to its ongoing movement; the developing of commissions within the structures of WEF; the possibility of regional structures for WEF; revisions of the WEF constitution; the naming of a full-time International Secretary; and the election of the new Executive Council. (For the first time what had been known as the "Executive Committee" was now called the "Executive Council," although no official action or explanation appears in the minutes for this change in nomenclature.)

One of the most significant steps taken at this assembly was the recognition that WEF could best carry out its mandate through the development of commissions. These would be made up of men and women from various parts of the world who were experts in, and directly involved in, the areas of concern of each commission. The Theological Assistance Program (TAP) had already come into existence under the leadership of Bruce Nicholls following the General Assembly of 1968 and had been officially constituted in 1969. Now consideration was given to expanding the ministry of TAP and making a more comprehensive Theological Commission.

Special attention was also devoted to the area of missions and that of communications, with plans to develop commissions for those areas. Each of these commissions will be considered in more detail in a later chapter, but it is important to note that the seeds from which these commissions sprang were sown at the sixth General Assembly.

Major portions of time were devoted to consideration of the significance of ICOWE and the ways for WEF to relate to whatever might be developing from that great congress. An expression of deep gratitude was recorded with the following action:

> RESOLVED: That the Sixth General Assembly of the WEF expresses:
>
> Our deep appreciation to God for enabling the International Congress on World Evangelization to meet in Lausanne.
>
> Our appreciation to Dr Billy Graham for his part in initiating ICOWE.
>
> Our desire to be involved in the follow up work of ICOWE and the urging of all WEF constituent bodies to seek maximum cooperation of all of "like precious faith" to carry out the Lausanne mandate, i.e. the evangelization of the whole world in our generation.
>
> Our determination to mobilize all available resources for the attainment of the object of the WEF.[3]

A Continuation Committee of ICOWE was to be appointed following the congress, composed of 49 men and women from the major regions of the world. While this committee had not yet met, it was felt by WEF that lines of communication should be kept open with it and that WEF should express its desire to cooperate and be involved in follow-up ministries. There was some concern expressed that another world organization could cause confusion among evangelicals. After lengthy discussion the following motion was passed:

> RESOLVED: That we communicate to the Continuation Committee of the International Congress on World Evangelization with a view to its consideration of the possibility that within the framework of the World Evangelical Fellowship the goals and wishes of the Congress which it is its objective to carry out, may be achieved and in particular, we express the following opinions:
>
> (1) That channels of communications should be kept open between the Continuation Committee and the Fellowship.
> (2) That individuals involved both within this Fellowship and the Continuation Committee should seek to keep both in concert.
> (3) That it is undesirable that there be any duplication of international organizations.
> (4) That this Fellowship is willing to consider proposals for the alteration of its by-laws more effectively to achieve the goals of the Congress within its Fellowship and constituent members.[4]

The possibility of encouraging the development of regional bodies were discussed. Several such bodies already existed, such as the European Evangelical Alliance, and the Association of Evangelicals of Africa and Madagascar. While neither of these had yet become formal members of WEF, both subsequently became active members. The organizing of such regional bodies elsewhere did not come until some years later with the founding of the Evangelical Association of the Caribbean, the Evangelical Fellowship of Asia, and CONELA (the Evangelical Confederation of Latin America).

*The Search for a Secretary*

The search for a full time International Secretary for WEF had been going on for some time without success. Clyde Taylor had hoped to step aside from this position at the General Assembly, but no successor had yet been found. Considerable time was spent in discussing a profile for the chief executive officer, trying to determine what type of person was actually needed, and who might meet these qualifications. Possible Third World locations for the WEF office were also considered in this context, although plans to move the office were postponed until the proper person could be found.

When it became apparent that no successor was in sight

the Executive Council asked Dr Taylor to continue as International Secretary on an interim basis for one year, or until an earlier appointment could be made. He agreed to continue temporarily on this basis. A minute was passed of special appreciation to Dr Taylor for his "life-long service to the evangelical cause and especially to the WEF," along with assurance of Christian love and prayers for him in the days ahead.[5]

The new Executive Council elected at the General Assembly was installed on 28 July, 1974, composed of the following:

| | | |
|---|---|---|
| President | Dr Hudson T. Armerding | (*USA*) |
| Vice President | Revd Stephanus Damaris | (*Indonesia*) |
| Recording Secretary | Dr Byang Kato | (*Zambia*) |
| Treasurer | Mr Gordon Landreth | (*England*) |
| Council Member | Revd Claude Noël | (*Haiti*) |
| Council Member | Revd C. L. Rema | (*India*) |
| Council Member | Rt. Revd A. J. Dain | (*Australia*) |

One of the delegates to the General Assembly was Mr Waldron Scott of The Navigators. He had been instrumental in persuading The Navigators to become associate members of WEF in 1973 and consequently had been named as their delegate to the General Assembly. During that week Scott had some conversations with Wade Coggins, Executive Secretary of the Evangelical Foreign Missions Association of the USA, in which it became apparent that Scott might be a candidate for the position of International Secretary or Administrator of WEF. The General Assembly had indicated that the job of the Secretary perhaps should be divided into two parts: International Secretary and International Administrator. The budget for 1975 had been drawn up to include two people in these roles.

Upon his return to Washington, D.C., Coggins had shared with Clyde Taylor the possibility that Waldron Scott might be available to replace him. Scott had been a missionary with The Navigators for many years in Asia and the Middle East and was well acquainted with the international scene. At ICOWE he had given a major presentation on the state of the church around the world. Preparations for this presentation had given him unusual contact with evangelical leadership on a worldwide basis, and the presentation itself at Lausanne had given him a high profile among such leadership. Taylor warmed immediately to this possibility and wrote to Scott to investigate.

Discussions between Clyde Taylor, Waldron Scott, and Lorne Sanny, president of The Navigators, took place during September. It became apparent that the appointment of Scott could be a felicitous solution to the long-standing problem of finding a full time chief executive officer for WEF. The Navigators graciously agreed to second Scott to WEF if he were called to this position.

## A New Era Begins

On 7 October, 1974, Waldron Scott met with the WEF/USA Corporation Board in Chicago. He was interviewed at length by this board, an experience which he described as "rather gruelling." But he was much encouraged by the warm words of support given by the board, especially by Dr Hudson Armerding, Dr Paul Toms, and Dr Billy Melvin of NAE.

As a result of this meeting the WEF/USA Corporation Board voted to recommend to the WEF Executive Council that Waldron Scott be appointed as International Administrator. This was followed through with a postal ballot, since the Executive Council would not be meeting again for an extended period of time. The results of the postal ballot were all affirmative. Thus Waldron Scott was named International Administrator of WEF in November, 1974, assuming his post officially on 1 January, 1975.

Early in 1975 another postal ballot was circulated to the WEF Executive Council requesting a change in the by-laws to change the title of Mr Scott from "International Administrator" to "General Secretary." This action was approved, and thus Waldron Scott carried this title throughout his tenure of office.

A new era was about to begin for WEF, as Scott became the first fulltime chief executive officer that WEF had ever had.

CHAPTER FOURTEEN

# Expansion and Frustrations

As the first full-time General Secretary of WEF Waldron Scott "hit the ground running." His vision for the need and the potential of WEF was strong, and he had progressive ideas about how to reach important goals. One of his first activities was to travel around the world with Dr Clyde Taylor, his predecessor, early in 1975 to become acquainted with the member bodies of WEF and with evangelical leadership in general. One wonders, with a smile, how some of the Third World churchmen must have viewed this pair as they travelled together: Clyde Taylor, a physical giant with huge hands, a stentorian voice, and outgoing style; Waldron Scott, small of stature, with a quiet voice and unassuming approach. Both men had been missionaries in their own right; both had travelled the world extensively; both were highly respected by their colleagues. But their appearance, style, and general demeanour produced an almost humorous contrast. Clearly WEF was under new leadership, and the manner of relating to the national members would be changing.

As a result of this trip Scott made several observations that led him to certain conclusions about his immediate priorities. First, he observed "that WEF, while appreciated by many evangelicals, had a poor image among others, including a surprising number of leaders within WEF itself." This was based on two factors, namely, "that WEF was not adequately

113

representative of the global evangelical community, and that it seemed preoccupied with structure rather than function."[1]

His second observation was that "organizing new national evangelical fellowships need not take precedence on my time and energies."[2]

He noted that there were approximately fifty national fellowships already in existence, most of which were directly or indirectly related to WEF. New fellowships were in the process of formation and did not seem to need much help from WEF at that stage.

He also noted, however, that among these bodies there were both strong and weak fellowships. The difference between the strong and the weak bodies was almost always related to whether or not they had full time executive leadership, or were depending on voluntary leadership.

## Working Out the Priorities

These observations led Scott to set certain priorities for his ministry and for WEF in general. He stated the following:

> (1) that our emphasis in the immediate future must be on developing the functional aspects of WEF and its constituent members; (2) that this would be accomplished best by strengthening the national and regional bodies and by developing international commissions; (3) that this in turn would require a greatly enlarged financial base . . . and (4) that this base could be developed most quickly in North America and later extended to other continents.[3]

Scott set about immediately to implement these concepts. During the next eighteen months he visited evangelical leaders in 27 countries, thereby raising considerably the profile of WEF and enhancing its credibility. He also placed special emphasis on the functional, rather than the structural, aspects of WEF, especially as demonstrated through its commissions. He gave attention to the Theological Commission, the Missions Commission, the Communications Commission, and the development of an international Women's Commission. (These commissions are described on pp.157–205.)

Administratively Scott responded to an average of 250

letters per month, an astounding output of work that greatly increased the visibility of WEF among evangelical leaders. He also increased the WEF mailing list from 700 names when he took over to 10,000 names by the middle of 1976.

He gave much time and thought to relationships with the Lausanne Committee for World Evangelization (LCWE). Having attended the Lausanne Congress of 1974 and seen the immediate aftermath at the WEF General Assembly at Chateaux d 'Oex, he felt that the development of closer contacts and cooperation between these two world bodies was indispensable for the cause of Christian unity. He recognized that the Lausanne Committee represented a broader evangelical spectrum than WEF, and it was his hope that closer cooperation would broaden the WEF constituency.

The small financial base of WEF was a major concern, as it had been to every one of his predecessors. Up to this point no one had been successful in developing a broad enough base to provide the kind of funds necessary to carry out the global visions which WEF had always represented. To this end he began to develop a programme known as "Global Deacons." His hope was to enlist laymen and women "who, like Stephen in Acts 6 and 7, are dedicated to Christ, ready to witness for Him, and prepared to assume financial responsibility in the worldwide evangelical community."[4] This was to be set up as a legal corporation under the name of "The Order of Saint Stephen." Articles of incorporation were developed, a certificate of membership was designed, and laypeople were recruited to commit themselves to this endeavour.

It was hoped that these men and women would contribute personally, would encourage their local churches to put WEF on the regular budget, would recruit others in the business and professional world to contribute, would travel occasionally overseas to become acquainted with the ministries of WEF member bodies, and in general would become responsible for a major portion of the needed finances of WEF.

In September, 1976, a full-time Director of Development for WEF, who also served as coordinator of the Global Deacons programme, was hired by Scott. There were high hopes that this appointment together with the vision of

Global Deacons would finally give the financial breakthrough that WEF had always needed. However, it was not to be. By April, 1977, Scott saw that the desired results were not being realized, and he found it necessary to terminate the services of the Director of Development. The programme of Global Deacons was continued for several years, but it never reached the potential levels which Scott had envisioned. (There were some similarities, both in purposes and in results, to the program of SHARE which J. Elwin Wright had initiated a quarter of a century earlier.) Scott had hoped that by 1980 he could enlist 2,000 Global Deacons who would help maintain contacts with 10,000 or more churches, and thus achieve an annual income of one million dollars. The goal was admirable, the method was legitimate, the efforts were herculean; but, sadly, the results were minimal.

One of Scott's hopes had been to establish the international headquarters of WEF in a Third World country rather than in the USA or Europe, where it had always been located. And so he secured an office in Beirut, Lebanon, where he had worked previously as a missionary under The Navigators. However, internal strife and turmoil were rampant in that land at the time, and the building where the office was located was blown up by a bomb, effectively nullifying Scott's endeavour. At that point Scott decided to locate the office in Colorado Springs, Colorado, where he was then residing. The headquarters of The Navigators, who had seconded Scott to WEF and who generously provided his full support, were in Colorado Springs, and it seemed logical and economical for him to remain there.

*Glen Eyrie*

The Executive Council of WEF, which had been elected at Chateaux d'Oex in 1974, held its first meeting on 20–22 November, 1976, at Glen Eyrie, headquarters of The Navigators. Present at the meeting were: Dr Hudson Armerding (USA), as president; Dr Claude Noël (Haiti), Dr Petros Octavianus (Indonesia), Mr Samuel Odunaike (Nigeria), Mr Gordon Landreth (United Kingdom), Mr Brian Bayston

(Australia), Mr Waldron Scott (*ex officio*), and Mr Melvin Taylor (staff). Time was spent discussing the activities of the General Secretary since he had assumed office on 1 January, 1975, the developments in the various WEF commissions, relationships with other Christian bodies, and the urgent financial needs including the development programme.

A major area of consideration brought to the Executive Committee by the General Secretary was the difficulty he was experiencing in combining three key functions, namely, administration, fund raising, and world travel. He expressed the need for relief in one or more of these areas if he was to function properly as the chief executive officer. It was agreed that world travel was essential for the promotion of unity and cooperation. The Council considered the possibility of naming regional vice-presidents who would supplement the work of the General Secretary by travelling on behalf of WEF in their respective regions. This was not implemented at that time.

In the area of fund raising a Director of Development, as mentioned above, had been hired, and there were hopes that this would solve the problem. Time was to show, however, that these hopes were not to be realized. It was also pointed out that 98.5 percent of the income of the past year for the international office had come from the USA. Thus the impact of development in other areas of the world had been almost nil. Membership fees from WEF members were so minimal that they were not distinguished as a separate item in the receipts. They comprised less than one half of one percent of the total income.[5]

At this meeting it was recognized that the Executive Council was not really in a position to function actively in the administration of WEF. "The structural weakness here is that the Executive Council is really not a body equipped to take executive action, scattered as it is over the world."[6] Therefore, it was agreed that more direct lines of authority and responsibility would be recognized between the President and the General Secretary. Since both of them resided in the USA, it was felt that there could be more frequent consultation between them, with the President serving as chairman of the board and the General Secretary reporting to him in his capacity as chief executive officer. Consultation with the Executive Council would be carried on more actively through postal ballots. In actual fact this was already the practice, as most of the decisions since Scott took office had been made through nearly two dozen postal ballots circulated to the Council.

*Taking Stock of Progress*

During 1977 Scott continued to encourage actively the various WEF ministries described above, but he was forced to do this almost single-handedly. It had been agreed that the Executive Council would meet again in January, 1978, but this meeting was cancelled due to financial difficulties. Therefore, Scott reported in writing to the Executive Council with a lengthy report on January 1, 1978, reviewing the previous year and looking forward to what lay ahead.

There had been encouraging developments in many Third World countries. New national fellowships had been formed in Thailand, Malaysia, Italy, Greece, Angola and several other African countries, most of which were considering joining WEF. Two regional fellowships, AEAM (Association of Evangelicals of Africa and Madagascar) and EAC (Evangelical Association of the Caribbean) were applying for membership in WEF. Some modest financial help had been channelled to several national fellowships for strategic projects. The General Secretary had paid regular visits to many member fellowships.

The Theological Commission, the Missions Commission, the Communications Commission, and the newly developing International Forum of Evangelical Women were all active and either carrying out specific programmes or laying plans for some.

In the area of publications 18 issues of *Global Report* containing news from around the world had gone out. The Theological Commission was publishing on a regular basis *Theological News, Theological Education Today,* and *Evangelical Review of Theology.* It had also published a number of monographs and reports on current theological issues, such as *Programmed Instruction* on theological education by extension, and *Karl Barth's Theology of Mission* by the General Secretary.

Good relations with the Lausanne Committee for World Evangelization continued to be a priority for Scott. He reported that "WEF has worked diligently toward establishing harmonious productive relations with LCWE, especially with Leighton Ford and Gottfried Osei-Mensah," Chairman and Executive Secretary respectively.[7]

Scott had also been active in relations with other evangelical bodies. He had played a significant role in alleviating tensions between AEAM and PACLA (Pan African Christian Leadership Assembly, held in Nairobi in 1977). He helped launch the "Love Africa" conference, scheduled for May, 1978, by introducing its sponsor, Brother Andrew, to the leaders of AEAM. He kept lines of communication open with the World Council of Churches, participating in some informal consultations with its leaders.

One area that was to cause considerable controversy later on was Scott's opening up of communication with the Roman Catholic Church. He reported:

> WEF's general secretary has established close contact with Cardinal Suenens and his International Correspondence Office in Brussels.
> Bruce Nicholls has established close contact with the Secretariat for Christian Unity in Rome.[8]

This triggered a reaction which came to the surface at the seventh General Assembly in England in March, 1980, as we shall see later.

*Crisis of Viability*

In the area of finances Scott had continued to work arduously to develop a strong base of support. He had been successful in increasing the mailing list to 15,000 names in North America and over 5,000 names in other parts of the world. The direct mail programme was showing signs of producing more adequate income. Scott had personally contacted nearly 100 churches, about twenty of which were now giving regular support to WEF. He was still hopeful that the Global Deacons programme would lead to increased stability in finances. The fact that The Navigators continued to provide Scott's full personal support was an important contribution and probably did as much as any other factor to keep WEF solvent during those years.

Nevertheless, WEF ended the year 1977 with a deficit of approximately $10,000, which, in view of its total budget of $263,000 for that year, was not as discouraging as it might have been. However, when one considered that the total income was only $118,580 it loomed more formidably.

Administratively Scott had taken some drastic steps to keep within budget. He had dismissed his personal secretary and his administrative assistant, and had moved the international office into his own home. He eliminated all travel except what was paid for by The Navigators or others, and had eliminated temporarily all grants to national fellowships and commissions. These actions caused him to report that "the general secretary's role has been reduced to simple clerical work."[9]

As he looked to the future he felt optimistic in terms of the vision and need of WEF, but apprehensive about the practical outworking of this. He wrote:

WEF is greatly needed in today's world. From the point of view of need its future is assured. The general secretary is committed thoroughly to the vision of WEF and would be happy to devote his life entirely to its ministry.

But from a practical point of view, whether WEF has a long-range future or not depends on whether we can develop substantial support from within the evangelical community, primarily in North America and secondarily in Europe and Australia. Unless we can do this it seems apparent that other evangelical groups with large incomes will take the initiative in promoting evangelical cooperation at various levels. While this may be acceptable it is not ideal, because each of these organizations has only a secondary interest in unity and cooperation, whereas WEF has evangelical unity and cooperation as its *primary* aim.[10]

In this context he spoke about how the general Christian public, including laymen and congregations, found it difficult to comprehend WEF. The difficulty of explaining the intangible concepts of unity and cooperation to churches and individuals who were more accustomed to hearing of tangible, visible mission activities, affected adversely WEF's financial base.

In a covering letter to the Executive Council sent with this report Scott concluded with these significant words:

> I want to thank each of you for your commitment to WEF and to me personally. Your support and advice have been invaluable. It has been a privilege to colabor with you. However, in view of my inability to resolve quickly enough the financial difficulties we face I want you to know that I stand ready to resign my post whenever you are agreed this would benefit WEF.[11]

Once again WEF was facing its recurrent crisis of viability. Every leader that WEF had had since its inception had understood the vision and need for WEF; every one of them was totally committed to the concepts and goals; and every one of them faced the frustration of lack of resources to enable him and his staff to carry out those goals.

# CHAPTER FIFTEEN

# "An Open Space"

Because it had been necessary, for financial reasons, to cancel the meeting of the WEF Executive Council planned for January, 1978, Waldron Scott continued in his duties as General Secretary without personal contact with the Council until it met again in September, 1979, in Wheaton, Illinois. Thus nearly three years had elapsed since the only other meeting Scott had had with the Council—which had been in November, 1976, at Colorado Springs. This inevitably placed him in a difficult position, as he tried to give leadership to an organization whose governing board was unable to meet with much frequency.

Scott's vision for WEF was strong and clear. His method of pursuing his goals did not always coincide with the viewpoints of some of the Council members. For example, he conceived of WEF as an "open space," a phrase he used to describe how WEF should function in providing a place for evangelicals of all persuasions to come together. He felt that evangelicals should be allowed to define for themselves what "evangelical" meant, and thus come under the umbrella of WEF in an "open space" without undue restrictions.

Others in the leadership of WEF, however, did not fully concur with this view. Some felt that certain limitations needed to be placed on the category of people permitted to function under WEF's umbrella. The fact that Scott was unable to meet for nearly three years with the full Council

undoubtedly contributed to the development of some tensions and frustrations, which might well have been cleared
up if more personal interaction had been possible.

During this period there were also some continuing
tensions between certain segments of the WEF membership.
There was a tendency for the European members to feel that
WEF was dominated by North Americans. This was probably
inevitable, given the fact that the office was in North
America, the General Secretary was a North American, and
much of the funding came from there. Funding for the
commissions, on the other hand, was coming largely from
Europe.

Scott, however, was rapidly gaining the reputation of
being much more Third World oriented in his own outlook.
He saw as one of his primary ministries the developing of
national leadership from non-Western countries. He spent
much time in the Third World and was successful in drawing
out various leaders from those countries into worldwide
exposure. In the process he managed, at times, to cause
misunderstanding among the North American constituency.
Some felt that he was "anti-missionary" or "anti-American"
in his strong emphasis on developing non-Western leadership. (There were some similarities to the problems which
Dennis Clark encountered along the same lines.) Others felt
that Scott was too broad in his "open space" concept, and
that he was making WEF too inclusive. This was a constant
point of tension, as Scott quite openly identified with some
from the Third World who felt as he did.

This was true in certain African countries, for example,
where WEF-related bodies did not include membership from
mainline denominations. Scott sided with the African brethren who felt that WEF should be more inclusive, while some
of the American constituency felt that the exclusive nature of
those bodies was to be applauded as a strength. They
wanted WEF to maintain certain restrictions.

## The Council Meets Again

It was with these tensions as a background that Dr Hudson

Armerding, President of WEF, convened the Executive Council in Wheaton, Illinois, USA, on 27–29 September, 1979. The following members attended the meetings: Dr Hudson Armerding (USA), Mr Brian Bayston (Australia), Mr Gordon Landreth (UK), Dr Claude Noel (Haiti), Revd C. Lal Rema (India), Mr Agustin Vencer, Jr. (Philippines), and Mr Waldron Scott. Mr Samuel Odunaike of Nigeria was unable to attend.

In preparation for this meeting Scott compiled a summary report of the present status of WEF.[1] He reviewed the situation in 1974 when WEF met at Chateau d'Oex, indicating a feeling of disarray and apathy. He spoke of the fact that WEF had inevitably acquired a North American image and orientation, and that the perception of many was that it represented only a minority segment within the global evangelical community. It was in this context that he had been appointed General Secretary.

He then outlined the progress which could be seen since 1974. He divided this into four categories: Identity, Unity, Cooperation, and Finance. Under *Identity* he spoke of grants made to cooperative projects such as BEST (Bangui Evangelical School of Theology in the Central African Republic) and CEEFI (Christian Education of the Evangelical Fellowship of India).

Under *Cooperation* he highlighted the ministry of the commissions, which he saw as WEF's primary tool for promoting cooperation at the international level.

When he came to *Finances* he called this "the biggest problem" that WEF was facing. He had been unable to find and keep a full-time director of development, and to him this was a "bitter disappointment." The most serious problem, however, lay deeper. He described it in this way:

> Underlying the financial problem, however, is a deeper one: pervasive apathy toward evangelical unity and cooperation in general, coupled with misunderstanding regarding the role of WEF in particular. For many ordinary Christians the strategic ministry of WEF is too vague and indirect to comprehend.[2]

This was a reflection of a difficulty about which (as we have seen) Scott had already written—the difficulty of defining in terms that could be grasped by the Christian public the concepts of unity and cooperation on which WEF was built. People could not be persuaded to give to an organization which they could not readily comprehend. The intangible concepts with which WEF was constantly dealing were very difficult for the pragmatic mind of most North American givers to visualize.

Scott also spoke of the problems faced because WEF was viewed by many as exclusive rather than inclusive, and as North American or missionary dominated rather than as a true global movement.

Speaking of the "general lack of comprehension of WEF" Scott gave vent to his frustrations by saying:

> But if there is one thing I have learned during the past four and a half years it is that unity and cooperation are close to the very bottom of the priority lists of most evangelical leaders. This apathy is intensified in the industrial nations by a general affluence that enables most churches, organizations and institutions to conduct and expand their programs with little or no sense of serious interdependence with others.[3]

If evangelical leaders in the nations that were capable of providing the necessary funding for WEF were not convinced of the importance of unity and cooperation—convinced enough to act specifically on behalf of these concepts in terms of hard cash—then there was little hope of building the needed financial base. Scott was therefore forced to say that "WEF's future is precarious, to say the least."[4]

In this context he held open the possibility that the seventh General Assembly, scheduled for March, 1980, might have to be cancelled, postponed, or convened as a meeting of Europeans and North Americans, a step which would destroy WEF altogether. He stated, "I myself am not interested in serving WEF if it cannot reflect the global evangelical community adequately."[5]

Scott reiterated his strong commitment to WEF as being Biblical and an urgent necessity for our time. But unless the decision makers in the evangelical bodies with financial resources could be persuaded of the need for WEF, he saw little hope for its future. Some of these men (denominational heads, para-church leaders, mission executives) he described as "not interested in WEF" and some as being "actively hostile" toward it.

## The Future of Waldron Scott

In concluding his report Scott spoke of his four and a half years in WEF as being "fulfilling in many ways," but he also described it as "a lonely experience and a frustrating one." The lack of funds and the distances involved, which had made it almost impossible for the Executive Council to meet, had kept the Council from playing an active leadership role and had compounded Scott's feelings of isolation.

Recognizing that some of the failures were of his own making and due to his lack of certain gifts, he nonetheless maintained that the nature of WEF itself was also responsible. He concluded this incisive report by offering to step aside.

> It may be best, therefore, to tender my resignation at the 7th General Assembly, or earlier if other arrangements can be made. Executive Council members should consider giving priority during the next six months to finding a replacement for me. In truth I would like to continue to serve WEF the rest of my life. But I probably cannot survive emotionally without evidence of (a) stronger commitment by evangelical leaders to the WEF vision, and (b) a shift in the understanding of the WEF vision itself—that is, a shift from an exclusivist to a more inclusivist view of WEF, and a shift from a disproportionate Western influence to a more balanced partnership. These changes do not seem to be on the horizon.[7]

In this report Scott also recommended that the next President of WEF should be a full-time person, preferably from the Third World, who could dedicate himself to representing WEF adequately.

When the Executive Council met these matters were taken seriously and discussed in depth. The possibility of a full-time president was accepted, and it was agreed to approach several different men as candidates for the position. It was also resolved to amend the constitution of WEF to provide for regional vice presidents for Africa, Asia, Europe, Latin America, and North America. These vice presidents would be requested "to devote up to one month of each year to travel and minister in his/her respective region in the interest of WEF."[7]

The council went into executive session to consider the General Secretary's report, and then voted unanimously "that the general secretary be invited and encouraged to continue in office."[8] When he was advised of this action by the President, Scott proposed "that the next six months be considered a further time of *evaluation* which might well determine the future of his own ministry as well as that of WEF."[9]

As the seventh General Assembly approached, these matters were paramount in the minds and activities of the leaders of WEF.

CHAPTER SIXTEEN

# "Serving Our Generation"

The Seventh General Assembly of WEF was a significant event in the life of the Fellowship. It was the most ambitious and progressive assembly yet held. In preparation for this event Waldron Scott compiled and edited a volume entitled *Serving Our Generation*, after the theme which had been chosen for the assembly. This was composed of well-prepared and thoughtful papers in three categories: (1) *Surveying the Globe*—surveys of the situation of the church in Africa, Asia, Latin America, Eastern Europe, Western Europe, and North America; (2) *The Commissions at Work*—reports of the progress and goals of the various WEF commissions; (3) *New Challenges*—6 papers on current issues facing evangelicals around the world. All of these essays were prepared by men and women who were deeply involved in the area or subject under discussion. Because WEF finances continued to be a problem Waldron Scott personally financed the publication of this book out of his own pocket.

Prior to the General Assembly six separate international consultations were held, in the same location. Four of them were referred to as "mini-consultations." They dealt with "Reaching Muslims," "Preparing Churches for Responsible Witness Under Oppressive Situations," "The Teaching of Missions in Theological and Church Education," and "International Accreditation." Two others were considerably larger and more ambitious in scope. They were: "Consultation on the

Theology of Development," attended by 41 people from 17 countries; and "Consultation on Simple Life Style," attended by 85 evangelical leaders from 27 countries. This latter was jointly sponsored by the Theology and Education Group of the Lausanne Committee for World Evangelization (of which John Stott was chairman), and the Unit on Ethics and Society of the Theological Commission of WEF (with Ronald Sider as convener).

Two volumes entitled *Evangelicals and Development* and *Lifestyle in the Eighties*, both edited by Ronald Sider, were published to share the results of the two latter consultations. Also, as a direct outgrowth of the Consultation on Simple Lifestyle, a further consultation was held in Grand Rapids, Michigan, USA, in June, 1982, on "The Relationship between Evangelism and Social Responsibility." Out of this significant gathering also came a volume entitled *In Word and Deed*, edited by Bruce Nicholls.

The four commissions of WEF—the Theological Commission, the Missions Commission, the Communications Commission, and the Commission on Women's Concerns—also held their own meetings just prior to the assembly.

## *The Seventh General Assembly*

The objectives of the Seventh General Assembly were spelled out as:

1. To understand better our global evangelical community in its unity and diversity, and to enjoy fellowship in Christ.
2. To anticipate the most significant issues of the eighties in the church and in the world, and to formulate evangelical approaches to them.
3. To develop more effective means for affirming our *identity* as evangelicals, expressing our *unity*, and enhancing our cooperation.[1]

The General Assembly met between 24–28 March, 1980, in the High Leigh Conference Centre in Hoddesdon, Hertfordshire, UK, a short distance outside London. It was attended by 141 persons from 48 countries representing 34 national evangelical fellowships affiliated with WEF. There were observers and guests from six Latin American countries and eight other countries.

President Hudson T. Armerding brought the keynote address on the theme of the conference, "Serving Our Generation—Evangelical Strategy for the 1980's." It was a statesmanlike and comprehensive survey of world evangelical thinking and strategy. In this important address he covered such items as the problem of truth *versus* error, Christ *versus* Caesar, the gospel and eclectic pluralism, obedience *versus* conformity, materialism, and the tension between structure and function. He concluded with a call to service that is rooted in fellowship, that has a commitment equal to the task, and a commitment to the Lordship of Jesus Christ. It was a fitting start and set the tone for the assembly.

The report of the General Secretary was a review of progress in WEF since the last General Assembly of 1974, a summary of the problems being faced, and a look at future prospects. The problems which Waldron Scott outlined here were similar to those he had described to the Executive Council in their meeting of September, 1979. He dealt with the lack of commitment of evangelical leaders to unity and cooperation, the resulting financial problems of WEF, the question of self-understanding, and matters of constitution and structure. He spoke honestly about the personal pressures under which he lived, saying, "The work of your general secretary is often lonely, usually tense as competing pressures from various parts of the evangelical community focus on his office, and frequently frustrating as meagre resources strive to fulfill a global vision."[2]

He concluded with a challenge which took each aspect of the name of the organization.

> Can WEF rise to this challenge? We must and we can, provided (1) we transcend our national predispositions and comprehend that great event of our era, the emergence of a *world* evangelical fellowship in all of its historical-cultural complexity; (2) we respond creatively to the fact that we are, in the final analysis, a world *evangelical* fellowship, with an obligation to be faithful to our past, critical of our present, and abreast of our future; and (3) we think through the implications of our desires to be a world evangelical *fellowship*: flexible in structure, modest in self-appraisal, and open to the whole people of God.[3]

Business sessions of the General Assembly included written and oral reports from many of the national fellowships that were members of WEF. Each of the four commissions also reported in detail on their progress and plans. Some of the observers and guests brought greetings. A number of the non-delegates were also given opportunity to make statements about their perceptions of the future of WEF.

## Controversial Issues

Considerable time was spent on constitutional revisions, the most crucial of which had to do with membership in WEF. Waldron Scott had been disturbed for some time that WEF membership structures were such that many evangelicals who wished to relate to the movement were excluded because they were members of churches that could not belong to WEF. An amendment was passed which opened up eligibility for membership considerably in the following way:

> The Executive Council may admit as participating members organizations other than national or regional bodies of evangelicals, including congregations, denominations, associations of congregations and denominations, parachurch organizations, and other voluntary associations of Christians organized for specific Christian purposes. A participating member shall meet the same membership requirements as a full member and shall have and enjoy all the rights and privileges of a full member other than those hereby reserved exclusively for a full member. Such participating members shall be admitted after consultation with the regional and/or national evangelical alliance involved.[4]

Two major issues came to the floor that occupied a significant portion of time and generated considerable discussion, some of it quite heated. The first was the relationship of WEF to LCWE (the Lausanne Committee for World Evangelization). Lengthy statements were made by various participants, many of whom, especially those from the Third World, felt that the existence of two world bodies representing evangelicals was intolerable. There were many who urged a merger between the two organizations. There was a recognition that the LCWE was rightly focussing on evangelization, and that this could make a significant contribution to WEF's ministry.

On the final day of the assembly the following resolution was presented:

> WHEREAS World Evangelical Fellowship has a deep and abiding

concern for world evangelization, and is convinced that evangelism must involve and relate to the local church; and

WHEREAS our desire is to accelerate and not impede world evangelization; and

WIIEREAS we are open to reasonable negotiations while reaffirming our commitment to the WEF Statement of Faith; and

WHEREAS it is our conviction that the time has come for initiatives to bring to an end the separate existence of two international evangelical organizations, to the satisfaction of both;

BE IT THEREFORE RESOLVED that we extend an invitation to the Lausanne Committee for World Evangelization to become the Evangelical Task Force of WEF, and that we empower our Executive Council to enter into such negotiations on our behalf.[5]

In June of that year this resolution came to the floor of the Consultation on World Evangelization, sponsored by LCWE in Pattaya, Thailand. It was given lengthy and detailed consideration by a "blue ribbon" Commission on Cooperation which had been named many months earlier and which had studied various documents and the possibilities of a merger between WEF and LCWE. The response of that Commission on Cooperation of LCWE was:

The invitation of the World Evangelical Fellowship (WEF) to LCWE to join this world body as its Evangelization Task Force or as its Commission on Mission and Evangelism was carefully studied. The principle that those united in the Truth of the Gospel should work in unity was noted. It is the opinion of the Commission that it would be premature for LCWE to enter into an organizational relationship with WEF either as a task force or as a commission at this time. It is, however, recommended that:

'A joint committee between LCWE and WEF be set up to explore ways and means further cooperation can be strengthened for joining endeavor in Evangelism, with progress reports presented to both the LCWE and WEF.'[6]

## Relating to Rome

The second major issue that rocked, and nearly divided, the General Assembly was the question of relationships with the Roman Catholic Church. Waldron Scott, with clearance from the Executive Council, had invited two observers from the Roman Catholic Church to attend and to bring greetings to the assembly. They were Mr Ralph Martin, a leader in the Roman Catholic charismatic renewal movement, and Msgr Basil Meeking of the Vatican Secretariat for Promoting Christian Unity. The presence of these two men, and especially their participation from the platform in bringing greetings, greatly disturbed some of the delegates.

It precipitated the most heated discussions of the week. Delegates from southern Europe (notably Spain, France and Italy), as well as some observers from Latin America, were especially agitated about the matter. They felt that the gesture was giving a stamp of approval to the Roman Catholic Church by recognizing it in this way in a world evangelical gathering. Because of the sensitivity of the issue the main session in which it was discussed was closed to all except official delegates.

In response to the question as to why the Executive Council had authorized an invitation to such observers, President Armerding stated that delegates to the WEF General Assembly were considered to be mature enough to tolerate the coming of outside observers who would thereby gain a more accurate understanding of the nature of evangelical identity. Some felt it was both acceptable and desirable to have such observers present, but not to have them speak from the platform. Others were adamantly opposed to any such representation.

After considerable discussion, General Secretary Scott, apologized for any offence that had been given, but he pointed out that as General Secretary he had to try to give balanced expression to all the various aspects of the global WEF community. He observed that in some parts of the world evangelicals were actively courting closer relationships with the Roman Catholic Church. He emphasized that we ought not to let one segment of the evangelical community determine WEF policy for the whole, possibly to the detriment of the whole.

The final action was as follows:

The WEF accepts as its first priority the maintenance and promotion of evangelical unity. It recognizes the need for sensitivity in any contacts with ecclesiastical, ecumenical or political bodies. Its duty to be a witness to the evangelical faith to such bodies should also be pursued.

But where some may be offended or misunderstand what is being done such witness may at times need to be made by individuals and not in the corporate name of WEF. In the General Assembly, the involvement of representatives or observers from ecclesiastical, ecumenical or political bodies shall have the approval of the majority of the full membership, if necessary by postal ballot.[7]

In spite of this action the Evangelical Alliance of Italy decided to withdraw from membership in WEF in protest over the issue. The Evangelical Alliance of Spain decided to hold in abeyance its future participation in WEF, depending on how this proposed action was to work out in practice.

As a result of the deep feelings and misunderstandings generated by this issue WEF appointed a carefully selected Task Force to study relationships with the Roman Catholic Church. This Task Force was composed of leading theologians from every major region of the world, with special attention given to those areas, such as southern Europe and Latin America, where the Roman Catholic Church has exercised special influence in the life of the nations. Under the leadership of Dr Paul Schrotenboer of the Reformed Ecumenical Synod the group met in Madrid, Spain, in October, 1985, and produced a first draft of a working document that would be presented to the Eighth General Assembly of WEF scheduled to meet in Singapore in June, 1986. This document was the result of well over a year of in-depth theological reflection on the implications of such relationships for evangelicals. At the time of this writing it is hoped that the issue will be satisfactorily resolved as a result of the effort of these men.

The new Executive Council elected at the General Assembly consisted of:

Dr Hudson T. Armerding (*USA*), who agreed to continue on temporarily in the office of President until the end of 1980 in the hope that a full-time president could be found.
Dr Tokunboh Adeyemo (*Nigeria*)
Mr Brian Bayston (*Australia*)
Mr D. John Richard (*India*)
Revd Agustin Vencer, Jr. (*Philippines*)
Dr Wade T. Coggins (*USA*)
Revd A. Morgan Derham (*UK*)
Dr Claude Noël (*Haiti*)

As the seventh General Assembly drew to a close there was a

renewed sense of optimism about the future of WEF, in contrast to the somewhat pessimistic feelings that pervaded the sixth General Assembly which had met immediately after the Lausanne Congress. The possibility of what might happen at Pattaya in June, 1980, and its effect upon WEF gave new hope and vision. Although the proposal presented to LCWE at Pattaya was not to be realized, the delegates did not know this in March, and their spirits were optimistic.

CHAPTER SEVENTEEN

# High Hopes and Interim Measures

Note: *From here onwards the author of this book becomes personally involved in the ministry of WEF. In order to facilitate smoothness of style the first person singular has been used.*

Immediately after the General Assembly closed, the newly-elected Executive Council held its first meeting in the offices of the Evangelical Alliance in London. The major items on the agenda were largely internal matters. Dr Tokunboh Adeyemo of Nigeria was elected Vice Chairman and Mr Brian Bayston of Australia was named Secretary-Treasurer "until further notice." The newly nominated members of the various commissions were confirmed by the council. There was discussion of the need for further contacts in Latin America and representation from that continent on the Executive Council, although no final action was taken immediately.

It was debated whether to present to the LCWE the resolution that had come out of the General Assembly with an invitation to LCWE to join with WEF as its Commission or Task Force on Evangelization. There was also discussion about how to react to a statement by a Norwegian evangelical

137

leader with a very negative attitude to WEF who was being quoted widely in the press. There was some consideration given to a new location for the WEF office, but no decision was taken.

The next formal meeting of the Executive Council was held just two months later (a rare event in WEF history, for two council meetings to be held so close together!) in Pattaya, Thailand, at the time of the LCWE-sponsored Consultation on World Evangelization. This was a convenient time to meet, since nearly all of the members of the Council had been invited to Pattaya anyway. The major item of consideration at that time was the recommendation, made previously, for WEF to elect a full-time President who would serve with the General Secretary in the representation of WEF internationally and in coordinating activities to help mould together the evangelical community worldwide.

## Dr Kamaleson Says No

After lengthy and prayerful consideration of this possibility, the Executive Council had decided to invite Dr Samuel Kamaleson of India (see ch. 6), who was now Vice-President of World Vision International, to become the full-time President of WEF. At Pattaya the Council met with Dr Kamaleson informally. He suggested that this be considered not as a job interview but simply as a time to discuss mutual concerns. Following this session, further private discussions were held with him by various individuals.

Finally it was agreed to extend a formal invitation to Dr Kamaleson. A letter was sent to him, dated 27 June 1980, from Pattaya, Thailand, signed by Dr Hudson T. Armerding as President of WEF and Mr Waldron Scott as General Secretary. It stated:

> On behalf of our international executive council we have the honour to extend to you an invitation to take up the office of ministry of President of the World Evangelical Fellowship.
>
> This invitation comes to you as a unanimous expression of the executive council after considerable discussion and fervent prayer. We believe you are God's man to lead his people into greater experiences of unity and cooperation during the portentous decade ahead.[1]

Dr Kamaleson had expressed his feelings about such a position during the discussion which had been held on 22 June at Pattaya. He indicated that he "belonged to WEF" irrespective of any formal relationships, and that he believed in its ministry. He had expressed some disappointment with the rigidity and exclusiveness that seemed to have been prevalent in the past in some quarters of WEF and expressed a hope for a broader WEF ministry by expanding the parameters of membership and influence. He also emphasized that WEF must re-evaluate its attitude towards the poor and powerless of the world, insisting that the decade of the 1980s belonged to them. As a basis for seriously considering this invitation he said that he would need "(a)a clear sense of calling from God; (b) the validation of a prayerful community of friends and associates; and (c) agreement on the part of his own family."[2]

On 19 August, 1980, Waldron Scott wrote a lengthy letter to Dr Kamaleson to elaborate further the vision and goals of WEF and how Dr Kamaleson would be able to help realize these goals. There was high hope that a man of his calibre, coming from a Third World nation yet enjoying a worldwide reputation and having extensive international contacts, possessing unusual gifts in communication and administration, could bring new life and broader outreach to WEF. And so it was a keen disappointment to WEF leaders when, after several months of prayer and thoughtful consideration, Dr Kamaleson indicated that he did not feel God was leading him to accept the invitation. This left WEF with no other immediate options for the important position of a full-time President.

## A Leadership Crisis

Then two events occurred which threw WEF into a temporary vacuum. Dr Hudson Armerding, who had agreed in March 1980 to continue as President temporarily beyond his term of office, now felt that he must conclude his term with effect from 31 December, 1980. His duties as President of Wheaton College, as well as other factors, made it impractical for him to continue beyond that date.

Then on 29 December 1980 Waldron Scott sent a telex, followed by a letter of the same date, to Dr Tokunboh Adeyemo, Vice Chairman of the Executive Council, presenting his resignation—to become effective on 31 December 1980. This was motivated by "compelling personal reasons." No further elaboration was given. Dr Adeyemo's response was not to accept the resignation but rather to request that Scott meet with the WEF Executive Council in Washington, D.C., in January, 1981.

The Executive Council convened in Washington on 30 January, 1981, but Scott was not present. Dr Adeyemo was elected as chairman to replace Dr Armerding and presided at the meeting.

The Council felt that they had no alternative but to accept the resignation, and so the following action was taken:

> That the Executive Council accepts the resignation of Mr. Waldron Scott as WEF General Secretary effective 1 January, 1981, to express our regret for such a great loss to WEF and to convey to him our appreciation for his commitment, contribution, and leadership in the visible growth and increasing influence of WEF as an evangelical witness worldwide.[3]

Arrangements were then made for managing the office procedures and the general leadership on an interim basis. Mr Glenn ("Buzz") Frum, who had joined the office staff as an assistant to Scott, was asked to become responsible, along with Miss Betty Froisland, for general administration. Miss Froisland was an exceptionally talented staff person who had worked with Scott as secretary and executive assistant. She and "Buzz" immediately took over these responsibilities. They had already moved the office from Scott's home to an office building in Colorado Springs, Colorado, and this action was ratified by the Council.

Dr Wade Coggins, executive secretary of EFMA and member of the Executive Council, was asked to become General Secretary on an interim basis until a new Secretary could be found. The interim period was set as being until 15 February, 1982.[4]

Since Dr Coggins already had a full time job with EFMA it was understood that this was at best a holding action, and that he could not be expected to give a major portion of his time to WEF. In order to relieve his burden of responsibilities, the Executive Council created an interim office of "Associate General Secretary", appointing every member of the Council to that position on a regional basis. Thus, there were eight regional Associate General Secretaries responsible for the regions of Europe, South Pacific, West and South Asia, East Asia, Africa, the Caribbean, Latin America, and North America. These offices were not budgeted items for WEF, and whatever expenses might be incurred were to be borne by the respective national fellowships represented by these Council members.

For the next year, working from his EFMA office in Washington, D.C., Dr Coggins carried on WEF responsibilities largely by correspondence and by phone consultations with Betty Froisland and "Buzz" Frum in Colorado Springs. In fact, so busy was Dr Coggins that he was never able to visit the WEF office.

*Revising the Structure*

On 24–25 April, 1981, a special committee composed of Dr Tokunboh Adeyemo, Dr Coggins, and Mr D. John Richard met in Amerongen, The Netherlands, to consider effective functional coordination of the various ministries of WEF. The executive secretaries of each Commission met with them, along with Jun Vencer of the Philippines, who was asked to provide management process for them.

In order to help relieve Coggins of some of the administrative duties of WEF three further positions were created during the meetings in Amerongen. Revd Theodore Williams of India was named Associate General Secretary for Fellowship Ministries; Revd Bruce Nicholls, also resident in India, was named Associate General Secretary for Commission Ministries; and "Buzz" Frum was named Associate General Secretary for Administration.

As a result of discussions held at those meetings an approach was made to myself, then working with Inter-Varsity Christian Fellowship of the USA, to become General Secretary. During the following weeks Wade Coggins consulted with me at length, both by phone and in person, concerning this invitation. However, I did not feel led of God at that time to accept the position. So Coggins continued with the responsibilities.

Approaches were also made to Dr Emilio Antonio Nuñez of Guatemala and to Dr Wingrove Taylor of Barbados to ascertain whether either of them would consider the position of General Secretary. However, neither of them was ready to accept.

The coming months were a time of frustration for Coggins, as he saw the enormous needs of WEF, the great potential it possessed, and the number of calls for help from many national fellowships. But his heavy responsibilities with EFMA made it impossible for him to give the time necessary to meet these needs in WEF. Thus by late 1981, he was feeling keenly the need for relief as soon as possible.

*Relief for the General Secretary*

It had been agreed in January 1981 that the Executive Council would meet again in February 1982 in Bangalore, India, for a full meeting. However, it turned out that a number of members of the Executive Council were also to attend the General Assembly of AEAM (Association of Evangelicals of Africa and Madagascar) to be held in Lilongwe, Malawi, in September 1981. Therefore Dr Tokunboh Adeyemo called for a special session of the Executive Council to meet in Malawi, along with WEF staff, at the same time. He stated that the purpose was not to hold a full "agenda" meeting. "Rather, it is a special (extra-ordinary) session of the ExCo (plus staff) to consider one agendum, filling the post of the General Secretary."[6] A fuller agenda would be prepared for the meetings in February, 1982.

Thus on 14–15 September 1981, five members of the Executive Council (Tokunboh Adeyemo, Claude Noël, John Richard, John Langlois, and Wade Coggins) met in Malawi along with three staff members (Bruce Nicholls, Theodore Williams, and "Buzz" Frum). Coggins reported that approaches to David Howard, Antonio Nuñez, and Wingrove Taylor had failed to produce a candidate for general secretary. In view of this the council resolved

> that Dr Wade Coggins be invited to be General Secretary for a period of up to two years and that the board of EFMA be requested to make Dr Coggins available for this assignment on a part-time basis. Dr Coggins accepted subject to the approval of the EFMA board.[7]

A further action was taken to help alleviate the administrative work for Dr Coggins as follows:

> It was resolved that the Revd Theodore Williams be invited to be Joint General Secretary on a part-time basis. Williams accepted the position.[8]

The rest of the time was spent in considering various matters related to the WEF Commissions, to financial reports, fund-raising efforts, and the consideration of a proposed conference on "The Nature and Mission of the Church" to be held in Wheaton, Illinois, USA, in 1983. (Further details of "Wheaton '83" will be given later.) A call was also issued through the membership of WEF to churches around the world to declare the year 1983 "Year of Church Renewal." A twelve-point commitment was drafted to be circulated to churches, to call them to specific action through the church for renewal in every area of life.

# CHAPTER EIGHTEEN

# Needed: A Bachelor with Unlimited Funds

The next meeting of the Executive Council was convened in Bangalore, India, on 1–3 February, 1982, with full attendance of the members. A heavy and detailed agenda lay before them with various reports from staff to be included. The Missions Commission had just met in Bangalore in an atmosphere of expectancy and optimism. The Theological Commission was enthusiastic about the plans for Wheaton '83, which were getting into gear by that time. The Communications Commission had been encouraged by the appointment of a full-time executive secretary, Miss Anne Ediger, resident in India, but had been deeply saddened by her untimely death later in 1981. Plans for a Relief and Development Alliance were also moving along well under the initiative of Jun Vencer. This was to be an alliance of relief and development bodies which were part of the national fellowships that belonged to WEF. Thus it was not to be a WEF commission, but rather an alliance of already existing organizations. Mrs. Beatriz Zapata of Guatemala had agreed to continue in the leadership of the Commission on Women's Concerns, which was still in its formative stages. Suggestions for a Commission on Church Renewal and Growth were being formulated.

In the search for a full-time General Secretary a new development was reported. An unexpected change in my own personal ministry, due to circumstances quite beyond my control, made it possible for me now to be available should WEF choose to call me.

Wade Coggins had been in contact with me and reported both that I was available and also that my full support for one year had been guaranteed by an outside source. There was discussion of "a substantial body of information" concerning my background and ministry that was laid before the Council. It was recognized that to appoint me would mean that four successive General Secretaries had come from the USA. There was also consideration given to the possibility of locating the WEF international office in a non-Western country to help alleviate the mistaken impression that WEF was an organization dominated by North Americans. After due consideration

> It was resolved unanimously (1) that Dr David Howard be appointed General Secretary of World Evangelical Fellowship; (2) that the appointment be subject to review by both parties after two years; (3) that the appointment date from the first day of March, 1982.[1]

It was also resolved to request Inter-Varsity Christian Fellowship of the USA to second me to WEF on a fulltime basis to serve in this capacity. This request was subsequently granted.

## Changes in Administration

The future administrative organization was then considered. Wade Coggins reported that he was now rescinding the appointment of all Associate General Secretaries, who had been assisting him during his interim term, in order to give the new General Secretary a free hand to build his own administration in accord with his own style and desires. Consideration was given to filling the office of President, now that a fulltime President was not available as originally conceived. After due consideration

> It was resolved that the office of president shall be non-administrative in character but the president shall help promote the ministries of World Evangelical Fellowship by a public ministry of biblical teaching.
> It was resolved unanimously that the Revd Theodore Williams be appointed president.[2]

There was a recognition that Theodore Williams' gifts in a public ministry of Bible teaching, representing WEF, could thus be utilized to the fullest possible extent. At the same time it was felt that the proper administrative lines of authority must be clarified. Two further actions were thus taken as follows:

> It was further resolved unanimously that we create the office of chairman of the executive council.
> It was further resolved unanimously that Dr Tokunboh Adeyemo be elected to the office of chairman of the executive council.[3]

This meant that the leadership of WEF was placed in the hands of a Chairman from Africa, a President from India, and a General Secretary from the USA.

The location of the international office was considered, but it was decided to leave a final decision on that in the hands of the new General Secretary. The office was still located in Colorado Springs. My wife and I were living at that time in Ft. Lauderdale, Florida.

In March 1982, shortly after I assumed the duties of General Secretary, the NAE (National Association of Evangelicals of the USA), through its Executive Director, Dr Billy Melvin, extended an invitation to WEF to occupy offices in the NAE headquarters in Wheaton, Illinois. NAE was the American member body of WEF and had been one of its most active supporters. Thus there was good reason, from an organizational standpoint, for WEF to be located near NAE. Wheaton had also become a major cross-roads for worldwide evangelical leadership. With the new Billy Graham Center recently opened at Wheaton College there was a steady stream of key leaders from Third World as well as Western countries passing through Wheaton. It was essential for WEF, as a worldwide body, to keep in touch with evangelical leadership from around the world, and Wheaton was as good a location for that as almost anywhere. As it happened, my wife and I still owned a home near Wheaton, where we had lived for some years prior to moving to Florida. And so after adequate consultation with the Executive Council, and after studying the pros and cons of a move, we moved the international office of WEF to Wheaton, Illinois, in August 1982, occupying space in the same building as NAE and World Relief. "Buzz" Frum and Betty Froisland carried the major responsibility for the move, since my wife and I did not arrive from Florida until a few weeks after the move took place. NAE graciously provided numerous services to WEF which made it unnecessary for the new arrivals to invest in much office equipment at a time when finances were especially tight.

Shortly after being appointed General Secretary I made my first trip for WEF. I travelled with my wife to England, where I consulted with leaders of the Evangelical Alliance, and with former WEF leaders such as Revd Gilbert Kirby and Dr John Stott, concerning the ministry of WEF. I also met with my good friend Gottfried Osei-Mensah, Executive Secretary of the Lausanne Committee for World Evangelization, to discuss future relationships between WEF and LCWE. We then went to The Netherlands, West Germany, Switzerland, and Spain for initial contacts with the leaders of the evangelical fellowships in those countries. We also spent a most interesting and valuable day in East Berlin. This trip served as an introduction for me to several WEF member bodies in Europe and to some of the key leaders; it proved to be very rewarding.

## Clear Lines of Authority

Upon my return from Europe I was able to meet for the first time with the WEF Executive Council on 16 June, 1982, at Hope College in Holland, Michigan. (Several members of the Council were attending another conference there, and it had been determined that this would be a good time to meet.) Since only half of the full Council was present, this meeting was declared to be *ad hoc*, with any decisions taken to be ratified by postal ballot with the other members. Its primary value was the opportunity for me to have personal dealings with the Council and to become better acquainted with its members, even though I had previously met all of those present and had known several of them for many years.

One of my first projects was to try to reorganize WEF's administration. I felt that WEF, as an international fellowship with loosely-related member bodies and commissions, needed a more firm structure. This was motivated also by the difficulty WEF had always experienced in defining itself and its role. As an international "umbrella" for national evangelical fellowships WEF has no administrative authority over any member, nor do the members have any administrative responsibility (other than a moral obligation) to WEF. While the Commissions were related directly through the staff of WEF (both full-time and part-time), the members of commissions are volunteers whose primary responsibility lies within their own vocations and does not belong to WEF. This makes for a certain looseness of structure and a blurring of the lines of authority.

In writing to the Executive Council I outlined my feelings on this matter as follows:

> I have been feeling for some time that we need a clarification of lines of authority and responsibility in WEF. We are a very loosely defined organization spread across the globe. This has both strengths and weaknesses. Our strength lies in our diversity and our worldwide representation within the body of Christ. One major weakness lies in the fact that our personnel are so spread out that we do not have adequate contact or interaction with each other. This makes for difficult supervision, which can lead on the one hand to feelings of neglect and insecurity, and on the other hand to unilateral or uncoordinated action by individuals.[4]

A new organizational chart was presented for approval by the Executive Council, showing more clearly the lines of authority and responsibility running from the Council through the General Secretary to the Commissions and staff.

The Executive Council studied the proposal and then, at a meeting in Wheaton, Illinois, on 17–18 June, 1983, took several steps. The recommended lines of authority outlined in the proposed chart were accepted. The title of General Secretary was changed to General Director. This reflected the feeling that in some areas of the world, notably North America where the international office is located, the term "secretary" connotes a different type of position to that connoted by the word "director" and is often misleading as to the function of the chief executive officer.

A new post of Assistant General Director was established to help the General Director in the overall administration of WEF. Dr Robert Youngblood was given this position. Dr Youngblood was located in The Netherlands, where he was

serving as project secretary for the Theological Commission
and was involved in fund-raising efforts for WEF in Europe.

Perhaps the most significant step taken was to name a
Working Group of the Executive Council, which was to meet
more frequently and would possess authority to act on
behalf of the Council. The Working Group is composed of
the officers of the Executive Council, namely, the Chairman,
the President, and the Treasurer, along with the General
Director. This step greatly facilitated my administrative
responsibilities, as it made it possible for me to have more
frequent and direct contact with a few men. Trying to deal
with the entire Executive Council, composed of ten men
scattered across the globe, had been a frustrating experience.
Now, however, the possibility of direct contact with just
three officers made the task much more manageable. By
phone and by mail, as well as some meetings, these three
men (Dr Tokunboh Adeyemo, Chairman; Dr Theodore
Williams, President; and Mr John Langlois, Treasurer)
became more active and were available to the General
Director for consultation and advice as needed.


*Tensions for the General Director*

Every one of my predecessors had experienced some
frustrations in fund-raising for WEF. For some of them this
was not a major burden, as they served only part-time in the
WEF position and their support was largely underwritten by
another organization. Also, some of them were by nature
more given to fund-raising. For me, however, this became
an area of constant tension.

First, I found it very difficult to define WEF's role in a way
that the general public could understand clearly. Since WEF
deals in intangible concepts, such as unity, cooperation, and
mutual identity, it is not easy to describe its functions to a
pragmatic person who wants to see specific results. WEF
cannot present visible projects such as orphans, refugees,
school buildings, or relief programmes. WEF is more nebulous
by its very nature than most other evangelical organizations.
When a goal-oriented businessman asks "What is happening

in the world today that would not be happening if WEF did not exist? And, therefore, why should I give to WEF?", one is hard pressed to give an answer that will satisfy such pragmatism.

Second, by nature I am not and never have been a fundraiser. I have shared these feelings with the Executive Council on various occasions from the very beginning of my term of office. I stated it most directly in a confidential memorandum in May, 1983:

> I have said before in communications with the Executive Council that I am not a fund raiser either by temperament or by training. But it is much deeper than that. I have some convictions of personal integrity related to my sense of the gifts and callings of God that prohibit me from making the kind of appeals that everyone says must be made if money is to be raised . . .
>
> . . . My personal convictions prohibit me from writing the kind of things that apparently must be written if WEF is to get the response that we need from the evangelical public . . .
>
> Consequently, I find myself in a dilemma described beautifully by a Spanish saying—caught "entre la espada y la pared," "between the sword and the wall." . . .
>
> I have never felt—and do not feel now—that my own personal ministry could revolve around finances. But the present situation in WEF seems to dictate that this is where the General Secretary must concentrate his efforts. We are increasingly stymied by lack of funds, but how to get those funds becomes a greater problem every day.[5]

Third, the amount of travel required to fulfill the functions of general director posed a constant dilemma for me. I will readily admit to enjoying the worldwide travel that is part of the responsibility of this position. However, the question of how to balance that travel and its expenses with responsibilities at home is one with which I have struggled for most of my adult life. My previous work, whether with the Latin America Mission, Inter-Varsity Christian Fellowship, or the Lausanne Committee, always required extensive periods of absence from home. WEF is no different. But how to balance my activities and still fulfill the goals of the job, as well as find the necessary funds for travel, is an unresolved issue. I have often said that the ideal person for this position would be "a bachelor with unlimited funds." If the General Director could spend eighty percent or more of his time on the road, with no limitation of funds or of family and home responsibilities, he could probably do a good job of coordinating and encouraging the work of the fifty member fellowships of WEF.

The travel itself has been a stimulating and rewarding experience. The opportunity to minister the Word of God to believers in many parts of the world, as well as to learn from them and share in their growth, has been wonderfully satisfying. In the first three and a half years following my appointment I was called upon to travel to an enormous number of countries, in addition to the European countries already mentioned: Bulgaria, Egypt, India, Pakistan, Sri Lanka, Bangladesh, Nepal, Thailand, Singapore, Australia, the Philippines, Guatemala, Nicaragua, Cuba, Colombia, Canada, South Africa, Zambia, Malawi, and Kenya. In every case I found my heart greatly blessed and strengthened as I learned from believers in such radically different cultures and political and social environments. It was a privilege to share with them and to minister God's Word.

# CHAPTER NINETEEN

# Financial Crisis

During the year of 1983 the financial situation of WEF worsened week by week. In spite of all efforts to match income with expenses, we were notably unsuccessful in doing so. In September 1983 I wrote to the Executive Council in an alarming way about the crisis.

> Here is what we face right now. We have spent all the deferred revenue funds that the Executive Council authorized us to draw on. In August we borrowed internally beyond what we have been authorized to borrow, and we have used up all such funds. . .
>
> At the end of this month, unless we get some major unexpected income, we will not have money to pay salaries of our office staff. This will be tragic, as most of these people have no reserves upon which to draw. I have just put through, in writing, an order for my salary to be cut in half beginning this month, but I cannot do this for the rest of the staff . . .
>
> As chief executive officer of WEF, I am responsible to the Executive Council for all that goes on in WEF, including over-sight of budget. I cannot authorize continued deficit spending, especially when there is no cash available even if we wanted to borrow it.[1]

On 5–6 October, 1983, the WEF/USA Corporation met in Chicago. This group was in the unreasonable position of having no administrative authority for WEF (that belonged to the Executive Council) but being legally responsible for WEF, before the US government. (Because of its tax exempt status, and because it needed to be able to issue tax deductible receipts to donors, WEF has to have a legal body recognized by the government. This body is the USA Corporation Board. If (God forbid!) WEF should ever be forced to declare bankruptcy—a scenario not at all beyond the realm of possibility in October, 1983—the USA Corporation Board would be held legally responsible for all WEF debts. Yet in 1983 this body had no administrative authority.)

The board meeting was a crucial one. An agonizing reappraisal of WEF finances was conducted and several major recommendations were made. Although I was not responsible administratively to the USA Corporation board, I felt under moral obligation to accept their recommendations, which were made in the finest possible spirit of desiring to help and support WEF. The primary recommendations were: that there be no more inter-fund borrowing within WEF; that the present office staff of six people be cut to three; and that the Executive Council establish the USA Corporation Board as the Finance Committee of the WEF/USA office operation.

It was with great agony of soul that I took action on these recommendations. I dismissed half of our staff, with effect from 31 October 1983. This was especially painful for me since two of them, John Liss and Carol Ann Paul, had worked closely with me for a number of years both in Inter-Varsity Christian Fellowship and LCWE as well as WEF. This left us with my personal secretary, Mrs Carol Messina, and our Director of Communications, Mr Harry Genet, who had moved into WEF responsibilities during that year from a secure position as Associate Editor of *Christianity Today*, thus giving up considerable job security and fringe benefits. Harry and Mrs Messina had to take over almost all the work being done previously by three other people, but they did so with efficiency, willingness, and a remarkable initiative, even though many of the jobs had not been in their original job descriptions.

### Eliminating the Deficit

These drastic measures were augmented by a special telephone and mail appeal programme aimed at member missions of EFMA, who had vital interests in the ministry of

WEF. This programme was carried out on a volunteer basis by Dr Vergil Gerber, who had recently retired from directing the Evangelical Missions Information Service. Dr Gerber personally called and pursued contact with approximately eighty mission organizations, requesting emergency financial help.

Dr Gerber's efforts, together with the austerity measures taken, allowed WEF to cut the deficit from approximately $70,000 in October to $28,000 by the end of December that year, and to eliminate it entirely by December 1984.

Emergency and austerity measures, however, do not build an ongoing financial base—something which WEF had desperately needed from its inception. In March 1984 a charitable foundation in the southeastern United States made a generous grant to WEF for the purpose of building a more permanent development programme. On the strength of this grant WEF hired Mark Lutz on a part-time basis as Director of Development, and Mrs Beth Brinson as a full-time assistant to him. A management consultancy firm, Management Development Associates, was also contracted to give direction and oversight to the programme The combination of these various efforts has provided a beginning for a more stable financial foundation.

However, at the time of writing, WEF is still struggling to find the direction in which it can go in order to develop a more permanent constituency. All too often over the years WEF has had to operate on an emergency basis in the midst of a severe financial crisis. Friends and mission organizations, especially the members of EFMA, have responded generously to repeated pleas for help. But one can "cry wolf" only so many times. And "crying wolf" is not the way to build a permanent foundation.

## A Statement of Mission

As part of the continuing effort to clarify the mission of WEF so that it can be described adequately to outsiders, a Statement of Mission was drafted by the USA Corporation Board and submitted to the Executive Council. At a meeting of the Working Group of the Executive Council held in Wheaton, Illinois, on 16–17 July, 1984, this was studied and revised.

The following Statement of Mission was accepted:

> World Evangelical Fellowship is an alliance of national and regional evangelical bodies formed with the purpose of encouraging, motivating, and enabling the local church to fulfill its scriptural mandates, constantly directing its work toward the local level. It does this by:
> - Strengthening national and regional alliances where they exist and building an evangelical presence and leadership generally.
> - Developing a sense of world movement by providing an international forum, ways for international fellowship to occur, and building a world evangelical identity.
> - Serving as a multi-directional conduit for information and resources thus enhancing the interdependence of churches.
> - Defining issues, articulating consensus, expressing compassion for the suffering church and humanity, and encouraging initiative through the work of its officers, commissions, and staff.

A long-range plan submitted by the General Director was also reviewed and revised by the Working Group in an effort to sharpen the focus of WEF's goals and purposes.

Plans for the eighth General Assembly of WEF were also discussed. The General Director was requested to take the initial steps for determining a suitable location and to begin programme planning. It was agreed that this General Assembly should be held in a non-Western country, especially since all previous Assemblies except one had been held in Europe or North America. Subsequent planning determined that the venue would be Singapore, with the dates being 22–27 June, 1986. The WEF Commissions would also hold meetings immediately following the General Assembly. The theme chosen for the assembly was:

RENEW THE CHURCH—REACH THE WORLD

This reflected a growing emphasis in WEF on the place of the local church, the need for renewal in the church, and the desire to fulfill more aggressively the third purpose originally stated for WEF, "the furtherance of the gospel."

# CHAPTER TWENTY

# "Defence and Confirmation of the Gospel"

In 1951 at Woudschoten the founders of WEF determined to organize their movement around four standing Commissions: Evangelism, Missionary, Literature, and Christian Action. While there was some activity involving these Commissions in subsequent years, none of them really developed into an active, continuing ministry. Other Commissions were suggested from time to time, and on a few occasions actually named.

In 1962 Dr Everett Cattell, President of WEF, wrote to Revd Gilbert Kirby, General Secretary, saying.

> My idea is that our task in commissions is not to start something new and carry on as a new agency. Rather our task is to coordinate or bring into cooperation those active bodies which are working in these specific areas of interest. Our task then is not to do the job ourselves but rather to secure cooperation between those who are heading organizations that are doing a job already. We have hoped that these chairmen might bring into their fellowship leaders of other organizations working in the same area and try to produce a greater kind of cooperation. These chairmen, therefore, would act as advisors to WEF on one hand; secondly, they would invite others in their field to become members of the commission . . . thirdly, they would seek to promote active cooperation where possible.[1]

This statement accurately reflects how WEF has always viewed its Commissions. However, it was not until 1969 that the Commissions actually began to function in a practical way and thus make an impact.

It was the area of theology that served as the catalyst for the WEF Commissions to become vital and active. As we noted in Chapter 10, at the General Council held in Lausanne in 1968 the two areas of theology and youth had been highlighted for special focus by WEF in the immediate future. Bruce Nicholls had been named as Theological Coordinator and C. Stacey Woods as Youth Coordinator. While the area of youth did not develop into a WEF commission, theological concerns became the basis for a vigorous and active commission under Nicholls' leadership.

The doctrinal issue of the WEF view on Scripture had been a point of contention, as we have seen, between the European Evangelical Alliance and WEF. But in 1968, a satisfactory answer had been worked out on this issue, and the European Evangelical Alliance had joined WEF. A Constitution Committee had recommended at the time that a Theological Commission be appointed. A motion was passed ". . . to approve the first section of the report authorizing the appointment of a Theological Commission to review and suggest necessary changes in the Confession of Faith for action at the next General Council."[2]

Thus, it was the matter of the Confession of Faith that stimulated the founding of the Theological Commission. However, it was evident from the very start that there were broader theological concerns which the church was facing in many parts of the world. Bruce Nicholls had presented a lengthy and well-thought-out paper at the General Council in 1968, articulating theological trends and problems that the church must face. And so when he was named Theological Coordinator it was quite appropriate for him to begin developing a programme to help the church grapple with the theological issues of the day.

## The birth of TAP

Out of this initiative was born TAP—the Theological Assistance Programme of WEF. Bruce Nicholls very quickly drew up an ambitious programme for TAP including such projects as theological publications, consultations on theological problems, leadership training, curriculum development for training schools, biblical library funds for schools, accreditation for theological colleges, evangelical research centres, programming for Theological Education by Extension and regional theological societies.

By December 1970 the Annual Report of TAP was able to report great progress in a variety of areas. The aims of TAP were outlined as:

1. To offer evangelical Bible schools, theological colleges and seminaries, churches, missions and fellowships in Africa, Asia and Latin America an information service of current developments and needs in theological education.
2. To encourage and sponsor, where desirable, specialist theological consultations, local and regional workshops and conferences in subjects of special concern to evangelicals in training of national leadership for the life and witness of the church.
3. To assist closer cooperation between evangelical theological schools in developing united training, common curricula and text-book programmes, and in sponsoring theological societies and centres for advanced study and research in evangelism and church growth.
4. To stimulate evangelicals to articulate their theological understanding of the historic evangelical faith in fulfillment of the Great Commission in terms and forms relevant to religious and secular cultures and to social change.[3]

The report then detailed ten projects in which TAP was already involved or had plans to become involved. They included an information service (for sharing of theological news and developments), staff consultative services, regional consultations (of which several had already been held and others were being planned), evangelical theological commissions and societies (on the regional and local levels), a centre for advanced theological studies in Asia (for training on B.Th., M.Th., and doctoral levels; possibly located in Singapore), evangelical research centres, workshops and study conferences (again, with several already held and others planned), Theological Education by Extension projects (cooperating with others working in this field), a Biblical Library Fund (to help strengthen the libraries of theological schools in the Third World), and short term teaching appointments (for theological teachers who could go overseas for the summer, or for a sabbatical, to teach in other schools).[4]

A staff of six people was listed as already involved in the

programmes of TAP. They included Bruce Nicholls, as general coordinator; Dr Saphir Athyal, general coordinator for Asia; Dr Bong Rin Ro, coordinator for S.E. Asia; Dr Eui Whan Kim, coordinator for N.E. Asia; Revd G. J. McArthur, coordinator for the South Pacific; and Mr John Langlois, administrator.

Nicholls' vision was for regional branches of TAP to be developed. Since he was located in Asia, and since most of those active in TAP represented Asia, it was only natural that TAP-Asia should soon come into being. Thus, by 1971 TAP-Asia had been formed, with the hope that similar regional branches would develop elsewhere. In September 1971, TAP-Asia produced a directory of theologians which covered thirty pages of double columns, listing names of theologians, professors, and training schools throughout the world. It was an ambitious beginning, to say the least.

As time went on it became evident that regional associations would like to retain their own identity while remaining loosely affiliated with the world-wide body. Thus Nicholls reported:

> . . . by 1974 a good number of the members of the Executive of TAP-Asia headed by the coordinator Dr Saphir Athyal wanted an independent self-image for TAP-Asia. They changed the name to Asia Theological Association and made it autonomous. This action did not change our working relationship, for I continued as a member of the Executive of TAP-Asia and then for the accrediting council when this was established . . .
>
> I think this development points to the fact that we must accept diversity as well as unity. This is well reflected in the WEF ethos of "fellowship." Regional bodies particularly those in the Third World do not want to be dominated by what they see as a largely Western controlled and financed body. We Westerners are generally concerned about organizational structures, our Third World brethren about inter-personal relationships.[5]

During this period of time Bruce Nicholls was also instrumental in founding TRACI—Theological Research and Communications Institute—in Yeotmal, India, where he was teaching at Union Biblical Seminary. Dr Saphir Athyal was the seminary's principal.

### Developing into a Commission

It became evident in the early 1970's that TAP should expand its interests and that a full Theological Commission should be formed under WEF. Shortly after Clyde Taylor assumed the office of International Secretary of WEF he began to give thought and attention to the development of commissions. His annual report for 1972 to the Executive Committee expressed interest in beginning their development. At a meeting of the Executive Committee held in Atlanta, Georgia, USA, on 2 July, 1973, Taylor reported:

> As we discuss the matter of WEF Commissions we need to give some guidelines as to the use of funds by Commissions, especially TAP as it is the most viable at the moment . . .
>
> With regard to projects, I am at times stunned by the fertile mind of our brother Bruce Nicholls who plans projects running into hundreds of thousands of dollars. Of course, the money isn't spent until in hand, but who finally approves these projects?[6]

At that same meeting the Executive Committee voted to "authorize the development of the following Commissions: Theology (TAP), Missions, and Communications."[7]

Then at the Sixth General Assembly held at Chateau d'Oex, Switzerland, Bruce Nicholls and John Langlois, as coordinator and administrator of TAP, reported on the progress of TAP since its inception in 1968. Reports were also given by theological associations in Asia (Dr Bong Ro), Africa (Dr Byang Kato), Latin America (Mr Peter Savage), Europe (Mr Daniel Herm), Australasia (Dr Neville Andersen), and North America (Dr Arthur Climenhaga). Dr John Stott addressed the assembly on the question of regional theological associations, suggesting that a fellowship of theologians should be encouraged nationally and regionally, and that theological education should be critically reconsidered.

Later in that assembly the Executive Committee agreed that they should establish a theological commission and "that the name of the commission should be the WEF Theological Association and that its principle programme shall be known as TAP (Theological Assistance Program)."[8]

Those named to serve on the commission were Neville Andersen (Australia), Peter Beyerhaus (Germany), Klaus Bockmuehl (Switzerland), Arthur Climenhaga (USA), Zenas Gerig (Jamaica), Daniel Herm (Germany), Byang Kato (*ex officio*), Gordon Landreth and John Stott (England), Philip

Teng (Hong Kong), and Paul White (Reunion Islands). Bruce Nicholls and John Langlois were asked to continue in their respective responsibilities of coordinator and administrator.

The first full meeting of the newly formed Theological Commission was held in London, 8–12 September, 1975, at the London Bible College. At that time several significant steps were taken. Dr Byang Kato of Kenya was named chairman and Dr Arthur Climenhaga of the USA vice chairman. It was recommended that an international council for accreditation of theological schools should be formed. This was later to be fulfilled in the formation of the ICAA (International Council of Accrediting Agencies).

It was also agreed that the name "TAP" should be dropped and that "WEF Theological Commission" should become the official designation. The Commission was to be expanded to include between 20 and 30 members, with an executive committee to be responsible for executive decisions. Staff portfolios were designated as Literature and Publications, and Finance and General Administration, under the direction of John Langlois; while Theological Education, and Theology and Research, were under Bruce Nicholls.[9]

To the credit of the Theological Commission it should be noted that following that first meeting the executive committee of the Commission met every year for the next decade. Much of the strength of the Commission and its programmes can be attributed to this fact.

One sad loss to the Commission early in its history was the untimely death of its Chairman, Dr Byang Kato, in December 1975. This left a vacuum that was difficult to fill immediately, as he was a perceptive African leader who was well abreast of theological trends not only in Africa but elsewhere in the world. Dr Arthur Climenhaga stepped up from Vice Chairman to Chairman and gave able leadership to the Commission for the next six years.

*Accrediting Agencies Combine Forces*

A valuable by-product of the work of the Theological Commission was the establishing of the International Council of Accrediting Agencies (ICAA). In March 1980, as one of the six consultations held just prior to the WEF General Assembly at Hoddesdon, England, five regional theological accrediting agencies met to form an international council. These were the Accrediting Council for Theological Education in Africa (ACTEA), the American Association of Bible Colleges (AABC), the Asia Theological Association (ATA), the (now) Caribbean Evangelical Theological Association (CETA), and the European Evangelical Accrediting Association (EEAA). These five associations formed the ICAA, with several other groups becoming associate members. Dr Paul Bowers, missionary of SIM International in Kenya, was appointed General Secretary.

The constitution stated ICAA's relationship with WEF as follows:

"II. Status. The Council operates with internal autonomy under sponsorship of the Theological Commission of the World Evangelical Fellowship."[10]

The purposes of the ICAA were spelled out in detail in the constitution:

1. To serve as a medium for contact and collaboration among accrediting agencies for evangelical theological education worldwide.
2. To promote a sense of community among participating agencies, for mutual stimulation and enrichment.
3. To promote among member agencies the improvement of accreditation services.
4. To promote a sense of community among institutions and programmes of evangelical theological education worldwide, for mutual stimulation and enrichment.
5. To promote the improvement of evangelical theological education worldwide.
6. To encourage the development worldwide of programmes of evangelical theological education which embrace in one integrated whole the spiritual, behavioural, practical, and academic formation of Christian leadership.
7. To encourage the development worldwide of programmes of evangelical theological education which are shaped by a deliberate attentiveness to the specific Christian communities being served, the specific vocations for which the students are being prepared, and the specific cultural contexts in which the students will minister.[11]

Over the next few years the ICAA was instrumental in encouraging and strengthening theological education through its various programmes on every continent. At its meeting in

Seoul, Korea, in September 1982, Dr Robert Youngblood, missionary of the Presbyterian Church of America and staff member of the WEF Theological Commission, was appointed General Secretary to replace Dr Bowers, who had resigned due to the pressures of other duties. Dr Youngblood was re-appointed for another three-year term at the ICAA meeting held in Hilversum, The Netherlands, in August 1985.

And so, to the gratification of the Theological Commission, an outgrowth of its efforts was able to serve the cause of theological education in a creative and practical way around the world.

# CHAPTER TWENTY-ONE

# Publications and Consultations

One of the areas in which the Theological Commission has led the way for WEF as a whole has been that of publications. From the early 1970's the Commission was active in sponsoring theological consultations on a variety of topics. Out of these came some valuable publications which have made a significant contribution to theological thought. Other publications have come as a result of the research and work of one or more individuals.

The first official publication to originate from the WEF commissions was "Theological News," a quarterly news release begun in 1969 as an information service of the Theological Commission. It has continued to the present time, providing news and views on contemporary theological trends and issues.

Another of the early publications was a small quarterly entitled "Programming News." This was initiated by John Langlois, administrative secretary of the Theological Commission, to meet a need in the field of Theological Education by Extension (TEE). A great deal of work was being developed at that time in TEE, but not much of a practical nature was available in programming materials. And so Mr Langlois and Bruce Nicholls asked Martin Dainton to become the first editor of a periodical on the subject, a task which he agreed to do. With the help of people involved in TEE in different parts of the world, such as Peter Savage in Latin America and

Patricia J. Harrison in Africa and Asia, Dainton published articles of a practical as well as theoretical nature to give guidance in TEE programmes. A selection of these articles was published in book form in 1977 under the title *Introduction to Programming*, with WEF as the publisher.

In 1976 this quarterly was expanded and renamed "Theological Education Today." Patricia Harrison became the editor. This publication, in turn, was merged with "Theological News" in 1983 and became a regular section of that quarterly. Also added at the same time was a special section of news on ICAA (International Council of Accrediting Associations), which we described in the foregoing chapter.

## Consultations and Publications

In 1975, as we have noted, the newly formed Theological Commission had held its first full meeting in London. It was an in-depth consultation of theological issues of the day. Major papers were given on the themes of "The Gospel and Culture," "The Church and the Nation," "Salvation and World Evangelization." In addition to the theological reflection embodied in these papers there were also numerous seminars on strategies and structures for theological education, research and publications, regional associations, and other related matters. The results of this consultation were published by WEF as a small book under the title *Defending and Confirming the Gospel*.

A major step forward in the production of publications was taken in October 1977, with the appearance of the first issue of the *Evangelical Review of Theology*. Originally published twice a year this journal carried a balance of selected articles from other theological journals, some original articles on current topics, and book reviews of publications in theology. In 1985 it became a quarterly and now covers such fields as theology and culture, mission and evangelism, ethics and society, pastoral ministry, TEE, local church education and hermeneutics.

In September 1976, the Theological Commission organized a consultation on "Church and Nationhood" held at St

Chrischona, near Basel, Switzerland. Four days of prayer, Bible study and theological reflection by approximately thirty theologians from various parts of the world produced "The Basel Letter," a communication to the churches summarizing the consultation's thinking on the biblical relationship of the church and the nation in today's world. The letter was circulated widely through WEF channels and elsewhere.

As the Theological Commission developed more fully other consultations were planned and organized, and these had an increasing impact on the church as a whole. One of the most significant was the International Consultation on Simple Lifestyle held at High Leigh Conference Centre in Hoddesdon on 17–21 March, 1980. Jointly sponsored by the Unit on Ethics and Society of the Theological Commission of WEF, and the Theology Working Group of the Lausanne Committee, this drew together 85 evangelical leaders from 27 countries. Out of this consultation came the most complete and biblically grounded statements which have ever appeared in evangelical circles on the question of simple lifestyle. The thorough and provocative papers presented at this consultation were edited by Dr Ronald Sider and published by Paternoster Press of Exeter, England (whom WEF had now chosen as its official publisher) under the title *Lifestyle in the Eighties: An Evangelical Commitment to Simple Lifestyle*.

Just prior to that gathering a smaller but still significant consultation on a related topic was held at the same location, 10–14 March, 1980, on the theme of "The Theology of Development." Forty-one people from seventeen countries, under the sponsorship of the Unit on Ethics and Society of the Theological Commission, wrestled with the theological implications for evangelicals of the problems of development in today's world. Strong and vigorous debate gave a creative beginning to reflection and action in this area. Again the results were published, edited by Ronald Sider, under the title of *Evangelicals and Development: Towards a Theology of Social Change*.

These two were part of the series of six consultations that immediately preceded the WEF General Assembly held at

Hoddesdon, on 24–28 March 1980. They were also the forerunners of two further consultations that grew directly out of what was begun there.

The first was the Consultation on the Relationship between Evangelism and Social Responsibility (CRESR) held at Reformed Bible College in Grand Rapids, Michigan, USA, 16–23 June, 1982. This also was jointly sponsored by WEF and the Lausanne Committee for World Evangelization. Bringing together 50 evangelical leaders from 27 countries, CRESR was the most ambitious consultation on that topic yet attempted in the evangelical world. Every effort was made to allow for legitimate differences of opinion and understanding of the teachings of the Bible in this critical realm. The participants represented a broad spectrum of theological perspectives. New ground was broken and great strides were taken towards defining an evangelical consensus in the area of social responsibility.

The final statement of the consultation appeared in 1982 as the Grand Rapids Report, *Evangelism and Social Responsibility: an Evangelical Commitment*, edited by John Stott. This was undoubtedly the most comprehensive statement on this topic ever produced by evangelicals. The full papers that formed the basis for discussion at the consultation were published in 1985 entitled *In Word and Deed: Evangelism and Social Responsibility*, edited by Bruce Nicholls.

A valuable summary of the thinking represented at CRESR is given in the preface written by Dr Bong Rin Ro (WEF) and Revd Gottfried Osei-Mensah (LCWE).

> Our conclusion was that there are at least three relationships between evangelism and social responsibility which are equally valid; namely, that Christian social concern is a *consequence* of evangelism, can be a *bridge* to evangelism, and should be a *partner* of evangelism. It was especially pointed out concerning the latter that in our Lord's ministry, proclamation and service went hand in hand. His words explained His works and His works dramatized His words. Both His word and works were expressions of His compassion for people.[1]

They then explain that "since Christian social concern is a consequence of evangelism, evangelism has a logical priority."[2] However, it was also recognized that

> Primacy does not necessarily imply priority in the sequence of time.

This too is obvious from the assertion that social concern can be a bridge to evangelism.[3]

There was also a distinction made between social service and social action.

> Social service covers activities related to relieving human need, philanthropy, seeking to minister to individuals and families, and works of mercy. Social action has to do with removing the causes of human need, political and economic activity, seeking to transform the structures of society, and the quest for justice.[4]

As a direct consequence of the consultations in Hoddesdon and CRESR in Grand Rapids a further and more ambitious conference was held at the Billy Graham Center of Wheaton College, Wheaton, Illinois, in June 1983, on "The Nature and Mission of the Church." Known as WHEATON '83 this consultation brought together 370 men and women from many walks of life and from many cultures in 60 countries. The planning committee was chaired by Dr William Shoemaker, who was at that time the Director of the Billy Graham Center. Bruce Nicholls served as coordinator. Although convened by the World Evangelical Fellowship WHEATON '83 enjoyed the cooperation of many groups such as the Lausanne Committee and World Vision (which provided generously both with funds and personnel).

## WHEATON '83

WHEATON '83 was divided into three "tracks" (areas of interest). Track I—"The Church in its Local Setting"—was chaired by Dr Pablo Pérez of Mexico. This track concentrated on how the church in its local setting is to fulfill its role as "God's primary agent in his mission for the world."[5] Case histories were used extensively to deal with how the church is to reach the unreached, respond to human needs, and build up the local church for the glory of God.

Track II—"The Church in New Frontiers in Missions"— was chaired by Patrick Sookhdeo of London. It concentrated on how the church needs to cooperate, within itself and with para-church agencies, in order to reach the unreached. "We ask both traditional and emerging missions to share resources with each other so that the whole body of Christ may be built up in unity and in faith."[6]

Track III—"The Church in Response to Human Need"— was chaired by Dr Tom Sine of the USA, along with others who worked closely with him. This track had already been planning its own conference independently of WEF, when it was discovered that there could be a mutually beneficial joining of forces into the three tracks. Again using extensive case studies, and involving the participants in vigorous interchanges, this track spoke with the conviction that "Christ's followers . . . are called, in one way or another, not to conform to the values of society but to transform them."[7] The word "transformation" became the key word for what had previously been referred to as "development." There was a strong call to repentance and faith, along with a call to challenge the forces of evil and injustice in society as part of the mission of the church in the world.

The results of WHEATON '83 have been published over a period of time (with more volumes still to come) in a series of books. There was also a "Letter to the Churches" which was carefully worked over with a drafting committee during the two-week consultation and published as a consensus of the participants as a message to evangelical churches around the world.

*Other Ventures*

Space does not permit an exhaustive chronicle of all the consultations and publications for which WEF has been responsible. Enough has been written to give some insight into the scope and type of studies which the WEF commissions have covered. Others will be mentioned in the chapters on other commissions. Further examples would be the Consultation on the Holy Spirit and Evangelism held in Oslo, Norway, in May 1985, jointly sponsored by the Theology Working Group of the Lausanne Committee and the Theological Commission of WEF; and two consultations on biblical hermeneutics held in Cambridge, England, in 1982 and 1984, sponsored by the Faith and Life Study Unit of the WEF

Theological Commission and coordinated by Dr Donald Carson. Two volumes entitled *Biblical Interpretation and the Church* and *The Church and the Bible in the World* edited by Dr Carson were published, giving the papers from these consultations.

In 1978 WEF in partnership with the Paternoster Press of England and InterVarsity Press, USA, initiated a monograph series known as the "Identity and Outreach" series. Six monographs were published over a period of seven years: *Karl Barth's Theology of Mission* by Waldron Scott; *The Biblical Doctrine of Regeneration* by Helmut Burkhardt; *Contextualization: A Theology of Gospel and Culture* by Bruce Nicholls; *Evangelicals and Social Ethics* by Klaus Bockmuehl; *Pornography: A Christian Critique* by John N. Court; and *Theology and The Third World Church* by J. Andrew Kirk.

*Transformation*

One publication that proved to be creative, progressive and at the same time controversial was first proposed by the Unit on Ethics and Society of the Theological Commission. Originally conceived as the "International Journal of Christian Social Ethics" its name was later simplified to *Transformation*. Edited jointly by Dr Tokunboh Adeyemo, Dr Ronald Sider, and Revd Vinay Samuel, it brought together an outstanding editorial board of men and women with a broad spectrum of viewpoints and of experience in the field of social ethics. Its purpose has always been to give a balanced presentation of perspectives on the burning social and ethical issues facing the church today, raising the issues, suggesting biblical solutions, and calling Christians to creative action. The first issue was dated January/March 1984, and received immediate acclaim as fulfilling a great need in a field which had been largely neglected by evangelicals.

Because this journal, by its very nature, dealt with controversial issues on which evangelicals hold legitimate differences of opinion, it was inevitable that some issues would cause misunderstanding. This was expected and faced from the beginning. It was also inevitable that some of the issues would be of a highly sensitive political or theological nature. Strong differences of opinion exist between evangelicals in different countries on political matters.

At a meeting of the WEF Executive Council in Hilversum, The Netherlands, in June 1985, this matter came to a head. There was unanimous agreement that *Transformation* was filling a very real need in evangelical literature and that it should be continued as a vital publication. However, there was disagreement as to whether or not WEF should be the publisher. Lengthy discussion produced the following summary in the minutes:

> General agreement was expressed that *Transformation* is successfully performing a valid and needed service. At the same time, a poll of each of the council members revealed broad agreement that an umbrella organization such as WEF, which seeks to hold together in basic unity a diverse grouping of believers—both between and within geographical regions—is poorly suited to sponsor a publication that must, to fulfill its function, be deliberately provocative or controversial on occasion. The strongest disclaimers about responsibility for views of the authors and the most scrupulous balance in content are insufficient to protect the sponsoring organization from divisive accusation.
>
> It was noted that a publication that presents a variety of positions vigorously is most credible if its editors are independent of any agency that exercises a censoring or inhibiting role.[8]

In view of this, and after vigorous discussion of the implications for WEF, it was moved and carried (with one dissenting vote and one abstention)

> . . . that in view of the nature and purpose of *Transformation*, we strongly recommend that the Theological Commission make arrangements for its continuing publication as an independent journal.[9]

This action was taken reluctantly, as all agreed on the valuable role that *Transformation* was playing; but the majority felt that it could do a more complete job if it did not speak for any specific organization.

CHAPTER TWENTY-TWO

# "The Furtherance of the Gospel"

The founders of the Evangelical Alliance and their successors in WEF had always had a worldwide vision as part of their purpose. This was spelled out specifically in 1951 when the first purpose of WEF was stated to be "the furtherance of the gospel." (See p. 31) One of the four commissions created at that time was the "Missionary Commission" under Clyde W. Taylor as chairman. While some limited initiatives were carried out, this commission, like the others named in 1951, did not become an active body.

However, Taylor and his colleagues did not lose their missionary vision, even though it was not as visible as might have been hoped in terms of specific action. After his appointment as International Secretary of WEF in 1971 Clyde Taylor made a trip to Asia in 1972 on behalf of WEF. Afterwards he reported to the Executive Board that he was impressed with the growth of missionary strength around the world.

> We eventually reached certain conclusions regarding evangelical mission strength in the world. There are only 9 evangelical missions associations in the world . . . The total missionary staff of these 9 fellowships approximates 20,000 overseas missionaries. For a total picture . . . there are at least 30,000 evangelical missionaries on active duty now. Of these two-thirds are directly or indirectly related to WEF.[1]

He then proceeded to propose the establishing of a Commission on Mission that could give leadership and capitalize on the desire for cooperation between these various mission efforts.

> With this in mind we feel that within the next two years, probably even before the next world meeting of WEF, a Commission on Missions will be established that can tie these agencies into one worldwide fellowship.[2]

In response to the recommendations of Dr Taylor the Executive Committee later passed the following motion:

> . . . that the Executive Committee authorize the development of the following commissions: Theology (TAP), Missions, and Communications; and that respective by-laws be prepared by each of these commissions . . . to be approved at the meeting in Lausanne next year.[3]

Dr Taylor followed up this action by a seven-day trip to Europe in October 1973, when he discussed with the European Evangelical Alliance the possibility of establishing these commissions. Taylor reported later that ". . . the establishing of both Commissions on Missions and Communications was warmly received and they indicated they would do all possible to help bring this about."[4]

## A Missions Commission

As a result, when the WEF General Assembly was held in Chateau d'Oex in July 1974, immediately after the Lausanne congress, there were specialized sessions which were built around each of the proposed commissions. The Missions Group which met recommended that a WEF Association of Missions be formed. The purposes were outlined as:

> 1. To provide coordination, services, and exchange of information to member associations.
> 2. To offer assistance and resources for seminars, study conferences and international meetings as desired.
> 3. To provide mutual assistance in developing missions, education, and exchange of personnel.
> 4. To encourage the establishment of national committees where none exists [sic].[5]

A steering committee was formed for this commission composed of Dr Wade Coggins of EFMA, USA; Dr David Cho of Korea International Mission, Korea; and Mr Ernest Oliver of Evangelical Missions Association, England.

This steering committee met in Seoul, Korea, 23–26 August, 1975, to lay plans for the proposed International Missions Commission (as it was then called). Waldron Scott, as General Secretary of WEF, met with them and presented his thoughts about the best way of setting up the commission. Scott saw three reasons for the commission's existence.

1. The World Evangelical Fellowship must keep the missionary task of the Church before the evangelical churches throughout the world.
2. The World Evangelical Fellowship needs a body to stimulate and provide guidance on strategy for mission in various forms.
3. There is the need for a bridge—building body between the new Third World Missions and the traditional Western Missions so that help can travel in both directions in the furtherance of the Lord's work worldwide.[6]

This meeting produced a lengthy list of recommendations for the WEF Executive Council, the major ones being that "The Missions Commission of the World Evangelical Fellowship" should be established, that it should be composed of not less than 20 members appointed by the Executive Council, that a steering committee of not more than 7 members should be named, and that steps should be taken to appoint a full-time executive officer of the commission, preferably "a youngish person of some missionary experience from the Third World, who would introduce refreshing Third World Mission concepts to the Commission's work."[7]

It was also recommended that three study conferences be held in the next five years. One would be for representatives of the 10 Missions Associations then existing in the world, one would be the inaugural conference of the Missions Commission, and one a conference on Third World Missions.

Following this initial meeting the Executive Council gave its approval for the establishing of the Missions Commission. The steering committee was expanded to include Revd Theodore Williams of Bangalore, India, who was Executive Secretary of the Indian Evangelical Mission. The committee also named as Executive Secretary Dr Chun Chae Ok of Korea. She was the first Korean woman in history to serve as a missionary, working in Pakistan for thirteen years. She also became the first woman in history to earn a doctorate in missiology when she completed her studies at the Fuller School of World Mission in Pasadena, California.

When the WEF Executive Council met in November 1976, Waldron Scott reported "that the Missions Commission had been constituted and that a key meeting of the heads of associations of missions will be held in Bombay early in 1977."[8]

*Bombay to Bad Liebenzell*

In January 1977, this happened. A total of 12 people attended representing the major associations of missions from different parts of the world. Out of this meeting came various suggestions for the Missions Commission's structure, programme, and future meetings.

As part of that larger meeting the steering committee of the Missions Commission also met. This was now composed of Wade Coggins (USA), as Chairman, David Cho (Korea), Theodore Williams (India), Ernest Oliver (UK), and Ernst Vatter (Germany), with Chun Chae Ok (Korea) as Executive Secretary, and Waldron Scott (USA) *ex officio*. Ernest Oliver was appointed Chairman to succeed Wade Coggins, who had requested to be relieved.

Two-year objectives were determined for the Missions Commission as follows:

1. Identify and establish contact with and extend fellowship to Third World missions . . .
2. Fraternal visits and interchanges . . .
3. Get help from various agencies to help us fulfill the above . . .
4. Provide information to mission executives on sources of information available . . .
5. Arrange a meeting of the full commission . . . possible date: January, 1979.[9]

That proposed meeting of the full commission was in fact held on 27–31 January, 1979, at the headquarters of the Liebenzell Mission in Bad Liebenzell, Germany. 27 mission leaders from all 6 continents gathered to hear papers, share ideas, and project future efforts of cooperation in the mission outreach of the church. Papers were given on "Unreached

Peoples," "Aid and Development," "Emerging Third World Missions," and "Strategy for Third World Mission."

This was a time of creative interaction between leaders from Third World missions and others from older, more traditional, Western missions. One of the participants described the event in colourful terms:

> Pens scratched and minds sifted what was being said. And as soon as opportunity for response was given, Liberia and Latin America disagreed in a flood of rhetoric while Korea and Norway marshalled thoughts and sat poised for the chance to express themselves.
>
> An unholy free-for-all? By no means. A collection of men and women . . . whom God has tapped for leadership wrestling with 'hows' and 'whens' of missionary outreach from Hong Kong, Singapore, or Holland.[10]

In a gathering where Third World leaders had full freedom to express their thoughts and feelings it was expected that Western missions would come in for some criticism. And they did. The above quoted report goes on to say:

> Inevitably, comparisons arose. Methods, and more, the attitudes of Western missionaries were soundly criticized. Strongest attacks were aimed at missionary control beyond the time when national Christians felt capable of leadership; at big business styled Christian organizations which impose their evangelism plans on a nation without listening to what local believers think about their schemes; and at the Westernizing which some missionaries appear to feel is synonymous with Christianizing.[11]

Nevertheless, in spite of these (largely deserved) criticisms, given openly and generally in a good spirit, there was a spirit of unity of purpose and thankfulness for what God had done through Western missions.

> But always before analysis degenerated into vituperation, someone would remember,
>
> "Yes, but if they had not come, I would not know Jesus. I thank God for those missionaries."[12]

Some changes in the Mission Commission's membership took place at this meeting. Ernest Oliver requested to be relieved of his role as Chairman, and Ernst Vatter of Germany was elected to succeed him. Dr Chun Chae Ok announced that, due to other pressing duties of teaching at Ewha Women's University in Korea, she could not continue as executive secretary. Revd Theodore Williams of India was chosen to succeed her. Revd Panya Baba of Nigeria was also elected to the commission. The addresses delivered at the Bad Liebenzell conference were published as a book entitled *World Missions—Building Bridges or Barriers.*

## Theodore Williams

The activities of the Missions Commission for the next few years were built largely around the ministry of the new Executive Secretary, Revd Theodore Williams. His gifts of Bible teaching and preaching caused him increasingly to be in demand all over the world. He used these opportunities to promote the vision of missions, the responsibility of the local church in world evangelization, and the formation of mission societies in Third World nations.

At the meeting of the WEF Executive Council held in Malawi in September 1981, Williams reported:

> One of the chief objectives of the Missions Commission is to encourage the emerging missions and to challenge the churches to realize their missionary responsibility. This is what we have been concentrating on this year and it has meant a lot of travel for me.[13]

He reported that in the course of the past year he had participated in conferences on missions in Mexico City, Guatemala, Brazil, Singapore, and Malaysia. Several of these, especially the meetings in Guatemala, were a "first" for the national church. Thus the impact of the Missions Commission was beginning to be felt in strategic locations on all continents.

## Together in Mission

In January 1982, the Missions Commission held its next full meeting in Bangalore, India—the home of Theodore Williams and, therefore, the office of the Commission. For five days (27–31 January) 40 leaders from five continents considered the theme "Together in Mission." The two dominant concerns of this conference were the training of missionaries and partnership between Western and "emerging" missions. Major papers were given by mission leaders such as Panya Baba of Nigeria, Petrus Octavianus of Indonesia, Chun Chae Ok of Korea, D. John Richard of India, Wade Coggins of the USA, Ernest Oliver of the UK, and others. These addresses were published in 1983 in a book edited by Theodore Williams entitled *Together in Mission*. An open letter from the participants was circulated to churches around the world, noting:

> (1) the need to reevaluate the quality and validity of missionary training programs; (2) the urgency to create avenues by which missions training programs become responsive to changing situations and needs; (3) the importance of stimulating spiritual development, prayer and holy boldness in facing human opposition and satanic forces; (4) the importance of conserving present personnel for the purpose of producing an increased percentage of long-term missionaries.[14]

Several units within the Missions Commission were also formed at that time. They were the Research and Information Unit, with Dr Lawrence Keyes of Brazil as coordinator; the Missions Education Unit, with Dr Lois McKinney of the USA as coordinator; the Missiology Unit, with two divisions— Theological Issues, with Dr Norvald Uri of Norway as coordinator, and Practical Issues, with Revd Panya Baba of Nigeria as coordinator.

Under Dr Keyes, the Research and Information Unit began publishing "Bridging Peoples," a small but extremely valuable bulletin containing up-to-date news on "emerging" missions in the non-Western world. This was published jointly by the WEF Missions Commission and Overseas Crusades, for whom Dr Keyes worked. (Later that year Dr Keyes became the president of Overseas Crusades and found it necessary to curtail some of his activities with the Missions Commission, although he continued to give encouragement and support.)

In 1984 Mr Tom Chandler, a missionary of Overseas Crusades who had worked for ten years in Singapore and Indonesia, joined the Missions Commission on a full-time basis as administrative assistant to the extremely busy Theodore Williams. Tom began to work closely with leaders in the Third World in developing missions conference and consultations. One of these was held in Nigeria in August of

1985, with a good representation of Nigerian church leaders who were leading the church out in missionary vision.

At the time of writing major plans are underway for COMIBAM, the Spanish acronym for Ibero-American Congress on Missions, to be held in Brazil in 1987. This will be the first continent-wide missions conference ever held in Latin America. The WEF Missions Commission has been deeply involved in the preparations for this congress, although it is not sponsored by WEF but rather by Latin American mission leaders.

It had taken over two decades for the third purpose envisioned by the founders of WEF—"the furtherance of the gospel"—to begin its realisation. But the decade from 1975 to 1985 has seen encouraging and rapid advance in this area. The spectacular increase in missionary vision and outreach from the non-Western world during that decade has been at least in part related to the ministry of the WEF Missions Commission. It has unquestionably had a significant influence in stimulating such vision and in encouraging the formation of Third World missionary associations and sending agencies. If so much progress can be made in ten years, how much more could the next decade achieve?

# CHAPTER TWENTY-THREE

# Communicating the Gospel

Webster tells us that communication is "the act of transmitting; a giving or exchanging of information . . . close sympathetic relationship . . . the art of expressing ideas, especially in speech and writing."[1] When one analyzes the three purposes for which WEF was founded—fellowship in the gospel, the defence and confirmation of the gospel, the furtherance of the gospel—one realizes quickly that communication is the key to all of these. Without communication there is no fellowship; without communication it would be impossible to defend and confirm the gospel; without communication the gospel will not be furthered.

The founders of WEF in 1951 saw this in embryo form when they decided to establish the four commission, one of which was on literature. During the decade of the 1950s and the early 1960s there was a growing emphasis in mission circles on literature, radio, films, audio visuals—in fact the entire field of communications. How did WEF respond to this developing discipline?

With the growing recognition that modern science and technology was placing in the hands of Christians new and creative means for transmitting the gospel, bringing the goal of achieving world evangelization into the realm of possibility, mission and church leaders began to wake up to the new potential for Christian witness.

The ministry of missionary radio had been recognized

181

since the founding of radio station HCJB in Ecuador, which broadcast the world's first missionary radio programme on Christmas Day, 1931. In the 1940s and 1950s other mission organizations followed the lead of HCJB and founded stations. As TV began to grow its potential was also seen. And already the field of literature had long been recognized as a major means of communicating the gospel; William Carey and his pioneer colleagues of Serampore, India, had seen the possibilities as far back as the late 1790s and early 1800s, with their great translation and publication programmes.

*An International Commission on Communications*

As the vision grew of what training in communications could mean for the advance of the gospel, leaders of WEF began to explore how this should relate to WEF's ministry. In May 1973, Clyde Taylor, as International Secretary, wrote some comments about "Potential Developments of the WEF." One part of this suggested an International Commission on Communications.

> It was felt years ago that ultimately one of the most important activities of world evangelism would center in this field. Now a number of national fellowships are active in the field of literature, radio, and TV and some in the use of films and audio-visual materials. There is enough interest in member fellowships with their communications committees to make such an international commission both possible and practical. Possibly literature committees will be brought together as a separate commission.[2]

Thus in July 1973, at its meeting in Atlanta, Georgia, the WEF Executive Committee authorized the development of three commissions: Theology, Missions, and Communications. In his report of October 8, 1973, to the WEF/USA Board, Clyde Taylor reported that the possibility of a Communications Commission was warmly received by European members of WEF.

The first specific steps for the formation of the Communications Commission were taken at the WEF General Assembly in Chateau d'Oex in July 1974.

Specialized groups in several areas of study met during

the assembly, and one of them concerned the issue of communications. This group reported to the assembly the following recommendations:

1. We hereby request the World Evangelical Fellowship to provide for a commission which would be known as the "World Evangelical Communications Association."

2. We suggest a seven continent committee, consisting of national communication bodies which presently exist and inviting others who may be formed to join.

3. We subscribe to the purpose, statement of faith of the WEF, and support the proposed bylaws and four purposes stated in the suggested nomenclature on pp. 1–4 (on file with the minutes).

4. We desire to implement the association by a three man steering committee consisting of Dr Ben Armstrong, Executive Secretary of the National Religious Broadcasters, Madison, N.J., USA: Mr Fred Magbanua, Philippines Director for the Far East Broadcasting Company, Manila, Philippines; and the Rev Horst Marquardt, Director of Evangeliums-Rundfunk, Wetzlar, West Germany.

5. The Association would include in basic principle, radio, TV, literature, audiovisuals, films, etc., but we feel immediate responsibility for the development of broadcasting concerns.

6. We envision that service organizations in the field of communications would be invited to participate, such as Evangelical Literature Overseas and International Christian Broadcasters.[3]

The recommended steering committee was approved by the Executive Council, who invited Dr Ben Armstrong to serve as Convener. Dr Armstrong made it a point to call a meeting of the Commission every year at the annual convention of the National Religious Broadcasters in Washington, D.C., even though it was only in its fledgling stage. During 1975 and 1976 initial steps were taken to publish a quarterly newsletter, to prepare a weekly broadcast of religious news, and to plan for a world congress on communications. The first issue of the WEF "Communications Report" was published in the summer of 1976.

In August 1976, Waldron Scott reported to the WEF Executive Council:

Progress has been achieved toward the development of a Communications Commission also. The Commission has published an International Directory of Christian Broadcasters and has begun publication of a quarterly newsletter. It has assumed responsibility for the weekly broadcast, World Religious News. And plans are being made for a World Congress on Communications in the Netherlands in October, 1978.[4]

When the Executive Council met in Colorado Springs in November 1976, this report was received with appreciation, and approval was given for co-sponsoring the proposed congress with the Lausanne Committee and the Evangelical Broadcasting Company of the Netherlands.

## From Congress to Conference

Lack of full-time personnel to direct the work of the Communications Commission meant that it had to depend entirely on the volunteer help offered by the members of the steering committee, all of whom were very busy with responsibilities in their own organizations. While these men had a vision for the Commission and wanted to do all they could to expand its ministry, they could not give it the attention they wished.

In his report of 1 January, 1978, to the Executive Council Waldron Scott stated concerning the Communications Commission:

> Although not as well developed as the other commissions, this commission has established good working relations with regional groups in Asia, North America and Europe.
> The commission was also active in planning the early stages of the forthcoming European Conference of Evangelical Communicators to be held in Amsterdam, October, 1978.[5]

The Executive Committee of the Commission met on 24 January, 1978, in Washington, DC. It was decided

> . . . that no World Communications Congress should be convened at this time. Rather, efforts will be made to encourage continental cooperation in fellowships of groupings, which should convene their own continent-wide consultations and conferences.[6]

It was also decided to "publish a quarterly international information sheet in English under the editorial direction of Dr Ben Armstrong as chairman of the commission."[7] Another significant step at this meeting was the appointment of Miss Gladys Jasper as a member at large of the Executive Committee. Miss Jasper, a missionary with the Christian and Missionary Alliance in Asia for many years, and a representative of Evangelical Literature Overseas, was destined to play a prominent role in the Communications Commission and eventually to become its Executive Secretary.

The European Evangelical Communications Conference (which replaced the global conference originally considered) was held in Amsterdam on 20–23 October, 1978. Members of the WEF Communications Commission participated actively in this conference, and strong links were established with European communicators who would give active leadership to WEF in subsequent years.

*Growing International Interest*

By 1979 the WEF "Communications Report" was being published monthly (except for July and August) with John Langlois of Guernsey, in the Channel Islands, serving as publisher for WEF, and Ben Armstrong of the USA as editor. This four page report gave news of mutual interest to communicators around the world, reported on new developments, and served as a channel for exchange of ideas.

The membership of the commission was expanded considerably in the first few years. In March 1980, at the meeting of the WEF Executive Council held in London, approval was given for membership in the commission of a total of 32 men and women, a goodly proportion of whom were from Asia, Africa, and Latin America. All of them were personally involved in the extension of the gospel through communications media of one sort or another. However, the Executive Council "noted the apparent absence from the Communications Commission of any representative of the important field of publications (e.g. *Christianity Today*) and instructed the General Secretary to convey its concern to Dr Ben Armstrong, chairman of the commission."[8] A study of this list of 32 people indicates that the majority of them were in the field of broadcasting or related media.

The full commission met just prior to the WEF General Assembly in Hoddesdon, England, on 21–24 March, 1980, with an ambitious agenda. The minutes of this meeting cover 52 pages plus 26 additional pages of appendices. Considerable time was given to discussing the future of the commission, to hearing reports from various parts of the world, and to considering the contributions the commission could make through publications, conferences, training programmes and other functions.

The Executive Committee chosen to serve for the next period was composed of Dr Ben Armstrong (USA), chairman; Revd Horst Marquardt (Germany), vice chairman; Drs L. P. Dorenbos (The Netherlands) treasurer; Mr D. John Richard (India), Miss Gladys Jasper (USA and Asia); Mr David Adams (UK).

Special study groups were set up to carry out the major work of the commission. These were, first, the Training Study Group (to seek the best ways of training those called to the use of media in presenting the gospel), with Mr Phill Butler as convener; second, the Theology Study Group (to develop a biblical theology of communication), with Mr David Adams as convener; third, the New Technology Study Group (to analyze frontier communications technology and determine how it can be used for Christian outreach), with Dr Ben Armstrong as convener; and fourth, the Ethics Study Group (to deal with ethical questions such as copyright laws in the use of the media), with Miss Gladys Jasper as convener.

*People and Achievements*

In January 1981, a major step forward was taken when Miss Anne Ediger, a Canadian missionary of the Mennonite Brethren Missions Service in India, was appointed Executive Secretary of the Communications Commission. There were high hopes of the quality of leadership which Miss Ediger would bring to the Commission, in view of her long years of missionary experience and her expert knowledge in the field of communications. Unfortunately, her activities were severely curtailed later that year due to illness. Then her life was sadly cut short by the illness, and she went to be with the Lord on 26 September, 1981.

Mr James Johnson of the USA had been elected chairman of the Communications Commission in January 1981 and was taking an active role in its leadership. The work left undone by Miss Ediger was taken up by Miss Gladys Jasper, who was appointed Executive Secretary in 1982. The Christian and Missionary Alliance generously seconded her to WEF on a fulltime basis, thus making it possible for her to concentrate entirely on the development of the Commission.

Gladys Jasper had performed missionary service for thirty-seven years in Asia (in India, Singapore, and the Philippines) and was known and respected throughout that continent as well as in other parts of the world, for her commitment to and her abilities in the field of communications. She had been instrumental in developing a wide variety of ministries in Asia.

It was decided that Miss Jasper would locate the Commission's offices in the Netherlands, where Dr Robert Youngblood already had an office of the Theological Commission. Here she could be close to some of the most active members of the Commission, such as Horst Marquardt, L. P. Dorenbos, and David Adams, and could also receive administrative help from Miss Betty Froisland who had moved to the Netherlands from Colorado Springs to help Dr Youngblood.

Miss Jasper concentrated her initial efforts in four areas. First, she worked hard on a revision of the constitution of the Commission, which was badly in need of attention. Second, she straightened out a lot of confusion on the membership lists of the Commission, developing guidelines for membership that would encourage more active participation by members.

And there were two other major projects which occupied a large portion of her time and attention. First was the development, in collaboration with the WEF Theological Commission, of a pilot curriculum for a Th.M. degree in communications for seminaries and training schools in the Third World, particularly in Asia. With the help of Mr Phill Butler and others a full curriculum was outlined and plans were laid to begin the course in January 1986 at Asia Theological Seminary in Manila. At the time of writing this course is being offered for the first time. Miss Jasper was present for its inauguration in Manila.

Her second major project was to prepare for the International Christian Media Conference (ICMC), scheduled to be held in the Netherlands in October 1986. Numerous changes in dates, location, sponsors, and programme made for great frustrations for her.

Several key groups that had originally agreed to undertake joint sponsorship—and thus financial responsibility—found it necessary to withdraw. This necessitated drastic changes in plans for such things as location, size of the conference, programme and dates. Miss Jasper, who was serving as coordinator for the ICMC, found herself caught in cross currents of argument and some misunderstandings that were difficult to sort out. However, at the time of writing she is still involved in the planning processes, along with other key leaders in communications.

In January 1985 Gladys Jasper was also instrumental in reviving the publication of the "Communications Report" on a quarterly basis. This was an important step forward in making the ministry of the Commission more effective.

And so another Commission began its strategic work. Now WEF looks to its Communications Commission to give increasing leadership to the church around the world in training others for the effective use of the media to communicate the good news of salvation.

CHAPTER TWENTY-FOUR

# "A Cup of Cold Water"

The leaders of WEF have always been sensitive to the biblical injunctions to serve the poor. They have always understood the obligation of Christians to reach out in love to those in need and give "a cup of cold water" in the name of Christ.

This can be seen consistently over the years of WEF's ministry. We have already mentioned several examples: J. Elwin Wright's concern for the refugees of Vietnam, for instance, expressed in the report of his trip around the world in 1954–55 (see pp. 41–2); Fred Ferris' concern for the refugees in Lebanon and Vietnam in 1957 (see p. 53); Dennis Clark's efforts in 1967 to help the poverty stricken people of Latin America in his desire to link a spiritual ministry with a compassion for the poor and hungry (see pp. 77–9); Clyde Taylor's efforts through DAS (Development Assistance Services), his cooperation with IIDI (International Institute for Development), and the formation of IDAC (International Development Assistance Commission) (see pp. 98–9).

This concern for social action was given specific form at a meeting held in Lausanne, Switzerland, on 25–27 August, 1969. Since it was not possible, for financial reasons, to convene the full Executive Committee, it was decided to take advantage of the presence of several WEF leaders at another neighbouring conference to convene an *ad hoc* meeting. Present were Dennis Clark, Ben Wati, Clyde Taylor, Ernst

189

Beck, Bruce Nicholls, and Stacey Woods, as well as Russell Self and George Hoffman, the latter two by the invitation of the president, Ben Wati. It was decided to form a committee that would be a channel for ministering to the poor and needy of the world. Minutes of that meeting state:

> International Christian Assistance (ICA). The International Secretary reviewed assistance given to Christians involved in the Southern Sudan civil war and the Nigeria/Biafra civil war, and stated that the British Evangelical Alliance had favourably looked upon a suggestion the Revd George Hoffman be appointed WEF ICA Co-ordinator.[1]

Considerable discussion produced a policy statement which was to serve as a guideline for WEF in its future outreach in social action.

> In assuming this new corporate responsibility the WEF reaffirms that the wholeness of man and the proper evaluation of all his problems can only be met by a right understanding of the Biblical perspective which focuses prior attention on man in his alienation and lostness from God and his consequent need for salvation.
>
> Allied with this we recognize afresh our responsibility to exercise a compassionate ministry in the name of Christ for those in need, particularly for those of the 'household of faith.'
>
> By means of our relief arm, the International Christian Assistance, we will seek to meet emergency needs, as requested by evangelical churches and affiliates.[2]

Mr George Hoffman was the coordinator of TEAR Fund (The Evangelical Alliance Relief Fund) of England. He had had extensive experience in relief and development work in many parts of the Third World. In reporting on this movement to the Executive Committee Dennis Clark wrote:

> WEF world plan of cooperation provides two main lines of partnership between evangelicals.
> 1. Emergency Consortiums [sic]. In the case of emergencies the cooperating agencies will receive phone, cable, and express letter information with request for finance/personnel/supplies. Mr Hoffman will coordinate programmes during the emergency. A permanent *Emergency Fund* and organizational network is necessary, and WEF hopes to consolidate such a fund.
> 2. The WEF co-ordinator will serve as a consultant to cooperating agencies, working with their nominee in the development of relief programmes aimed at informing Christians of needs. The WEF coordinator will also provide an information service to supporting

agencies of overseas relief needs related to trustworthy Christians in developing nations.

Finance may be forwarded through the WEF office at Lausanne.[3]

This was an ambitious and laudable programme. Its foundations were biblical, its goals were clear, and its methods were honest. However, for a variety of reasons, not all of which are entirely clear in the historical records, it did not develop as fully as had been envisioned.

## Relief and Development

By 1976 Clyde Taylor was writing to Waldron Scott to express some of his frustrations in this area and the difficulty which WEF had experienced in putting its plans into practice. He said:

> You bring up this matter of a commission on development—this is a long story and one that is a great disappointment to me because I felt that it was really under way. I would hate to try to put all this down on paper. It's going to take too much secretarial time to do it. Suffice it to say that this thing was approved by the International Board of WEF. We went ahead with it in this country. We did have some difficulties due to personnel in operating the Commission on International Development but the action that killed it was a proposal brought up by [name withheld] of the Evangelical Alliance in Great Britain who is so much of a Socialist that he opposes anything that savors of the free enterprise spirit and he has other people backing him . . . In any case he proposed to the Executive Council of WEF that they withdraw authorization for the WEF to have a commission on international development and that they would hope that if such a thing were needed that the NAE would sponsor it in this country and take it out of the hands of WEF.[4]

Taylor then goes on to explain that the NAE operated through the World Relief Commission and in cooperation with the Institute for International Development. He then adds,

> I think there's a real potential here and I concur with you that it shouldn't be all relief. We should be involved in development.[5]

At a meeting of the WEF Executive Council in September 1979, Waldron Scott reported that plans were moving ahead for establishing a Relief and Development Commission. He mentioned that prior to the General Assembly in March 1980 there would be a consultation on the Theology of Develop-

ment, which would form the basis for such a commission.
The purposes of the Commission were given as:

> To develop more effective relationships between relief agencies and
> national evangelical associations.
> To assist in the development of more effective relationships between
> Western relief agencies and Third World receptors.
> To evaluate ethical issues in relation to competition, or perceived
> competition, between agencies.
> To consider the possibility of some relief and development funds
> being used to develop national infrastructures reflective of national
> constituencies.
> To investigate the extent to which relief and development agencies
> diminish funds available for missions generally.[6]

Scott was encouraged by the Council to proceed with the
Relief and Development Commission in anticipation of the
General Assembly.

At the General Assembly itself a recommendation was
made to establish a Commission on Social Responsibility. The
Executive Council requested Jun Vencer of the Philippines to
convene a meeting with the help of the General Secretary, to
consider this whole matter.[7]

The meeting was held at the time of COWE (the Consultation
on World Evangelization) in Pattaya, Thailand, on 20 June,
1980, with the following in attendance: Jun Vencer (Philippines), as chairman; John Richard (India); Claude Noël
(Haiti); Jerry Ballard (USA) and Waldron Scott *ex officio*.
Consideration was given to the recommendations of the
General Assembly. It was decided that it would be premature
to establish a Commission on Social Responsibility. Rather
the committee recommended to the WEF Executive Council
"the immediate organization of a Commission on Relief and
Development, primarily among WEF-related relief and development agencies."[8]

It was also proposed

> . . . to recommend to the executive council that WRC (World Relief
> Corporation of NAE/USA) and TEAR Fund, UK, call for a consultation of
> WEF-related relief and development agencies to: (a) discuss closer
> relations among these agencies, and to (b) consider the possibility of
> creating a WEF Commission on Relief and Development.
> An agenda committee was suggested to be composed of: Jerry Ballard
> (WRC), George Hoffman (TEAR Fund, UK) and Jun Vencer (PCEC) to plan
> for the consultation.[9]

These recommendations were approved by the WEF Executive Council at Pattaya, and the nominated committee organized a full-scale consultation to be held in Hong Kong in October 1980.

*Steps Towards a Commission*

From 29 October to 1 November, 1980, the chief executive officers of 18 WEF-related relief and development agencies met in Hong Kong to consider ways and means of more effective cooperation under the theme "Workers Together with Christ." Waldron Scott brought the opening greetings on behalf of WEF. He stated that

> Without doubt the growth of relief and development operations has been one of the most creative innovations to emerge in evangelical circles since World War II. In addition . . . relief and development agencies have helped evangelicals recapture some of the social dimensions of the gospel lost sight of during the modernist-fundamentalist controversy . . .
>
> To my knowledge this is the first time representatives of WEF-related relief and development agencies—donor and delivery—from all parts of the world have met together to discuss mutual problems and explore more effective ways to work together.[10]

Those days were spent in intensive discussion of the various ministries of the agencies represented, all of which were related to the national evangelical alliances of their countries. This consultation proposed the formation of a Co-ordinating Committee to follow through on the recommendations of the consultation for more effective cooperation between the agencies represented. The committee chosen was composed of:

| | |
|---|---|
| Jun Vencer | East Asia (Chairman and Convener) |
| Jerry Ballard | The Americas |
| George Hoffman | Europe |
| Samuel Yameogo | Africa |
| Ron Mathews | Southern Asia |

This committee held its first meeting in Wheaton, Illinois, on 31 July 1981, with all members present. It was their conclusion that the recommendations from the previous consultations in Hoddesdon and in Hong Kong could best be realized by a formal alliance of these agencies.

> The Coordinating Committee recommends to the Executive Council of WEF the formation of a WEF Relief and Development Alliance (Commission) to be composed of the Hong Kong Consultative Body's member agencies.[11]

This recommendation came before the WEF Executive Council at its next meeting two months later. After consideration the council voted

> . . . to authorize the Coordinating Committee to proceed with plans to establish a relief and development alliance under WEF, in conjunction with the General Secretary, for submission to the Executive Council . . . and that the Coordinating Committee to be encouraged to make provision for similar evangelical agencies to cooperate in the project.[12]

Thus on 30 January, 1982, at a special meeting in Bangalore, India, the Executive Council approved the establishment of a Relief and Development Alliance of WEF composed of the 18 bodies that had met in Hong Kong in 1980. The interim executive committee mentioned above was authorized to act on behalf of the Alliance.

This committee met immediately in Bangalore, supplemented by the presence of Wade Coggins (*ex officio*), Neville Andersen (Australia), Claude Noël (Haiti), and "Buzz" Frum (of the WEF staff). Two days were spent in discussing how the Alliance should be formed, how it should function, and how it would relate to the various member bodies, each of which was responsible to its national evangelical fellowship. It was decided that the Alliance would have no legislative authority over the member bodies but rather would serve to coordinate activities related to fund raising, disaster and emergency relief, and other such matters.

The name chosen was Inter-Church Relief and Development Alliance, known as IRDA. It was pointed out that WEF's constituency is the national church in each country, and that it was important, therefore, to highlight the church-related status of IRDA. The word "alliance" was carefully chosen also to distinguish it from a specific commission. It was an alliance of already existing agencies which were active in relief and development in representation of their national evangelical fellowship. However, it was agreed that for administrative purposes IRDA should be considered on an equal plane with the other WEF commissions.[13]

At the meeting of the Executive Council that same week action was taken to authorize IRDA as an official WEF body.[14]

A further meeting of the IRDA Executive Committee was held in Bangkok in October 1982. Strong efforts were being made to build a working, viable alliance that would contribute significantly to better cooperation and coordination of relief and development efforts around the world.

At the time of writing it remains to be seen what will be the results of the creation of IRDA. When a typhoon hits the Philippines, or an earthquake shatters Mexico City, or a volcano buries a town in Colombia, or a famine devastates Ethiopia and other parts of Africa many of the member agencies of IRDA are on hand immediately to provide help and relief. This takes tremendous amounts of time, energy, personnel, and money.

Perhaps it is because the members of IRDA have been so busy meeting urgent needs that they have been unable to give time and thought to the organization of IRDA as an effective body. There is full agreement on the need for such an alliance. How to make it an effectively operating body still remains to be determined.

CHAPTER TWENTY-FIVE

# "The Women who Proclaim the Good Tidings"

"The Lord gives the command; the women who proclaim the good tidings are a great host" (Psalm 68:11, NASB). Throughout history women have always played an important part in the development of God's plans for the spread of the gospel in the world. This can be seen in both the Old and the New Testaments as well as in the history of missions since.

This is not the place to develop a full scriptural analysis of the role of women in the fulfillment of God's plans. That has been done more completely in many other books. But one need remember only such people as Sarah, Deborah, Ruth, Hannah, the widow of Zarephath, Esther, the virtuous woman of Proverbs 31, the Virgin Mary, Elizabeth, Mary the mother of James and John, Martha, Lydia, and Priscilla, to realise quickly how important women have been in God's plans. And, like the writer of Hebrews, we could add that "time would fail me to tell" of the exploits of countless women who over the years have been God's special instruments in pioneering outreach with the gospel to previously unreached peoples.

Throughout most of the years of WEF's ministry one must recognize with some shame that women were largely ignored. References to women in WEF documents, either in any roles of significance or in terms of the special needs of women, are few and far between. Various women such as Elizabeth Evans and Betty Froisland played a very important

197

part behind the scenes in indispensable office work and administration to keep the machinery in motion. But their role was largely hidden, and concern for the unique needs of women did not come to the fore until the late 1970s.

The first indications of such concern began to appear during Waldron Scott's tenure as General Secretary. On 27 August, 1976, Scott prepared a report to the WEF Executive Council in which he summarized the present status of WEF and plans for the future. Among his concerns for the immediate future he listed:

> Expanding the ministries of our present commissions, including the development of an international Women's Commission. I find great enthusiasm for the latter wherever I travel, both within the Third World and Western countries. With respect to a timetable for the Women's Commission, I would suggest developing this commission to the point where it would be able to make a significant contribution at a global level by 1980. That is when the United Nations will be sponsoring its second International Women's Year.[1]

As a follow up to this suggestion, and in preparation for a meeting of the Executive Council to be held in November, Scott prepared a further paper the following month. In this he mentioned the fact that the United Nations had sponsored its first International Women's Year (IWY) in 1975 and would be focussing again on women in 1980. He added, "Because of the unique role and importance of women in the evangelical movement worldwide WEF has set 1980 and the second IWY as a target for the development of its international Women's Commission."[2]

He envisioned two steps in this process. First, "the formation of a steering committee of six women drawn from six continents." Second, "the formation of a 30-woman commission and the organization of a half-dozen regional task forces" which would "identify the concerns of evangelical women in the various continents, stimulate cooperation between existing evangelical women's groups, and prepare an agenda for 1980."[3]

He then went on to say that "the ultimate objective of the Women's Commission is to unite evangelical women worldwide and help them identify their special concerns so that unitedly they may make a more effective impact both within the evangelical community and in society at large."[4]

*A Vision Grows*

When the Executive Council met in Colorado Springs in November 1976, Scott reported that a number of women had spoken to him during his world travels urging that WEF form a commission that would focus on women's concerns. It was then resolved

> That the general secretary, after consultation, convene a meeting of select women to act as a study group to draw up terms of reference of a possible women's commission.[5]

During the next several years Waldron Scott's work was shared by his wife, Joan, and she took a special interest in planning the development of the women's commission.

By the time of his annual report to the Executive Council in January, 1978, Scott had already coined a full name for the proposed commission. He referred to the "International Forum of Evangelical Women." This name was to persist for the next two years. In his report he said,

> Approval for this commission has been received from the WEF Executive Council and a steering committee of five ladies has been organized.
>
> The steering committee is now corresponding with national evangelical associations to obtain names of key women in each country. There has been a good response to date.[6]

During the next two years plans were laid for a meeting of the commission to be held in England in conjunction with the WEF General Assembly. During 1979 a steering committee met in Elburn, Illinois, USA, to prepare for this meeting. They were Miss Mary Wang (England), Mrs Lydie Noel (Haiti), Miss Joy Hansell (Canada) and Mrs Joan Scott (USA).

From 20–23 March 1980, the International Forum of Evangelical Women (IFEW) met in London just prior to the General Assembly. Attending were women from Africa, Latin America, Europe, Asia, Australia, and North America. While the Forum was not a large group it was composed of women who were active in ministry in their own lands and who had a vision for uniting with each other around the world for the advance of the gospel. They discussed at length the purposes, structure, and programmes that IFEW should develop.

An ambitious organizational chart was drawn up, showing the relationship between IFEW and WEF in general, plus various sub-units of IFEW to cover such things as "Theology of Women," "Information and Communication," "Evangelism and Pastoral Care," "Social Concern and Human Development," Women and Family," "Education," "Missions," and "Finance."

By the kind of unfortunate turn which can happen in history nearly all the records of this meeting of IFEW in 1980 were destroyed, leaving very little for the historian to depend upon for an accurate portrayal of what transpired. Thus, while the meeting was a significant one, there is no reliable way to reconstruct it completely today.

## Organizing and Reorganizing

Following this meeting of IFEW and the General Assembly, the WEF Executive Council met in London on 28 March, 1980, and took several actions which affected the Commissions. IFEW had recommended names for the Commission on Women's Concerns, and a list of fourteen women were approved for membership on the Commission. They represented thirteen different countries, spread across all the continents. Mrs Beatriz Zapata of Guatemala was nominated International Coordinator of the commission.

When Waldron Scott resigned as General Secretary at the end of 1980 his wife, Joan, who had been a leader in the Commission, also withdrew from active participation. This left a vacuum which was hard to fill, since she had carried much of the administrative load behind the scenes. Mrs Zapata continued with her burning vision for the work among women, but she was hampered by lack of finances, lack of personnel to help, and the heavy responsibilities of her own work with her husband Virgilio in a variety of ministries in Guatemala.

Following Waldron Scott's resignation, and during the interim leadership of Dr Wade Coggins, Bruce Nicholls was appointed Associate General Secretary for commission ministries. At the meeting of the Executive Council held in Malawi in September, 1981, Nicholls recommended the following:

> That the Women's Commission be disbanded and the present members be considered for transfer to other commissions, and that each commission should have a minimum of 10% women members and work towards a goal of 20—30%.[7]

This recommendation was not accepted. Instead the Executive Council voted

> . . . to retain the Commission on Women's Concerns and that we encourage (a) male participation in the commission and (b) increased female participation in the other commissions.[8]

In March and April, 1982, Bruce Nicholls made a tour through Latin America during which he visited Mrs Zapata in Guatemala to discuss the future of her Commission. Following that visit he wrote to me with a series of proposals for the future reorganization of the Commission, suggesting names for membership, new structures, areas of concern for study, and other items. The most significant recommendations were:

> That WEF disband the Commission on Women's Concerns and replace it with a Commission on the "Christian Family."
> That the commission include both women and men—we suggest 9 women and 6 men.
> That Mrs. Zapata be the chairman or executive secretary of this commission.[9]

On 8 May, 1982, Mrs Zapata and her husband Virgilio visited my wife and me in Ft. Lauderdale, Florida. We discussed at length the future of this commission. Beatriz agreed at that time with the recommendations of Bruce Nicholls to reorganize the commission as a Commission on the Christian Family. She hoped to plan a conference for approximately thirty people to be held in conjunction with WHEATON '83 on the theme "Biblical Basis for the Family." The commission would concern itself with such issues as the sanctity of human life, the sanctity of marriage, the social abuses of the family, and work and leisure in the family.[10] I encouraged Beatriz to move ahead aggressively with these plans.

### *"Women" or "The Family"?*

In June 1982, Mrs Zapata was invited to attend the *ad hoc*

meeting of the WEF Executive Council held in Holland, Michigan, USA. At that time she presented the proposal to reorganize the commission as a Commission on the Christian Family. The Executive Council accepted the recommendation and moved

(1) to appoint a steering committee to investigate the formation of a Commission on the Christian Family with a view to disbanding the Commission on Women's Concerns and that such committee report to the next executive council meeting; (2) to appoint Mrs. Zapata as convener and Mrs. Lydie Noel, Miss Ruth Lichtenberger and two men to be selected by Mrs. Zapata and the General Secretary . . .[11]

At WHEATON '83 there were a number of women in attendance from many parts of the world. Throughout the two weeks of the consultation there was an increasing dissatisfaction among the women for what they felt was an ignoring of women in leadership, in participation, and in influence, and a general insensitivity on the part of the men to the role of women.

On 29 June, 1983, a group of 35 of these women met during WHEATON '83 in an informal caucus to discuss the place of women and how WEF should respond to their needs. Although no formal minutes were kept of this gathering, it was reported to me by some of them that there were tears, anger, frustration and deep feelings expressed that the men in leadership of WHEATON '83 were insensitive to the women. There was also keen disappointment that WEF was probably going to dissolve the Commission on Women's Concerns and change it into another form. They feared that the unique needs of women would be buried among other issues.

At the end of WHEATON '83 the WEF Executive Council met at Wheaton for further deliberations arising out of the consultation. Mrs Zapata reported the feeling of the women, expressed two days earlier. It was then clarified by the Executive Council that the Commission on Women's Concerns was not to be disbanded but rather that the membership was to be discontinued and a new slate of members to be chosen. It was moved

That the present membership of the Commission on Women's Concerns be discontinued; that Mrs. Beatriz Zapata be appointed executive secretary. She is to consult national alliances and fellowships for recommendations for members of the commission. The list of proposed members is to be presented to the general director with authority to act.[12]

## Starting Again

During the coming year Mrs Zapata received invaluable administrative help from Mrs CarolAnn Paul of the USA. Mrs Paul was working as my administrative assistant in the WEF office and took a keen interest in the work of this commission. She was among those whom I was forced to release in October 1983, for financial reasons, but she continued to work closely with us, especially on matters related to this commission. I was able to help secure for her a position on the staff of Wheaton College, so that she was close to our office and available for consultation work on mailings and other matters.

During 1984 Mrs Zapata and Mrs Paul worked closely together to plan a crucial meeting of a carefully selected steering committee to lay some foundations for the Commission's ongoing ministry. A friend in North Carolina provided a generous grant to cover the costs of bringing this group together from the four corners of the earth. CarolAnn Paul did extensive preliminary preparation both in logistics (travel, housing, and the like) and programme planning, drawing up a detailed statement of purpose including goals and objectives.

From 11–14 November, 1984, this steering committee met at the Fellowship Deaconry in Elburn, Illinois, USA. It consisted of Mrs Beatriz Zapata (Guatemala) as executive secretary; Miss Dorothy Dahlman (USA), Mrs Ingrid Kern (German Democratic Republic), Mrs Lydie Noël (Haiti), Mrs Juliet Thomas (India), Mrs Agnes Walker (Australia) and Miss Florence Yeboah (Ghana), with Mrs CarolAnn Paul (USA) as administrative secretary. Also present for some parts of the meetings were Mrs Fran Wolfley (USA) as observer, Mr Harry Genet as WEF Director of Communications, and myself.

Much time was spent in personal fellowship, sharing of

what God is doing among women in different parts of the world, study of the Scriptures to find a sense of direction for this special ministry to women, and discussion of the purpose, goals, and programmes of the commission. A detailed purpose statement was drawn up as follows:

*Purpose Statement and Objectives*
The Commission on Women's Concerns of the World Evangelical Fellowship will seek to meet the unique needs of women around the world. This can be accomplished by:

(A) *Encouragement*—to encourage Christian women to reach their full potential in Jesus Christ.

(B) *Fellowship*—to serve as a catalyst in the formation of national women's movements and provide for national and international fellowship and interaction.

(C) *Communication*—to provide vehicles of communication for Christian women, listening to and offering solutions for other women's needs.

(D) *Outreach*—to present the whole Gospel to the whole person.[13]

Following this statement came a lengthy list of objectives and goals under each of the main four headings, with specific projects suggested in order to carry them out. A budget of $15,000 for the year 1985 was drawn up to implement these goals.

Subsequently, the WEF Executive Council approved by postal ballot the eight women on the steering committee as the official members of the Commission on Women's Concerns.

In June 1985, CarolAnn Paul produced the first issue of *Intercom*, an "in-house" quarterly news sheet for the members of the commission to exchange news, views, personal needs, prayer requests, and ideas. Each member of the Commission sends in items to be included, Mrs Paul collates and edits them, and then she prepares an issue of *Intercom* to be circulated to all members.

At the time of writing plans are under way for the Commission on Women's Concerns to play a significant part in the eighth General Assembly of WEF in 1986. The Commission will be in charge of one major plenary session at the assembly and then will hold a meeting of the full commission immediately after the assembly.

There is good reason to believe that this commission will

make a vital contribution in the coming years by encouraging women to "proclaim the good tidings" along with the great host of women who have played a part in fulfilling God's plan of redemption since biblical times.

CHAPTER TWENTY-SIX

# "Renew Our Days as of Old"

The prayer for renewal among God's people is timeless. It is as old as the Psalmist who prayed, "Renew a right spirit within me" (Ps. 51:10), as old as Jeremiah who cried out, "Renew our days as of old" (Lam. 5:21), and as old as Paul who called for "the renewing of your mind" (Rom. 12:2). The Scriptures are full of exhortations to renewal. The history of the church is a history of renewal movements in every era, when the Spirit of God touched the people of God to bring new life and fresh vision.

Throughout the history of WEF one finds references to calls for renewal scattered throughout its documents. WEF has always recognised that if the church is to fulfill its mission in the world it must be renewed in spirit and in vision. However, this sense of the need for renewal did not take visible form in the structuring of WEF until the decade of the 1980s.

On 30 January, 1981, when the WEF Executive Council met to discuss the resignation of Waldron Scott (see p. 140), Bruce Nicholls was present as a member of staff to discuss the integration of WEF commissions with the movement. At that time Nicholls expressed himself "very strongly for pastor care and the renewal of the church (ethical credibility, training of laity, and accreditation) as the direction evangelicals should go."[1] After some discussion the Executive Council moved

That Dr. Pablo Pérez (convener), Theodore Williams, Bruce Nicholls, Tokunboh Adeyemo, and Wade Coggins be appointed as members of a special committee to develop a WEF Commission on Evangelism to be submitted to the Executive Council during its September 14, 1981, meeting for approval.[2]

In April 1981, a special meeting was called in Amerongen, in The Netherlands, as a planning consultation for the relationship of the commissions to the entire ministry of WEF. During this time recommendations for possible new commissions were discussed, and a proposal was made for a Commission on Church Renewal and Evangelism. The steering committee nominated in January was felt to be the appropriate group to continue the planning processes. Certain goals for the commission, along with a proposed programme for 1981–1983 including study themes, were recommended. No formal action was taken but the steering committee was encouraged to continue its study and make recommendations for how to proceed.[3]

## A Commission on Church Renewal

When the Executive Council met in Malawi in September 1981, Bruce Nicholls recommended that the proposed Commission on Evangelism be concerned instead with "Church Renewal and Mission." In response to this the Executive Council voted

> . . . to appoint a steering committee of seven persons to prepare detailed plans for formation of a Commission on Church Renewal and Growth for presentation to the Executive Council, steering committee to consist of Tokunboh Adeyemo (chairman), the WEF general secretary (*ex officio*), the joint general secretaries (*ex officio*), John Richard (secretary), Pablo Pérez and Peter Kuzmič.[4]

A twelve-point "Call to Church Renewal" was approved and it was agreed to designate 1983 as 'A Year of Church Renewal."

In November 1981, four members of the steering committee (Adeyemo, Pérez, Richards, and Coggins) met in Wheaton, Illinois, to discuss further steps. They drew up these suggested objectives for the commission:

a. To build up a network of regional and national bodies interested in church renewal and growth.
b. To stimulate, encourage and support all bodies involved in church renewal and growth.
c. To create concern for church renewal and growth in areas where there are no specific bodies to care for this concern.[5]

These objectives and other plans were reported to the Executive Council meeting held in Bangalore, India, on 1–3 February, 1982. The report was "received with gratitude" and the steering committee was "requested to continue." [6]

As plans for WHEATON '83 began to develop, it became increasingly evident that much of what would come out of that consultation—especially from Track I on "The Church In Its Local Setting"—must of necessity relate to church renewal. Thus the members of the steering committee became closely involved in the planning for WHEATON '83. John Richard and Pablo Pérez took leading roles in the preparations for and realization of Track I. It was a logical development for this proposed commission to become responsible for the follow-up to Track I too.

On 1 July, 1983, immediately after the close of WHEATON '83, the Executive Council met. They recognised that the follow-up to the consultation would be extensive and crucial, and therefore more people would be needed to make it effective. Action was taken to expand the steering committee to eighteen people, representing every continent, "to function until the commission is officially established."[7]

Subsequently the steering committee was organized more closely with Dr Pablo Pérez (Mexico), as chairman, John Richard (India) as coordinator, and Mrs Mary Lou Wilson (USA) as associate coordinator. The Executive Council gave permission for the steering committee to be expanded as needed, and several more persons were added in May, 1984. John Richard, as coordinator, wrote to the new members to explain the purposes of the committee.

This is part of an effort to facilitate church renewal worldwide which in short is to see that the church ministers to God in worship, to the saints in nurture and to the world in witness and service.

Of necessity, this will involve serious study of issues such as Theology of Church Renewal; Resources for Church Renewal; various

Ingredients of Church Renewal; Models of Church Renewal and other related topics.

The Steering Committee will also seek to reinforce Biblical basis for the nature and mission of the church in its local setting.[8]

In November 1984, Mrs Mary Lou Wilson, who was taking an active role in the administrative procedures for developing the commission, sent out a three-page questionnaire to members of the steering committee seeking their response to areas of need, possible programmes, potential new members, and other matters.

## *Inauguration*

In December 1984, the executive committee, composed of Pérez, Richard, and Wilson, met in the WEF offices in Wheaton to lay detailed plans for the formal inauguration of the full commission in the Netherlands in June 1985. Harry Genet represented WEF as a consultant in this meeting and I was able to attend briefly for the opening part.

The steering committee met in Amerongen, the Netherlands, from 3–7 June, 1985. Nine members of the committee were present, Dr David Kornfield of World Relief (USA) as an invited guest and Mr Harry Genet representing the WEF administration. I had been requested to attend but had received a rare invitation to minister the Word of God in Cuba that same week and felt that I should not pass up such an opportunity.

And so, on 6 June 1985, the WEF Commission on Church Renewal came officially into being.

Nine new members were invited to join the commission, and an Executive Committee of 8 was appointed. Revd John Richard was elected chairman. Three others were chosen as secretaries: Dr Pablo Pérez, executive secretary; Dr David Kornfield, assistant executive secretary and treasurer; and Mrs Mary Lou Wilson, assistant executive secretary.

The following statement of purpose and definition was adopted:

1. The purpose of the World Evangelical Fellowship Commission on Church Renewal is to encourage, motivate, and enable the local church to obey the biblical call to renewal.

2. Church renewal is the people of God turning to Him in repentance, and walking together in fresh response to the indwelling Spirit in obedience to God's Word, glorifying Christ in worship, in fellowship and mutual ministry and in witness and service so as to bring all things under His Lordship.
3. The local church is the community of Christ's saving rule made up of those who bear and confess the name of Christ in a particular area for the purpose of ministering to God in worship, to members in nurture and to the world in witness and service.[9]

Considerable attention was also given to developing objectives that would guide the commission in carrying out its purpose. The objectives were:

1. Strengthening the vision and the efforts of national and regional alliances as they assist local churches in renewal.
2. Serving as a network for information and resources, thus enhancing the interdependence of churches in renewal.
3. Defining issues, seeking biblical guidelines, articulating consensus and developing resource materials to facilitate the renewal process.[10]

The following week the WEF Executive Council also met in the Netherlands. Dr Pérez reported to the council on the formation and deliberations of the Commission on Church Renewal the previous week. It was moved and carried "that the formation of the commission be ratified."[11]

*Rapid Action*

The members of the Executive Committee moved into action rapidly. On 22 June, 1985, John Richard, Pablo Pérez, Mary Lou Wilson, and David Kornfield met in Wheaton, Illinois, to draw up job descriptions, assign areas of responsibility, work on a budget, and outline procedures for advance. It should be noted here that World Relief of the USA had agreed to release Dr David Kornfield for part-time work with this commission and to underwrite his expenses for a limited period of time. This was a great step forward. Mrs Wilson was also appointed on a part-time basis and began to operate from the WEF offices. Dr Pérez and Revd John Richard were both serving on a volunteer basis.

Again on 9 September 1985, Pérez, Kornfield, and Wilson met for a day at Midway Airport in Chicago. David Kornfield reported on an extensive trip he had just completed in Brazil, working with local churches in renewal ministry. David had grown up in Latin America as the son of missionaries in Bolivia and Peru, and so he spoke Spanish fluently and understood the Latin culture. Because of this I had recommended that he concentrate his efforts primarily in Latin America during the early stages of the formation of the commission. We felt that if he could develop some models of renewal ministry in a culture in which he felt at home, these models could then be expanded and adapted to other areas of the world.

Mrs Wilson actively pursued administrative matters such as preparation of the budget, plans for a brochure for the commission, and plans for the full meeting to be held in conjunction with the 1986 WEF General Assembly.

The Executive Committee met again in Wheaton, Illinois, on 6 December, 1985. Further plans were crystallized and momentum was gained.

The WEF Executive Council recognized that the matter of church renewal is integral to our entire ministry. For this reason when plans for the eighth General Assembly were being drawn up it was unanimously agreed that the theme for that assembly should be:

RENEW THE CHURCH—REACH THE WORLD

The entire programme for the assembly was developed around this theme, and the Commission on Church Renewal was asked to play a major role in the programme's development.

If WEF can be instrumental in stimulating renewal of the local church, the possibilities for worldwide impact are limitless. The Commission on Church Renewal could well become a key element in this renewal process, and be the catalyst for God to "renew our days as of old."

# CHAPTER TWENTY-SEVEN

# "I Know not what the Future hath . . ."

It was the godly poet, John Greenleaf Whittier (1807–1892), who wrote from his heart these haunting words:

> I know not what the future hath
>   Of marvel or surprise
> Assured alone that life and death
>   His mercy underlies.
>
> And if my heart and flesh are weak
>   To bear an untried pain,
> The bruiséd reed He will not break,
>   But strengthen and sustain.
>
> And so beside the silent sea
>   I wait the muffled oar;
> No harm from Him can come to me
>   On ocean or on shore.
>
> I know not where His islands lift
>   Their fronded palms in air;
> I only know I cannot drift
>   Beyond His love and care.

It will be evident to the reader who has persevered to this final chapter that there have been times in the history of WEF when its leaders have felt like a "bruiséd reed." Some have shared Whittier's feeling that "my heart and flesh are weak." There certainly have been times when they stood "beside the silent sea." WEF'S history has not been one glorious trium-

213

phant advance from victory to victory. Yet there has always been the underlying confidence of those who are "assured alone that life and death/His mercy underlies."

Today as we survey the past, analyze the present, and look to the future of WEF we can certainly agree with the poet that, while we "know not what the future hath," we do know that we "cannot drift beyond His love and care."

The vision of the original founders of the Evangelical Alliance in 1846, and subsequently of the World Evangelical Fellowship in 1951, was valid and biblical then—and is just as valid and biblical today. The concepts of "fellowship in the gospel," "defence and confirmation of the gospel" and "the furtherance of the gospel" express eternal, unchanging truths and challenges.

There are few Christians today, at least in evangelical circles, who would condemn the idea of fellowship in the gospel with others who are members of the body of Christ. While there may be differences of opinion as to how the parts of the body of Christ can best cooperate in defending and advancing the gospel, few would contend that these are not legitimate and biblical goals.

The World Evangelical Fellowship was raised up by God to be a channel through which this fellowship could be expressed and this cooperation realized. The activities which WEF has carried out to express "spiritual unity in action" (as Gilbert Kirby so well expressed it) have been chronicled here as a reminder of our great heritage and as a challenge for the future.

A famous and oft-quoted dictum of George Santayana says, "Those who refuse to learn from history are condemned to repeat it." History can be either a *prison* or a *pedestal*. As a prison it can confine us unnecessarily within the past and thus hinder progress. But as a pedestal it allows us to stand on the platform erected by our forebears and see the future more clearly than they could because of our enhanced perspective.

In these pages I have tried to record the past as accurately as possible. It is my hope that this will instil in us today a greater appreciation of the men and women who have preceded us, of the vision which God gave to them for "spiritual unity in action," and of the heritage which they have left us.

I have also tried to analyze the past strengths and weaknesses evident in the growth of WEF. If we can learn from this history, mindful of Santayana's warning, we can profit from the strengths and avoid the mistakes. We can stand on the pedestal they have built and look further into the future.

I do not possess the gift of prophecy. Therefore I cannot pretend to predict what the future of WEF will see. With Whittier I say, "I know not what the future hath/Of marvel or surprise . . ." However, I am confident that "the Lord will fulfill His purpose" for WEF (Psalm 138:8). There is no doubt whatsoever that the Lord gave the original vision for WEF to His people. It is our task today to find God's ways for us to carry out that vision, so that the body of Christ in our generation may enjoy true "fellowship in the gospel." may be faithful in the "defense and confirmation of the gospel," and may move ahead aggressively in "the furtherance of the gospel."

May God give us the strength, courage, and perception we need.

# Of Elephants and Crocodiles

Shortly before finishing this book I was in Southern Africa for several weeks. One afternoon by the Zambesi River, which forms the border between Zimbabwe and Zambia, I was talking with a boatman near Victoria Falls. He told me of a fascinating incident which he had witnessed just a few days before I was there, and it struck me as a parable of WEF.

Late in the afternoon a herd of elephants crossed the Zambesi River. Since the current is swift in places the bull elephants line up in the form of a dam, thus stopping enough of the swift water to allow the baby and female elephants to cross below them. Suddenly a large crocodile grabbed the leg of one bull elephant under water. The elephant reached down with his trunk, grabbed the snout of the crocodile, tore it off his leg, and lifted the crocodile up in the air.

The other bulls saw the attack and immediately came to the aid of their companion. Together they grasped the crocodile by the jaws and literally ripped him down the middle, tearing him in two. Then they calmly returned to the business of getting the herd across the river.

In this story I saw several parallels (bizarre as it may seem) to the ministry of WEF. First, cooperation is indispensable in the work of the church around the world. Individually and corporately we need the strength and encouragement of others who will stem the tide to allow us to progress in the

217

midst of swirling currents. This is "fellowship in the gospel."

Second, "the furtherance of the gospel" requires entering Satan's territory, and this can be dangerous. The crocodile considered that the river was his territory. It was being invaded by hostile forces, and he was not willing to allow this. Those who reach out into territory as yet unclaimed for the gospel are placing themselves in dangerous waters. Thus cooperation in the effort is more indispensable than ever.

Third, when one member of the body has placed himself in a vulnerable position on behalf of others, and is attacked, he needs the help of others to counter-attack. Few creatures on earth could be more dangerous or devastating than the crocodile. Who would care to engage him in combat? But the cooperative effort of bull elephants served not only to deliver the one under attack, but also to keep the way clear for the smaller members of their herd to cross in safety.

So it is in the body of Christ, as members join together for the defence and confirmation of the gospel with those who are reaching out in fellowship and in the furtherance of the gospel.

## New Directions for WEF

In January 1986 the Working Group of the Executive Council of the World Evangelical Fellowship met for three days of uninterrupted prayer, study of the Word, and seeking the face of God for the future of WEF. Gathering in the quiet atmosphere of the Fellowship Deaconry in Elburn, Illinois, USA, they asked God how WEF could best fulfill its mission of fellowship, defence, and furtherance of the gospel. Mindful of the "Statement of Mission" that had been developed in 1984, they focussed their attention on discovering what tasks are necessary to fulfill that mission, what WEF is best equipped to do, and where and how this can best be done.

The group consisted of Dr Tokunboh Adeyemo, as Chairman; Dr Theodore Williams, as President; Mr John Langlois, as Treasurer; and myself as General Director. The Chairman had also co-opted for this meeting Attorney Jun

Vencer from the Philippines, Mr Morgan Derham to represent Europe, and Dr Wade Coggins as Chairman of the USA Corporation Board. During the three days there developed an unusual recognition of the presence of God, a profound sense of unity, and a renewed vision of "a dream that would not die." All of those present expressed their feeling that in all their years of experience in WEF (and some of them dated back two decades in their involvement), they had never experienced such a clear sense of God's presence and leading in an executive meeting.

Several major decisions were taken during those days. One of the most far reaching in its implications was the decision to move the international headquarters of WEF from the Western world, where it had always been located, to a Third World location. It was felt that, since WEF is truly an international and not a North American organization, it must be sited at a major crossroads of the non-Western world. A number of key cities of the world were studied in order to evaluate their suitability for the ministry of WEF. At the time of writing a final decision has not been made, because of the need for careful study *in loco*, but the weight of preference and evidence points to a location such as Singapore. It is hoped that in the near future WEF can transfer its operations, internationalize its staff, and begin to focus its ministry on the needs expressed by its member bodies.

A second decision was to ask me if I would accept reappointment as General Director following the fulfillment of my term, which was to expire at the General Assembly in June 1986. I responded affirmatively and was reappointed for four years starting on 1 July 1986, with the stipulation that the appointment would be reviewed by both parties in June 1988. Inherent in both these decisions was the understanding that I would move to the new location.

A third decision was to reexamine the ministries of WEF in order to see how WEF can best serve its constituent bodies. It was decided that the primary focus should be in five areas: (1) Publications and Information Services; (2) Leadership Development; (3) Missions and Evangelism; (4) Global Issues and Human Need; (5) Discipleship and Church Renewal.

These might eventually develop organizationally into specific departments, with the existing commissions serving each department according to their special expertise.

A fourth decision was to establish regional offices in several parts of the world to expand the financial foundation upon which WEF can develop its ministries. While nearly all WEF financing has come from the USA and Europe, this does not adequately reflect the international character of the movement. It is hoped that WEF can indeed become international not only in concept but also in personnel and resources.

Our Lord, who Himself prayed "that they all may be one . . . that the world may believe" (John 17:21), gave the original dream to His people in 1846. He has kept that dream alive for nearly a century and a half, in spite of frustrations, failures, and difficulties. It is our prayer today that "a dream that would not die" may be fulfilled by His people around the world, so that our Lord's prayer for oneness leading to belief may be answered in our day.

# Notes to Chapters

*Chapter One:* WHO IS AN EVANGELICAL?

1. R. V. Pierard, "Evangelicalism," in *Evangelical Dictionary of Theology*, ed. Walter A. Elwell, Grand Rapids, MI, Baker Book House, 1984, p. 379
2. John H. Gerstner, "The Theological Boundaries of Evangelical Faith," in *The Evangelicals*, ed. David F. Wells and John Woodbridge, Nashville, Tenn., Abingdon Press, 1975, pp. 21–23
3. Harold Lindsell, "Who Are the Evangelicals?", *Christianity Today*, 18 June, 1964, p. 3
4. Pierard, *op. cit.*, p. 381


*Chapter 2:* THE EVANGELICAL ALLIANCE

1. Ruth Rouse and Stephen C. Neill, *A History of the Ecumenical Movement 1517–1948*, Philadelphia, The Westminster Press, 1967, p. 324
2. *ibid*, p. 319
3. *Report of the Proceedings of the Conference Held at Freemasons' Hall, London, 1846*, London, Partridge and Oakey, 1847, p. 5
4. J. B. A. Kessler, *A Study of the Evangelical Alliance in Great Britain*, Netherlands, Oosterbaan & LeCointre N.V.—Goes, 1968, p. 17
5. *ibid*, p. 29
6. *Proceedings, op. cit.*, p. 44
7. Kessler, *op. cit.*, p. 36, 37
8. Rouse and Neill, *op. cit.*, p. 322
9. *ibid*, p. 323
10. Kessler, *op. cit.*, p. 42

11. *Proceedings, op. cit.,* p. 189
12. Kessler, *op. cit.,* p. 42
13. *ibid,* p. 43
14. *ibid,* p. 45
15. *ibid,* p. 46, 47
16. John H. Ewing, *Goodly Fellowship: A Centenary Tribute to the Life and Work of the World's Evangelical Alliance 1846–1946,* London, Marshall, Morgan and Scott, 1946, pp. 22–24
17. Rouse and Neill, *op. cit.,* p. 256

*Chapter 3:* CONTRIBUTIONS OF THE EVANGELICAL ALLIANCE

1. Stephen Neill, *The Church and Christian Union,* London, Oxford University Press, 1968, p. 340
2. Kenneth Scott Latourette, *A History of the Expansion of Christianity,* Vol. IV: *The Great Century,* New York, Harper and Brothers, 1941, pp. 41–42
3. Norman Goodall, *The Ecumenical Movement,* London, Oxford University Press, 1961, p. 6
4. Kessler, *op. cit.,* p. 54
5. *ibid,* p. 61
6. Rouse and Neill, *op. cit.,* p. 346
7. Goodall, *op. cit.,* p. 178–179
8. William Richey Hogg, *Ecumenical Foundations,* New York, Harper and Brothers, 1952, p. 36
9. Arthur P. Johnston, *World Evangelism and the Word of God,* Minneapolis, Minnesota, Bethany Fellowship, 1974, p.45
10. Ewing, *op. cit.,* p. 98
11. *Evangelical Christendom,* Vol. I, January, 1847, p. 3
12. *ibid,* p. 2
13. Rouse and Neill, *op. cit.,* p. 635
14. J. Edwin Orr, *The Second Evangelical Awakening in Britain,* London, Marshall, Morgan, & Scott, 1949, p. 216–217
15. Rouse and Neill, *op. cit.,* p. 632
16. *Evangelical Christendom,* Vol. CIV, May, 1950, p. 34
17. *Evangelical Christendom,* Vol. CVIII, September, 1954, p. 75
18. Rouse and Neill, *op. cit.,* p. 638

*Chapter Four:* THE FOUNDING OF THE WORLD EVANGELICAL FELLOWSHIP

1. The history of the ecumenical movement has been ably traced in a scholarly way by Ruth Rouse and Stephen Neill in their definitive work, *A History of the Ecumenical Movement 1517–1948,* Philadelphia, The Westminster Press, 1967, and will not be duplicated in this book.
2. Bruce L. Shelley, *Evangelicalism in America,* Grand Rapids, Michigan, William B. Eerdmans Publishing Co., 1967, pp. 72–73

3. *ibid.*
4. *ibid*, pp. 80–82
5. *ibid*
6. "The Relationship of the National Association of Evangelicals to the World Evangelical Fellowship," unpublished paper in files of NAE and WEF, no date.
7. "Evangelical Christendom," Oct.-Dec., 1948, p. 108
8. Kessler, *op. cit.*, p. 95
9. *ibid*, pp. 95–96
10. Billy Graham Center Archives, Wheaton, Illinois; accession #83–24, Box 3 Folder 73. Records of WEF (not processed).
11. Billy Graham Center Archives, Wheaton Illinois; accession #67–17, Box 20, "Summary of the International Conference at Woudschoten, Holland, Aug. 4–10, 1951," unpublished minutes of NAE.
12. *ibid*
13. *ibid*
14. *ibid*
15. *ibid*
16. *ibid*
17. "Evangelical Christendom," Nov. 1951, pp. 109–110
18. Billy Graham Center Archives, Wheaton, Illinois; accession #83–24, Box 1, Folder 30 "Travel Reports." Records of WEF (not processed).
19. *ibid*

*Chapter Five:* EARLY GROWTH

1. Billy Graham Center Archives, Wheaton, Illinois; accession #83–24, Box 1 Folder 30, "Travel Reports." Records of WEF (not processed).
2. There is some discrepancy in early reports and records on nations that either applied for or were received into membership at Clarens. The facts cited here are found in *Evangelical Christendom*, Vol. CVII, Dec. 1953. Dr Wright's report to the NAE Commission on International Relations dated 12 October, 1953, indicates that Belgium, Formosa, and Greece were also members, although he omits Germany, perhaps by oversight since Germany was listed on the programme for a report as a member.
3. J. Elwin Wright, "Report of the Executive Secretary, Commission on International Relations of N.A.E., Minneapolis, Minnesota, Oct. 12, 1953"
4. "The World Evangelical Fellowship—Founded 1951." Unpublished paper, no date, p. 2
5. Wright, *op. cit.*, p.2
6. "The World Evangelical Fellowship . . . What Is It?" A study paper, 1966, pp. 5, 7
7. J. Elwin Wright, "The World Journey of Dr. Wright and Mr. Keck," unpublished report, no date but probably written in early 1955, p. 4

8. "The Relationship of the National Association of Evangelicals to the World Evangelical Fellowship," unpublished paper, no date but probably written in 1957, p. 3
9. *ibid*
10. "World Evangelical Fellowship (American Section) Report of the Executive Secretary, Hollenden Hotel, Cleveland, Ohio, April 9, 1956," p. 1

*Chapter Six:* EMPHASIS ON PEOPLE

1. "Minutes of the Second Meeting of the General Committee of the World Evangelical Fellowship, Held at Barrington, Rhode Island, U.S.A., 27–31 August, 1956," p. 2
2. *ibid.* "Appendix I, World Evangelical Fellowship By-Laws", Clause 9
3. "Minutes . . . " *op. cit.*, p. 2
4. *ibid.*
5. "Appendix I . . ." *op. cit.*, Clause 1
6. "Appendix II . . ." *op. cit.*, pp. 1, 2
7. *ibid.*
8. "World Evangelical Fellowship *Bulletin* (American Edition)," October, 1956, pp. 1–2

*Chapter Seven:* CHANGING THE GUARD

1. "World Evangelical Fellowship (American Section) Report of the Executive Secretary, Hollenden Hotel, Cleveland, Ohio, April 9, 1956," p. 2
2. Notes of 4–6 December, 1958, meeting, unpublished
3. Billy Graham Center Archives, Wheaton, Illinois; accession #83–24, Box 1, Folder 30, "Travel Reports." Records of WEF (not processed), Report of the W.E.F. Tour of Revd Fred G. Ferris, p. 1
4. *ibid.*
5. *ibid.*
6. *ibid.*
7. *ibid.*, p. 3
8. *ibid.*, p. 4
9. *ibid.*
10. Report of the Executive Director, NAE Commission on International Relations, World Evangelical Fellowship, Los Angeles, California, 6 April, 1959, p. 7
11. *ibid.*
12. *ibid.*
13. Letter from Fred Ferris to A. Jack Dain, 15 July, 1960
14. Letter from Fred Ferris to John Bolten, 13 October, 1961
15. Letter from A. J. Dain to Fred Ferris, 12 April, 1960
16. Letter from Fred Ferris to John Bolten, 13 October, 1961
17. Report of the International Secretary, World Evangelical Fellowship, Hong Kong, 25 April to 2 May, 1962, p. 4

*Chapter Eight:* "SPIRITUAL UNITY IN ACTION"

1. Gilbert Kirby, "A Britisher Writes A Letter To Americans," *United Evangelical Action*, September, 1962, pp. 12–13
2. *ibid.*
3. *ibid.*
4. *ibid.*
5. *ibid.*
6. World Evangelical Fellowship *Bulletin*, No. 1, 1964, p. 1
7. Letter from Everett Cattell to Gilbert Kirby, May 31, 1962. Accession # 84–34, Box 4, Folder 8, Records of WEF (unprocessed). Archives of the Billy Graham Center, Wheaton, Illinois.
8. World Evangelical Fellowship *Bulletin*, No. 2, 1964, pp. 1, 2
9. *ibid.*
10. Letter from Gilbert Kirby to Everett Cattell, 6 May, 1965. Accession # 84–34, Box 4, Folder 8, Records of WEF (unprocessed). Archives of the Billy Graham Center, Wheaton, Illinois.
11. World Evangelical Fellowship *Bulletin*, No. 1, 1965, p. 1
12. *ibid.*
13. Everett L. Cattell, "National Association of Evangelicals and World Evangelical Fellowship," *Christianity Today*, January 29, 1965, pp. 13–14
14. *ibid.*
15. WEF Executive Council Minutes, London, 21 and 22 September, 1965; accession # 84–34, Box 4, Folder 8, Records of WEF (unprocessed). Archives of Billy Graham Center, Wheaton, Illinois.

*Chapter Nine:* TENSIONS AND PROGRESS

1. WEF Executive Council Minutes, Berlin, 27–30 October, and 1 November, 1966; accession #84–34, Box 4, Folder 8, Records of WEF (unprocessed), Billy Graham Center Archives, Wheaton, Illinois
2. Dennis Clark, "The Ethos and Objectives of WEF—Berlin 1966," *op. cit.*, Billy Graham Center Archives
3. *ibid.*
4. *ibid.*
5. Letter from Clyde Taylor to Dennis Clark, 12 May, 1967, *op. cit.*, Billy Graham Center Archives
6. Letter from Kenneth Downing to E. L. Frizen, 5 July, 1967
7. Minutes, Special Discussion Committee, C & MA Headquarters, New York City, 6 September, 1967
8. A. Morgan Derham, unpublished "General Report—USA-Final Stage" November, 1967. Personal diary kept during trip around the world
9. *ibid.*
10. A. Morgan Derham, personal letter to the author, 14 September, 1985
11. Memo from Jack F. Shepherd to General Directors of the Latin America Mission, "Report on the November 27–28 WEF meeting," 1 December, 1967

12. Report from Dennis Clark, "WEF and Social Action," Billy Graham Center Archives, *loc. cit.*
13. Letter from Everett Cattell to Dennis Clark, 6 April, 1967, Billy Graham Center Archives, *loc. cit.*
14. Letter from Dennis Clark to Clyde Taylor, 21 November, 1966, Billy Graham Center Archives, *loc. cit.*
15. Letter from Dennis Clark to Clyde Taylor, 24 April, 1967, Billy Graham Center Archives, *loc. cit.*
16. Minutes of the United States Committee of WEF, Chicago, 16 May, 1967, Billy Graham Center Archives, *loc. cit.*

*Chapter Ten:* INTERNATIONALIZING THE WEF

1. Letter from Dennis Clark to Carl Henry, 16 November, 1967, file 8, Box 18, folder 51, WEF Records (unprocessed), Billy Graham Center Archives
2. Letter from Dennis Clark to Carl Henry, 28 November, 1967, *ibid.*
3. International Secretary's Report to General Council (not dated but apparently prepared in April, 1968), Billy Graham Center Archives, *loc. cit.*
4. *ibid.*
5. *ibid.*
6. General Council Report, Lausanne, 1968, p. 20; Billy Graham Center Archives, *loc. cit.*
7. Letter from Gilbert Kirby to Everett Cattell, 30 July, 1962, Billy Graham Center Archives, *loc. cit.*
8. Letter from Gilbert Kirby to Everett Cattell, 2 October, 1962, Billy Graham Center Archives, *loc. cit.*
9. "Statement on Holy Scripture adopted by the European Evangelical Alliance," General Council Report, Lausanne, 1968, Billy Graham Center Archives, *loc. cit.*
10. Minutes of WEF Council Business Sessions, Lausanne, Switzerland, May 4, 1968, Billy Graham Center Archives, *loc. cit.*
11. *ibid.*
12. *ibid.*
13. *Christianity Today*, June 7, 1968, p. 38

*Chapter Eleven:* FROM LAUSANNE TO LONDON TO WASHINGTON

1. Dennis Clark, Open Letter to the Executive, 2 May, 1970
2. Dennis Clark, telephone conversation with the author, 9 September, 1985
3. WEF "World News," Press release, 10 July, 1970
4. Letter from Dennis Clark to Gordon Landreth, 22 March, 1971. Accession # 85–91, Box 2, Folder 39, Records of WEF (unprocessed), Billy Graham Center Archives, Wheaton, Illinois

5. *ibid.*
6. "World Evangelical Fellowship—by the editors," *loc. cit.*, folder 27
7. *ibid.*
8. *ibid.*
9. *ibid.*
10. "1972 Report on the WEF," *loc. cit.*, folder 27

*Chapter Twelve:* INTERNATIONAL AMBASSADOR

1. Minutes, WEF/USA Board, 12 April, 1972, St. Louis, Missouri
2. Memo from Clyde Taylor to members of the WEF/USA Board, 12 December, 1971
3. By-Laws of IDAC. Filed with minutes of WEF/USA Board, 1972
4. Minutes, WEF/USA Board, 8 October, 1973, Chicago, Illinois
5. Minutes, WEF Executive Committee, 2–4 July, 1973, Atlanta, Georgia
6. Clyde W. Taylor, Report to WEF Executive Board, "Asia Tour—October 11 to November 16, 1972"
7. Donald E. Hoke, Letter of invitation, 20 February, 1973
8. *ibid.*
9. A. J. Dain, Letter to Clyde W. Taylor, 19 February, 1973
10. Papers for Post-Congress World Organization Consultation, Atlanta, Georgia, 29 June—2 July, 1973. In WEF files, Wheaton, Illinois
11. *ibid.*
12. *ibid.*
13. *ibid.*
14. Minutes, WEF Executive Committee, Atlanta, Georgia, 2–4 July, 1973
15. Clyde W. Taylor, Letter to A. J. Dain, 6 March, 1974
16. Clyde W. Taylor, Letter to Donald E. Hoke, 19 March, 1974
17. Donald E. Hoke, Letter to Clyde W. Taylor, 30 April, 1974
18. Wilhelm Gilbert, Letter to A. J. Dain, 17 April, 1974
19. A. J. Dain, Letter to Wilhelm Gilbert, 1 May, 1974
20. A. J. Dain, Letter to Clyde W. Taylor, 13 May, 1974
21. *ibid.*
22. *ibid.*
23. *ibid.*
24. Arnold T. Olson, Letter to Clyde W. Taylor, 29 March, 1974
25. Clyde W. Taylor, Letter to Arnold T. Olson, 5 June, 1974

*Chapter Thirteen:* IS THERE LIFE AFTER LAUSANNE?

1. Rev. Dr I. Ben Wati, President's Report, Sixth General Assembly of WEF, Chateaux d'Oex, 25–29 July, 1974
2. Dr Clyde W. Taylor, Report of the International Secretary
3. Minutes of the WEF Sixth General Assembly, Chateaux d'Oex, 25–29 July, 1974
4. *ibid.*
5. *ibid.*

*Chapter Fourteen:* EXPANSION AND FRUSTRATIONS

1. Waldron Scott, "Report to the WEF Executive Council, August 27, 1976"
2. *ibid.*
3. *ibid.*
4. *ibid.*
5. Minutes of the WEF Executive Council Meeting, Colorado Springs, USA, 20–22 November, 1976
6. *ibid.*
7. Waldron Scott, "Report to the WEF Executive Council, January 1, 1978"
8. *ibid.*
9. *ibid.*
10. *ibid.*
11. Letter from Waldron Scott to WEF Executive Council, 6 January, 1978

*Chapter Fifteen:* "AN OPEN SPACE"

1. Waldron Scott, "General Secretary's Report," 25 September, 1979
2. *ibid.*
3. *ibid.*
4. *ibid.*
5. *ibid.*
6. *ibid.*
7. Minutes of WEF Executive Council Meetings, Wheaton, Illinois, USA, 27–29 September, 1979
8. *ibid.*
9. *ibid.*

*Chapter Sixteen:* "SERVING OUR GENERATION"

1. Record of Proceedings and Minutes of the Seventh General Assembly of the World Evangelical Fellowship, High Leigh Conference Centre, Hoddesdon, Hertfordshire, UK, 24–28 March, 1980
2. General Secretary's Report, Seventh General Assembly of WEF
3. *ibid.*
4. Minutes of Seventh General Assembly of WEF
5. *ibid.*
6. David M. Howard, "The World Evangelical Fellowship (WEF) and the Lausanne Committee for World Evangelization (LCWE): A Study of Past, Present, and Future Relationships," December 15, 1982, p. 31
7. Minutes of Seventh General Assembly of WEF

*Chapter Seventeen:* HIGH HOPES AND INTERIM MEASURES

1. Letter from Hudson T. Armerding and Waldron Scott to Samuel T.

Kamaleson, 27 June, 1980. Appendix B in Minutes of WEF Executive Council Meeting, Pattaya, Thailand, 21–24 June, 1980

2. Summary of meeting between Dr Samuel Kamaleson and the WEF Executive Council, Pattaya, Thailand, June 22, 1980, Appendix A, *op. cit.*

3. Minutes of WEF Executive Council Special Meeting, Washington, D.C., USA, 30 January, 1981

4. The minutes actually state "February 15, 1981," but it is evident that this is a typographical error, as the Council obviously did not feel that a new general secretary could be found in two weeks. Action on a new general secretary was officially taken in February, 1982

5. Letter from Tokunboh Adeyemo to Wade Coggins, 25 June, 1981

6. Minutes of the WEF Executive Council Meeting, Lilongwe, Malawi, 14–15 September, 1981

7. *ibid.*

8. *ibid.*

*Chapter Eighteen:* NEEDED: A BACHELOR WITH UNLIMITED FUNDS

1. Minutes of the WEF Executive Council Meeting, Bangalore, India, 1–3 February, 1981

2. *ibid.*

3. *ibid.*

4. Memo from David M. Howard to WEF Executive Council, 22 March, 1983, on "Administrative Reorganization of WEF"

5. Memo from David M. Howard to WEF Executive Council, 23 May, 1983, on "Responsibilities of the General Secretary"

*Chapter Nineteen:* FINANCIAL CRISIS

1. Memo from David M. Howard to WEF Executive Council, 22 September, 1983, on "Financial Status of WEF"

*Chapter Twenty:* "DEFENCE AND CONFIRMATION OF THE GOSPEL"

1. Letter from Everett L. Cattell to Gilbert W. Kirby, 16 August, 1962

2. Minutes of the WEF Council Business Sessions, Lausanne, Switzerland, 4 May, 1968

3. "Programme for the Seventies"—Annual Report of the Theological Assistance Programme for the year 1969–70 and the programme for the coming year; Annual Report No. 1, December, 1970

4. *ibid.*

5. Letter from Bruce Nicholls to David M. Howard, 19 July, 1985

6. Report of the International Secretary to the WEF Executive Committee, Atlanta, Georgia, 2 July, 1973

7. Minutes of WEF Executive Committee, Ramada Inn, Atlanta, Georgia, 2–4 July,1973
8. Minutes of WEF Executive Committee, Chateau d'Oex, Switzerland, 25–29 July, 1974
9. WEF Theological Commission, Consultation held in London, England, 8–12 September, 1975
10. Constitution of the International Council of Accrediting Agencies
11. *ibid.*

*Chapter Twenty-One:* PUBLICATIONS AND CONSULTATIONS

1. Bruce J. Nicholls, editor, *In Word and Deed*, Exeter, The Paternoster Press, 1985, p. 8
2. *ibid.*
3. *ibid.*
4. *ibid.*
5. News Release from WHEATON '83, 19 July, 1983
6. *ibid.*
7. *ibid.*
8. Minutes of the WEF Executive Council, Hilversum, The Netherlands, 11–14 June, 1985
9. *ibid.*

*Chapter Twenty—Two:* "THE FURTHERANCE OF THE GOSPEL"

1. Clyde W. Taylor, Report to the WEF Executive Board, "Asia Tour", October 11 to November 16, 1972
2. *ibid.*
3. Minutes of the WEF Executive Committee, Ramada Inn, Atlanta, Georgia, 2–4 July, 1973
4. Clyde W. Taylor, Report to the WEF/USA Board, O'Hare Airport, Chicago, 8 October, 1973
5. Minutes of the Executive Council, WEF General Assembly, Chateau d'Oex, Switzerland, 25–29 July, 1974
6. Notes on meeting of Steering Committee for the Proposed International Missions Commission of the World Evangelical Fellowship, held in Seoul, Korea, on 23, 25, and 26 August, 1975
7. *ibid.*
8. Minutes of WEF Executive Council meeting, Glen Eyrie, Colorado Springs, USA, 20–22 November, 1976
9. Minutes of the Steering Committee, Missions Commission of World Evangelical Fellowship, Bombay, India, 21 January, 1977
10. Mrs Caroll Ferguson Hunt, WEF Missions Commission Conference, Bad Liebenzell, Germany, 27–31 January, 1979
11. *ibid.*
12. *ibid.*

13. Theodore Williams, Report to WEF Executive Council meeting, Lilongwe, Malawi, 14 September, 1981
14. WEF News Release on Meeting of Missions Commission, 3 February, 1982

*Chapter Twenty-Three:* COMMUNICATING THE GOSPEL

1. *Webster's New World Dictionary*, New York, The New World Publishing Company, 1970
2. Clyde W. Taylor, "The World Evangelical Fellowship—1973," 1 May, 1973
3. Minutes of the Executive Council, WEF General Assembly, Chateau d'Oex, Switzerland, 25–29 July, 1974
4. Waldron Scott, General Secretary's Report to the WEF Executive Council, 27 August, 1976
5. Waldron Scott, Report to the Executive Council, 1 January, 1978
6. Minutes of the WEF Communications Commission Executive Committee Washington, D.C., 24 January, 1978
7. *ibid.*
8. Minutes of the Executive Council, London, 28 March, 1980

*Chapter Twenty-Four:* "A CUP OF COLD WATER"

1. Report to the WEF Executive Committee on the WEF Officers, Staff, and Co-ordinators Consultation, Lausanne, Switzerland, 25–27 August, 1969
2. *ibid.*
3. Annual Report of the International Secretary to Members of the World Evangelical Fellowship, 1 October 1968–30 September, 1969
4. Letter from Clyde Taylor to Waldron Scott, 24 March, 1976
5. *ibid.*
6. Minutes of the WEF Executive Council, Wheaton, Illinois, USA, 27–29 September, 1979
7. Minutes of the WEF Executive Council, London, 28 March, 1980
8. Minutes of WEF Executive Council, Pattaya, Thailand, 21–24 June, 1980, Appendix C
9. *ibid.*
10. Minutes of the World Evangelical Fellowship's Consultation for Inter-Church Relief and Development Agencies, Hong Kong, 29 October-1 November, 1980
11. Minutes of the Coordinating Committee of the Consultative Body for Inter-Church Relief Agencies, Wheaton, Illinois, USA, 31 July, 1981
12. Minutes of WEF Executive Council Meeting, Lilongwe, Malawi, 14 September, 1981

13. Minutes of the Coordinating Committee of the Inter-Church Relief and Development Alliance, Bangalore, India, 30–31 January, 1982
14. Minutes of WEF Executive Council Meeting, Bangalore, India, 1–3 February, 1982

*Chapter Twenty-Five:* "THE WOMEN WHO PROCLAIM THE GOOD TIDINGS"

1. General Secretary's Report to the WEF Executive Council, 27 August, 1976
2. Report on "Women's Commission, September, 1976."
3. *ibid.*
4. *ibid.*
5. Minutes of the WEF Executive Council, Colorado Springs, USA, 20–22 November, 1976
6. Waldron Scott, Report to the WEF Executive Council, 1 January, 1978
7. Bruce Nicholls, Report to WEF Executive Council, "Agenda Malawi 1981," 24 July, 1981
8. Minutes of WEF Executive Council, Lilongwe, Malawi, 14 September, 1981
9. Memo from Revd B. Nicholls to Dr D. Howard, "Proposal for a new WEF commission to replace the Commission on Women's Concerns" (no date, but probably written in May 1982)
10. Letter from Mrs Beatriz Zapata to David Howard, 14 April, 1982
11. Minutes of a meeting of members of the Executive Council held at Hope College, Holland, Michigan, USA, 16 June, 1982
12. Minutes of WEF Executive Council Meetings, Wheaton, Illinois, USA, 1 July, 1983
13. Report of the Steering Committee of the WEF Commission on Women's Concerns, Elburn, Illinois, USA, 11–14 November, 1984

*Chapter Twenty-Six:* "RENEW OUR DAYS AS OF OLD"

1. WEF Executive Council Special Meeting, Washington, D.C., USA, 30 January, 1981
2. *ibid.*
3. World Evangelical Fellowship Planning Consultation, Notes on the Proceedings (not formal minutes), Amerongen, the Netherlands, 21–24 April, 1981
4. WEF Executive Council Meeting, Lilongwe, Malawi, 14 September, 1981
5. Notes on Preliminary Meeting of the Steering Committee, Commission on Church Renewal and Growth, Wheaton, Illinois, USA, 13 November, 1981 (Appendix 0 in Minutes of WEF Executive Council, Bangalore, India, 1–3 February, 1982)
6. WEF Executive Council Meeting, Bangalore, India, 1–3 February, 1982
7. Minutes of World Evangelical Fellowship Executive Council Meeting, Wheaton, Illinois, USA, 1 July, 1983

8. Letter from D. John Richard to new members of Steering Committee, 15 May, 1984
9. The Commission on Church Renewal of World Evangelical Fellowship, Report on the Steering Committee Meeting, Amerongen, Holland, 3–7 June, 1985
10. *ibid*.
11. Minutes of the World Evangelical Fellowship Executive Council Meeting, Hilversum, the Netherlands, 11–14 June, 1985

# Index

235